John LeMay

THE BIG BOOK OF JAPANESE GIANT MONSTER MOVIES
Volume 1: 1954-1982
Revised and Expanded 2nd Edition

BICEP BOOKS

© 2017 by John LeMay. All rights reserved.

ISBN-13:978-1974442713
ISBN-10:1974442713

*For my parents who introduced me to these films,
and for Scott who discovered them alongside me.*

CONTENTS

PREFACE TO THE NEW EDITION

"A Revised and Expanded Edition already, isn't it too soon?"

Yes, it is a little soon for a 2nd Edition already I suppose, but let me explain why. I wrote the first draft of this book back in 2013 for a publisher that specialized in titles on niche movie genres. I thought for sure they would be interested in a book covering that most respected of niche film genres: the Japanese giant monster film (or dai kaiju eiga for the more educated fans). But alas, my proposal was either rejected, or lost in the mail. Though I hope it was the latter and not the former, in any case, I'm glad it was. Publishing the book myself allotted me more freedom, and, in the process, more fun. When I released the book through Amazon's Createspace platform in 2016, I had no idea the reception would be so positive. It was, after all, a guide book of movie reviews and trivia with no photos.[1]

But back to the question at hand: Why a Revised and Expanded Edition so soon? The answer is simple, in my haste to publish, the first edition of this book was somewhat rudimentary. As some astute reviewers pointed out, it lacked page numbers in the Contents for starters. And, as Nicholas Driscoll of Toho Kingdom pointed out in his review on the aforementioned website, I had neglected to cover a few very important films. So, I suppose the main reason I jumped on a 2nd Edition so soon was a chance to review some of the films I missed the first time around—most of which I simply hadn't seen yet like *Abominable Snowman* (1955), Daiei's *Yokai Monsters* trilogy, *Great Prophecies of Nostradamus* (1974), and *The Bermuda Depths* (1978) among many others.[2] This would

---

[1] For those unfamiliar with Godzilla fandom, Fair Use typically does not apply to Godzilla, Gamera or Ultraman in the case of publishing photographs. For the sake of being respectful to the creators of the aforementioned monsters/sentai this book has no photos to illustrate it, and the cover—now in wrap around form as the artist, my good friend Shane Olive, originally intended—is graced by a giant ape battling a plesiosaurus.
[2] As to why movies like the 1967 *Ultraman* movie aren't included the answer is simple: I still haven't seen it.

probably be a good time to also fess up that most of the other newly added films aren't technically dai kaiju eiga.

But then again, the criteria for these films can be a tad bit hard to pin down sometimes. For instance, what officially makes a movie a part of Dai Kaiju Eiga? For starters, technically *Legend of Dinosaurs and Monster Birds* and *The Last Dinosaur* both focus on prehistoric beasts. However, the prehistoric beasts in question are actually larger than their real-life counterparts and are thusly monster-sized. And then there are films such as *Atragon*, about a futuristic submarine which battles the lost continent of Mu for supremacy of the world. Though not a dai-kaiju eiga in the same sense as the Godzilla and Gamera films, it does feature a dai kaiju in it: Manda. And as every good fan knows, Manda was eventually spun into the Godzilla series, as were several other kaiju, via 1968's *Destroy All Monsters*. *The Mysterians* due to giant robot monster Mogera is also included. And then there are the giant slugs in *Great Prophecies of Nostradamus*, which are certainly giant when compared to their real life counterparts but I suppose they are not necessarily "giant monsters" when compared to people. Furthermore, does the giant swarm of bees that appears in Shochiku's apocalyptic insect thriller *Genocide* (1969) pass for the criteria? Who can say? But, in the end, I kind of doubt anyone will complain about such matters. Chances are if you love dai kaiju eiga, you probably also love the other fantastical outputs of Toei, Daiei and Toho. The same goes for the Shaw Brothers' *Mighty Peking Man*, not a Japanese Dai Kaiju Eiga, but considering the SPFX were done by none other than Godzilla stalwart Sadamasa Arikawa, I think it counts. But, for the sake of purists, and in keeping with this book's title, movies with a loose connection to the genre are listed as "Bonus Reviews."

As for the main entries, each is listed under its official English language title (more on that later) followed by alternate titles in other countries and its theatrical release date in Japan. Though I pondered including American release dates and Japanese re-release dates as well, I decided not to, as it was too exhaustive. In the instance that a film's American version deviated enough from the Japanese version, it gets its own separate entry as with *Godzilla, King of the Monsters!*, *Half Human* and *Varan the Unbelievable*. However, when the alterations were still fairly minor, as was the case with *King Kong vs. Godzilla* or *Gammera the Invincible*, the alterations are discussed though they don't warrant a separate entry.

Each film's director, SPFX director, screenwriter and music composer are listed followed by members of the cast, with the name of their characters listed in parenthesis. When possible, suit performers are listed though many times they went uncredited. Aspect ratio and runtimes are also listed, though only the Japanese runtimes, as the films sometimes had a different run-time in each country depending on what the foreign distributer decided to cut out. Following that is a synopsis of the film, which you are encouraged to skip if you have already seen said film, and exists solely to inform those who possibly haven't seen the entry in question. After this production background, as well as a critiquing of the film, is given. And, as an added bonus, interesting bits of miscellaneous information are listed under Trivia after each entry. This is likely the portion that most well-informed fans will enjoy, and hopefully, learn something new.

To return to the ever confusing issue of titles, each are listed under their official English language title bestowed upon them by their respective studios in Japan. Example: *Godzilla's Revenge*, the popular American title for what in Japan was called *March of the Monsters*, here goes under the official title chosen by Toho, *All Monsters Attack*, even though no one really likes that name. Similarly, though the 1966 Godzilla movie is popularly known as *Godzilla vs. the Sea Monster* in America, and *Godzilla, Mothra, Ebirah: Big Duel in the South Seas* in Japan, in this book it is listed as *Ebirah, Horror of the Deep*.

So, with no further ado, I hope you enjoy this revised and expanded edition of *The Big Book of Japanese Giant Monster Movies Volume 1: 1954-1982* which contains over 25 new films, plus new trivia for many of the original entries.

John LeMay
July 7, 2017

FOREWORD

I first came to know John LeMay in 2005 through a fan letter written by him to me about my Godzilla stories published in *G-Fan* back in the 90s. By then I figured those stories had been forgotten and was delighted to find out that not only did someone like them, but they remembered them! They say the best way to reach a man's heart is through his stomach. With writers, the fastest way is through their ego. Compliments are food for the writer's soul and John's letter was quite a feast. Of course we became friends.

Since 2005, John became a prolific writer himself with an impressive collection of non-fiction works—covering everything from the Roswell UFO Crash to Billy the Kid—through Arcadia Publishing and The History Press. More relevant to this work though; you may have seen his name in issues of *G-Fan, Mad Scientist,* and *Xenorama.* He has done retrospectives for *Godzilla vs. The Sea Monster* (*G-Fan #87*), *Godzilla vs. Mechagodzilla* (*G-Fan #104*), and *Godzilla vs. Space Godzilla* (*G-Fan #105*). He has written about real life kaiju (*G-Fan #81*) and real life Rodans (*G-Fan #82*), and compared the parallels between Hammer and Toho studios (*G-Fan #87*). He has even delivered articles on more obscure topics such as Toho's vampire films ("Toho's Bloodthirsty Trilogy" -*Xenorama* #17) and *Sayonara Jupiter* ("*Sayonara Jupiter.* A Disaster Among Disaster Films"- *Xenorama* #19).

This is an amazing accomplishment, considering the fact he was fresh out of high school in 2005. Few people have this many published credits to their name by the time they reach 30, especially books. Any author will tell you that writing a book is an investment in time. A year of your life, at least—Poof!—gone. I am very proud of him.

OK, so we have this new work from Mr. LeMay, *The Big Book of Japanese Giant Monster Movies.* What do you have to look forward to? *The Big Book of Japanese Giant Monster Movies* is a reference guide to the kaiju films produced by the

Japanese film industry. A lot of books of this nature have come and gone. To make his book stand out, John mined Japanese language sites for information which would not be available in the West. For instance, he had found that Ishiro Honda cut the Frontier Missile scene from the Japanese version of *Mothra vs Godzilla*, contrary to what we have been told in North America. Common knowledge says the scene was filmed for the U.S. market. Now is this true? I cannot say. But that is what some people claim in Japan. As a lifelong Godzilla fan, I have read all kinds of material on the subject starting with Robert K. Davidson's *Great Monsters of the Movies*, which was published in 1978, to the articles written by Ed Godziszewski and Guy Tucker for *G-Fan* in the 90s. I have to admit feeling apprehensive toward this new book about an old topic. Was it going to be interesting or was it going to feel like walking down a path I have walked down so many times before? John has pulled a rabbit out of the hat. I enjoyed the book. His prose speaks as one fan talking to another. He recognizes that the Japanese filmmakers often presented their monsters as characters, which is what I liked the most. If you understand that aspect of kaiju films then, in my opinion, you understand what makes kaiju movies special. I hope you enjoy *The Big Book of Japanese Giant Monsters Movies*. I certainly did.

Neil Riebe
May 2016

Neil Riebe is an author and illustrator living in Madison, WI. He is the author of several beloved fan-fiction stories in the early days of G-Fan, before fan-fiction was banned from the magazine's pages, and thus Neil's new stories appear on FanFiction.net.

INTRODUCTION

Kaiju Eiga: Calling Monster Island

The 1960s were a wild and offbeat time for cinema exports. Rome introduced the world to Sword and Sandal epics and Spaghetti Westerns via Cinecitta Films, Mexico made up colorful lucha-heroes, China showcased the Shaw Brothers and Kung Fu, England gave the gothic Hammer horrors of Peter Cushing and Christopher Lee, and the Japanese had their "rubber suited giant monsters." All of these genres carried their fair share of notoriety, but none have been drubbed quite so mercilessly as the poor Japanese monsters. Unfortunately to most Americans, Japanese monster films, called dai kaiju eiga (big monster epics) in their home country, are something only to laugh at with their bad dubbing and men in rubber suits trashing "card board boxes" made up to look like buildings, when in fact the films are testaments to Japanese ingenuity. They are also artful representations of nuclear anxiety, interracial romance, ecological terror, and comedy (be it intentional or otherwise). Nor are the buildings made of cardboard. The miniature sets perfected by Eiji Tsuburaya from Toho Studios could go head to head with the miniatures in American productions of the time any day, and often could surpass them. The actors that starred in these films took them just as seriously as any other production they were in, and more often than not they were A-Listers. *Seven Samurai*'s Takashi Shimura had several roles in the sci-fi and kaiju films of Toho, as did Akiko Wakabayashi and Mie Hama (Bond girls in *You Only Live Twice*), and even Toshiro Mifune himself battled a giant dragon in *The Birth of Japan*.

This will come as a surprise to many, but the first Japanese dai kaiju was not 1954's *Godzilla*, but 1933's *Wasei Kingu Kongu* (*King Kong: Made in Japan*), which was followed by 1938's *King Kong Appears in Edo* (Edo being the original name for Tokyo). Not surprisingly all three films (*Edo* came in two parts) utilized a man in a suit to bring Kong to life rather than stop-motion, making for a sort of prehistoric precursor to what Japanese monster films would become in the 1950s.[3] Ironically enough, the *Edo* Kong suit was created by Fuminori Ohashi who would later create the first Godzilla suit with Eiji Tsuburaya. In yet another ironic twist both *Kong* films were lost in the bombing of Hiroshima, one of the very events that later birthed the Godzilla series.

The bombings of Hiroshima and Nagasaki were still fresh in the minds of many Japanese in 1954 during *Godzilla's* inception. In March of that year the fishing vessel Lucky Dragon No.5 drifted into contaminated waters during the testing of the H-Bomb on Bikini Atoll resulting in the radiation poisoning of the crew. The death of the first crew member, Aikichi Kuboyama, and the contaminated tuna soon sparked an international incident between Japan and the U.S., which eventually paid a $2 million settlement to the families of the crew.

Later that April, Toho Studios producer Tomoyuki Tanaka had just been denied visas to shoot his next epic, *In the Shadow of Glory*, on location by the Indonesian government. En route to Tokyo by plane from Jakarta, Tanaka looked to the turbulent seas below and imagined a prehistoric monster lurking beneath their depths awakened by the H-Bomb. It would be the perfect feature to replace the one he had just lost. Tanaka was keenly aware of the American film *The Beast from 20,000 Fathoms* wherein a stop-motion dinosaur is awakened by nuclear tests. This shows in the story draft Tanaka cooked up on the flight home titled *The Giant Monster from 20,000 Leagues Under the Sea*, or so studio legend says. Other reports suggest the idea was dreamed up in studio rather than on the plane in the heat of the moment. Whatever the case, Tanaka's production would have meaning and depth the American monster films lacked. The kaiju, that had yet to be designed or named, would be a true allegory for the horrors of nuclear war Japan had been

---

[3] In the interest of being thorough, *King Kong Made in Japan* was a comedy short about a man creating a King Kong stage play, and the ape in *King Kong Appears in Edo* is human-sized despite what the publicity materials imply.

tragically reminded of only too recently during the Lucky
Dragon incident.

The Four Godzilla Fathers

Tanaka was one of only four men integral to bringing
Godzilla to life. The other three were director Ishiro Honda,
composer Akira Ifukube, and special effects director Eiji
Tsuburaya. Tsuburaya was born in 1901 and began his film
career at 18, when he was hired as a scenario writer for Japan
Natural Color Film Co. Tsuburaya's true love was Special
Effects (SPFX), which he learned the basics of at the studio
which had since merged with Kokatsu. However, a 1933
showing of *King Kong* in Japan inspired him to perfect his
new craft. By 1936 he debuted as the SPFX director for *The
New Soil*, a Japanese-German co-production which employed
Tsuburaya's method of rear projection. The innovative
SPFX work caught the eye of Iwao Mori, president of a film
studio called PLC that would soon become the Toho Movie
Company. Before he could do much at the new studio,
Tsuburaya was drafted into the Imperial Army Air Corps
where he made flight training films. This eventually led to
him doing WWII propaganda films featuring miniature
recreations of various naval and aerial battles, notably *The
War at Sea from Hawaii to Malaya* (1941). By 1954, long after
WWII was over, Tsuburaya was now the head of SPFX at
Toho Studios. When Tanaka approached him to handle the
effects on the new production (simply titled "G"), Tsuburaya
had coincidentally already written his own story treatment
about a giant octopus attacking Japanese vessels at sea. That
other Ray Harryhausen classic, *It Came from Beneath the Sea*,
had not yet been released for the record.

Tsuburaya's collaborator on the war picture *Eagles of the
Pacific*, Ishiro Honda, was brought in to direct the film, now
called *Gojira* after the monster. Honda was born in 1911 in
Yamagata and raised in a monastery. He too began a career
in film that was interrupted by the onset of WWII. In 1945,
during the bombings of Nagasaki and Hiroshima, Honda was
a POW in China. Upon his return to Japan, Honda began
directing several feature films and documentaries. He was
also a friend and collaborator of Akira Kurosawa, Japan's

greatest filmmaker. In the 1980s Honda would serve as associate director on Kurosawa's films such as *Ran* and *Rhapsody in August* to name a few. Honda notably directed the entire Tunnel segment in *Akira Kurosawa's Dreams,* a series of artful vignettes. Though Kurosawa was the better known of the two, in 1954 both men had releases dealing with post-war nuclear anxieties. Kurosawa's was the Toshiro Mifune film *I Live in Fear*. For once, Honda emerged the victor, with his *Gojira* not only beating *I Live in Fear*, but also surpassing the box office grosses of Kurosawa's seminal *Seven Samurai.*

Providing the mood of *Gojira* was Akira Ifukube, part of a very distinguished family in Japan, born in 1914. Ifukube was self-taught in the composition of music outside of a few violin lessons. Remarkably, he wrote his first composition, *Japanese Rhapsody,* at 19. Even Ifukube saw service in the war in the most unlikely of ways. Having written a thesis on wood vibration in terms of creating new musical instruments, Ifukube was as a result assigned to study the captured all wood British war plane *DeHavilland Mosquito.* By the late 1940s Ifukube joined Toho Studios. His first film for them was *The End of the Silvery Peak*—it would be followed by over 200 other film scores over his forty plus years in the industry. In 2007 he won a Lifetime Achievement Award from the Japanese Film Academy.

Suitmation

Aside from the bad dubbing (the films are better if one watches them in the original Japanese with subtitles), the most picked upon aspect of kaiju eiga is suitmation, a technique still used today in the ongoing *Ultraman* franchise from Tsuburaya Productions. Although the concept sounds simple, a great deal of hard work, and even danger, goes into suitmation.

Back in 1954 it was decided that despite Tsuburaya's love of stop motion effects (and the arduous amount of time it would take to create Godzilla using this technique) the studio would use a man in suit instead. Although it sounded primitive, it cut the production times drastically. Ray Harryhausen's masterpieces like *The Seventh Voyage of Sinbad* (1958) and *Jason and the Argonauts* (1963) each took around a full year to complete the effects work on. With Tsuburaya's technique Toho could churn out several SPFX pictures per year, which they effectively did in the 1960s.

While Godzilla was not the first kaiju brought to life via suitmation, Tsuburaya and his team arguably perfected the process. Suitmation acting works most effectively when paired with miniature sets, optical effects, matte shots, and high speed filming. Despite being called high speed filming, it translates to the filmed images moving slower due to more frames being photographed per second therefore giving an illusion of size. As for the miniatures, their scales depended on how big the studio wanted to portray the monsters. In the case of the original *Godzilla*, a 50 meter monster, the sets were reproduced at a one-twenty-fifth scale. Due to the high speed filming when the buildings crumble they look normal sized.

Typically to build a monster suit a small clay model was produced, or merely a design sketch, for suit makers to model their creation from. In the case of *Godzilla*, the first suit made couldn't even move it was so stiff, but most sources say the suit was intended only as a trial version. The G-suit produced for filming ended up weighing around 220 pounds and was made of urethane foam and covered with liquid plastic. Inhabiting the suit wasn't an easy job for the two men who portrayed Godzilla in his first outing, Haruo Nakajima and Katsumi Tezuka. Under hot studio lights temperatures inside the suit would rise to over 130 degrees Fahrenheit, and as a result the two men could only stand to stay inside the suits for limited amounts of time. Also, if the suits were not tailored for the actor wearing them they could end up being too tight which resulted in painful chaffing and blisters. Most actors entered suits through a zipper in the back, usually along Godzilla's dorsal fins.

Usually, the actors' heads would be situated in the monsters' necks, and tiny holes were drilled allowing them limited vision so they could at least have an idea of where they were going. In the future, the heads of the monster suits became radio controlled allowing the mouths and eyes to open and close on command. Occasionally actor's real eyes were made use of in the case of humanoid monsters. In *War of the Gargantuas* slits in the eyes allowed for a wider range of emotion from the more human monsters, as did a similar method in Daiei's *Daimajin* series. Even up to the 1990s suit acting remained unchanged for the most part, the only innovations were mechanical additions to the suits' heads allowing for the snarling of lips and other details. For the original *Godzilla*, Nakajima operated the mouth of the suit manually from inside. Nakajima went on to portray Godzilla for the next consecutive 11 films, calling it quits after 1972's *Godzilla vs. Gigan*. Nakajima also portrayed many of Toho's other well-known kaiju including *Rodan*, *Varan*, Baragon in *Frankenstein Conquers the World*, the title star in *King Kong Escapes*, and Gaira in *War of the Gargantuas* to name a few. Nakajima coincidentally battled his own successor, Kengo Nakayama, in *Godzilla vs. Hedorah* in which Nakayama portrayed the title villain. Nakayama would also play Gigan in two consecutive films, but would not become Godzilla until 1984. He played the monster in every entry of the Heisei series up to *Godzilla vs. Destroyah* in 1995.

Suit acting was particularly hazardous when it came to water scenes set in Toho's big pool. If an actor were to trip in the heavy suit, they would be at risk of drowning. In the case of *Ebirah, Horror of the Deep* (1966), wherein Godzilla battles a foe underwater, Nakajima was outfitted with a special breathing apparatus. Other hazards included scenes involving fire and pyrotechnics, usually during confrontations with the military or other kaiju. On several occasions suits accidentally caught fire which resulted in burns to the actors. More often than not these exciting sequences remain in the final cuts, notably in *Mothra vs. Godzilla* wherein Godzilla's head catches fire. Even more hazardous were confrontations with the military in Toho's big pool. During the filming of *The Return of Godzilla* Nakayama (by then going by the name of Kenpachiro Satsuma) suffered an electrical shock! This also happened on the set of Daiei's first *Gamera* film when a lamp fell into a water tank nearly electrocuting the man inside the suit. During another incident, a flame thrower placed in the Gamera suit's mouth malfunctioned and caused the suit to explode. Needless to say it, was empty at the time.

Perhaps the most unfortunate aspect of monster suits is that they don't last forever. If they did they would be prime candidates for museum displays, but they decay rather quickly over the course of several years until eventually nothing recognizable is left. In the case of the massive plant monster from *Godzilla vs. Biollante*, it became a shelter for stray studio cats!

Monster Successes

Gojira (later anglicized as Godzilla in the U.S.) garnered an attendance of 9.6 million people in Japan, 11% of the population at the time. Toho quickly cranked out a sequel which was released in April of 1955, *Gojira No Gyakshu* (*Godzilla's Counterattack*), which sold over 8 million tickets. A standard 1950s "monsters on the loose" affair featuring a new Godzilla battling an Ankylosaurus, it didn't hold a candle to the original film's artistic endeavors. A year later in America *Gojira* was released as *Godzilla, King of the Monsters!* which integrated footage of Raymond Burr as reporter Steve Martin into the proceedings for U.S. audiences. The film was a big success, and garnered even more American exposure when it aired on television soon after.

Back in Japan, Toho released two more monsters onto the public in the 1950s with the classic *Rodan* (1956), and the not so classic *Varan* (1958), a creative and financial disappointment. After a three year hiatus, Dai Kaiju Eiga re-birthed itself when a colorful mammoth moth emerged from her cocoon in 1961's massively successful *Mothra*. Followed by the even bigger hit *King Kong vs. Godzilla* in 1962, Toho found themselves on a roll with giant monsters and soon began experimenting with off-shoots like *Dogora the Space Monster* (1964), *Frankenstein Conquers the World* (1965), and *War of the Gargantuas* (1966) alongside non-stop Godzilla sequels. In addition to this were more SPFX spectaculars such as *The Mysterians* (1957), *Battle in Outer Space* (1959), *Gorath* (1962) and *Atragon* (1963), sci-fi films that occasionally featured giant monsters, but not always. The films were successfully exported to countries all over the world, including the all-important American market. In 1965

Toho would even import American starts like Nick Adams to star in their Kaiju Eiga.

By 1965 the genre had reached its zenith after the creations of Godzilla's two greatest nemeses: King Ghidorah, Toho's golden space dragon, and Gamera, Daiei Studio's flying turtle and friend to all children. Unlike King Ghidorah, Godzilla's many battles with Gamera would only take place at the box office as the turtle became his #1 competitor. However, Godzilla's eventual undoing would come from the most unlikely of sources with good intentions: Eiji Tsuburaya and his dai kaiju TV series *Ultraman*. Featuring a human hero who could transform into the giant Ultraman to battle the monsters, the show was so successful it would eventually result in an oversaturation of kaiju battling superheroes on TV in the early 1970s. Tsuburaya Production's kaiju killing superheroes had a hand in killing monsters on the big screen as well. When kids could see kaiju on TV for free, there was less incentive in paying to go to theaters to see the same thing. Ironically in an early 1966 episode of the series Ultraman kills a monster named Jirass which was created from a Godzilla suit.

1966 was an interesting year for the genre as it saw the birth of another famous monster, *Daimajin*, and in its wake a sub-genre of Dai Kaiju Eiga set in feudal times. Daimajin was a statue that came alive to punish evil feudal lords in a successful trilogy produced by Daiei Studios. Preceding the *Daimajin* trilogy the same year was Toei's *The Magic Serpent*, based on a folktale which featured kaiju and ninja. It was 1967 that served as the biggest year for Dai Kaiju Eiga though, as nearly every major Japanese studio got into the game. Toho's offerings were *King Kong Escapes* and *Son of Godzilla*. Shochiku unleashed *The X From Outer Space*, and Nikkatsu let loose *Gappa the Triphibean Monster*. Even Korea produced a giant monster film called *Yongary, Monster from the Deep*. The Godzilla-like monster brought to life by technicians imported from Japan even had a child character cheering it on inspired by *Gamera*. That year Daiei released their seminal Gamera film, *Gamera vs. Gyaos*. After this, Gamera's popularity would rise and Godzilla's would begin to fall. The twisting terrapin would go on to star in four more profitable vehicles for Daiei: *Gamera vs. Viras* (1968), *Gamera vs. Guiron* (1969), *Gamera vs. Jiger* (1970) and *Gamera vs. Zigra* (1971) after which Daiei filed for bankruptcy.

Toho, though still going strong compared to other studios, was in dire straits somewhat themselves in the early 1970s which saw the disbanding of the old studio system. Whereas Tomoyuki Tanaka used to produce five to six films per year, the number dropped to only two big pictures per year, one of which more often than not starring Godzilla; though none of these sequels managed to garner attendances of over two million people, and a couple of entries actually drew less than a million. Taste in SPFX films in Japan began to temper towards disaster epics such as *Submersion of Japan* (1973), *Conflagration* (1975) and *Deathquake* (1980) which became big hits. Some of these, such as *Great Prophecies of Nostradamus* (1974), dabbled in kaiju but were not giant monster films. Toho even produced a trilogy of bloody vampire films in the early 1970s in competition with Hammer Studios.

1975 saw the release of Toho's last Godzilla film, *Terror of Mechagodzilla*. In a touch of irony, *Ultraman Leo*, to be the last Ultra series for some time, ended its run the same year. There were no kaiju films in Japan after the last G-film save for a few. Ultraman made the jump to the big screen in his first original feature *6 Ultra Brothers vs. the Monster Army* (although the film was actually a 1974 Thai co-production with Chaiyo Studios) released in Japan in 1979. Toei produced *Legend of Dinosaurs and Monster Birds*, a sort of Japanese attempt at *Jaws* in 1977 and Tsuburaya Productions made *The Last Dinosaur* starring Richard Boone and a rubber-suited T-Rex the same year.

On the Other Side of the Pacific

Consequently, Godzilla's popularity was soaring in the U.S. after his retirement in Japan in the late 1970s. The monster had his own Marvel Comic's (yes, *that* Marvel Comics) series where he sparred with the Avengers, and also a successful Hanna-Barbera cartoon which ran for two seasons. His most popular film at the time, financially speaking, was *Godzilla vs. Megalon*, ironically one of the series' biggest flops in Japan.

In an attempt to cash in on Dino de Laurentiis' upcoming 1976 *King Kong*, U.S. distributer Cinema Shares created a poster falsely depicting Godzilla and his insectoid nemesis atop the World Trade Centers. The poster caused monster fans to flock to theaters even if the end results left them bitterly disappointed.

Godzilla films had an interesting track record in America, and were often released out of sequence. For instance, 1956's *Rodan* beat 1955's *Godzilla Raids Again* to American theaters. *Rodan* was released successfully in 1957 while the Godzilla sequel wasn't released until 1959 as *Gigantis the Fire Monster*. This was after an aborted Americanization of the film called *The Volcano Monsters* failed to materialize. It would've taken the re-editing of *Godzilla, King of the Monsters!* a step further by eliminating all footage of the Japanese cast to replace them with American actors utilizing only the SPFX footage. Instead, the film was released as it was dubbed into English and did moderately well for Warner Bros which seemed to fear using Godzilla's name in the title, hence *Gigantis*. Godzilla's name would return in the Universal release of *King Kong vs. Godzilla* in 1963.

The mid-1960s were Godzilla's heyday in America, as *Godzilla, King of the Monsters!* played frequently on TV, encouraging many kids to venture to theaters whenever a new G-film was released. *Mothra vs. Godzilla* came to America swiftly by September of 1964, only five months after its Japanese release. It was the first G-film released by Samuel Z. Arkoff's American International Pictures (AIP), though Hollywood legend claims Arkoff had tried to obtain the rights to *Godzilla* in 1955. Fearing Mothra (whose solo film had a successful release from Columbia in 1962) was a laughable opponent for Godzilla, they billed the film as *Godzilla vs. the Thing*, and posters featured Godzilla battling a giant question mark. The film was a success and was quickly followed by its sequel, *Ghidrah, the Three Headed Monster* in 1965 released by Continental. In some cases it was double billed with Elvis Presley's *Harum Scarum* with ads touting "The Beat and the Beast make a holiday feast!" Unfortunately, this would be the last Godzilla film in U.S.

theaters for several years. By 1966, Daiei's giant turtle made it to American movie screens as *Gammera the Invincible*. It would be the only of Gamera's adventures to play in theaters. The sequels were snatched up by AIP-TV which didn't even have enough faith in the turtle to put his name in the titles. *Gamera vs. Barugon* became *War of the Monsters* and *Gamera vs. Viras* was called *Destroy All Planets*. Nor would Daiei's 1966 *Daimajin* trilogy be widely distributed to U.S. theaters, though the first film did receive a limited release. Likewise, Shochiku's *The X From Outer Space* went straight to TV in the states. So too did Nikkatsu's *Gappa the Triphibean Monster* (ironically produced in Japan solely with the hopes of a U.S. theatrical release) as *Monster From a Prehistoric Planet*. Oddly, at the same time, Toho's non G-films were all getting big theatrical releases, from marketable films like *Frankenstein Conquers the World* and *King Kong Escapes* to offbeat fare such as *Atragon*.

1965's *Monster Zero* was beat to the states by the television broadcast of its 1966 sequel *Godzilla versus the Sea Monster* in 1968 by AIP TV who didn't think the film warranted a theatrical release. This was followed by the 1969 TV premiere of 1968's *Son of Godzilla* and the theatrical release by AIP of *Destroy All Monsters*, the zenith of the Japanese monster film which was a success. Finally, *Monster Zero* was released on a double-bill with *War of the Gargantuas* in 1970 raking in around $3 million for distributor Maron Films, which also released *Godzilla's Revenge* (1969) in 1971. 1972 would see a successful AIP release of 1971's *Godzilla vs. Hedorah* as *Godzilla vs. the Smog Monster*. It would be the last G-film released in the states until 1973's *Godzilla vs. Megalon* in 1976, a film which some die-hard G-fans despise. Although *Megalon* was enjoyed by its intended child crowd, it soured adult audiences' taste in G-films in America. It was even aired by NBC in a prime time slot (hosted by John Belushi in a Godzilla suit no less) garnering huge ratings, resulting in even more people seeing it. In 1977 Cinema Shares tried to release 1974's superior *Godzilla vs. Mechagodzilla* as *Godzilla vs. the Bionic Monster*, but were forced to change the title due to a lawsuit from Universal who claimed they were infringing upon their TV series *The Bionic Woman*. As a result the film was released as *Godzilla vs. the Cosmic Monster* and never gained the wide exposure that *Megalon* did. Following this was 1972's *Godzilla vs. Gigan* (which AIP mysteriously never released in 1973 despite planning to do so) by Cinema Shares as *Godzilla on Monster Island* in 1977. As for the "last" Godzilla movie, released as *The Terror of Godzilla*, it didn't stand a chance after the 1977 release of *Star Wars* which permanently nudged Japanese monster films to second run theaters.

Monsters with Morals

In the same way that Spaghetti Westerns greatly differed stylistically from their American inspirations, so too did Dai Kaiju Eiga, but most people in the west failed to grasp the differences. Most only noticed that American films employed stop motion animation (or currently computer graphics) while the Japanese always used suitmation. In truth, the differences between the two genres differ more deeply than just on the technical level. Many American audiences loved the jaded morality of the Spaghetti Western, but they failed to notice the similar layers of kaiju eiga. The biggest difference between the kaiju and the animalistic American monsters was that that the kaiju were not merely mindless engines of destruction, but rather characters with functions and moral dilemmas within the stories.

The Brown Gargantua, Sanda, in *War of the Gargantuas* is finally reunited with his long lost brother, Gaira, only to discover he is a murderer. While Sanda was raised by kindly humans, Gaira was left to his own devices and eats them. Sanda must choose between defending the human race (most of which will try to destroy him anyway) and his evil brother, the only of his kind. Godzilla himself goes on a cinematic journey of moral discovery through his many sequels. A beady eyed evil menace in 1964's *Mothra vs. Godzilla*, the monster kills the giant moth, yet in the sequel, *Ghidorah, the Three Headed Monster*, he takes pity on an outmatched Mothra larva and comes to its rescue. For the next several entries he was something of an anti-hero, saving the world only because it coincided with his own agenda. By the 1970s the monster had evolved into a full on selfless superhero, frequently rescuing Japan from alien invaders out of the goodness of his heart. In the 1990s he went through a similar transformation as an evil villain until he again becomes a hero in 1994's *Godzilla vs. Space Godzilla*. In the 2000s he was both the harbinger of nuclear destruction in *Godzilla, Mothra and King Ghidorah: Giant Monsters All Out Attack* and again a "superhero" in *Godzilla: Final Wars*. In this sense one could argue that Godzilla is as much an actor as a special effect, changing his character and performance from film to film. Daiei's turtle Gamera as well functioned as a fully fleshed out character in most of his outings with clear cut motivations and sympathies. Daiei's Daimajin was somewhat ambiguous, invoking the fears of both the heroes and the villains alike making for a complex, if not mysterious, monster.

When the giant monster film gained a surprising resurrection in America during the late 2000s, it was Japanese monsters that served as the inspiration, not classic American creations. It began with J.J. Abram's found-footage opus *Cloverfield* (2008), which was followed by Gareth Edward's docu-drama style *Monsters* (2010). In Guillermo Del Toro's *Pacific Rim* (2013), in which giant robots battle monsters, the creatures are actually referred to as kaiju. Not only that, the designs of the robots and the kaiju were distinctly Japanese. Even J.J. Abrams stated that he intended for *Cloverfield* to capture the post 9/11 anxieties of the American peoples in much the same way that *Gojira* did for the Japanese in 1954. *The Beast from 20,000 Fathoms*, the American film which *Godzilla* is sometimes considered to be a "rip-off" of, was never mentioned.

THE FILMS

Godzilla (1954)

Alternate Titles: *Japan: The Terror of the Monster!* (Spain) *The Monster of the Pacific Ocean* (Portugal) *Godzilla: Monster of the Sea* (Sweden) *Godzilla, the Monster of the Century* (Greece)
Release Date: November 03, 1954

Directed by: Ishiro Honda
Special Effects by: Eiji Tsuburaya
Screenplay by: Takeo Murata, Shigeru Kayama & Ishiro Honda
Music by: Akira Ifukube
Cast: Akira Takarada (Ogata) Momoko Kochi (Emiko) Akihiko Hirata (Dr. Serizawa) Takashi Shimura (Dr. Yamane) Fuyuki Murakami (Prof. Tanabe) Sachio Sakai (Hagiwara) Toyoaki Suzuki (Shinkichi) **Suit Performers:** Haruo Nakajima/Katsumi Tezuka (Godzilla)

Academy Ratio, Black & White, 96 Minutes

Story
A wave of ship disappearances off the coast of Japan are followed by the emergence of a gigantic creature on Oto Island called Godzilla. An investigation is led by paleontologist Dr. Yamane accompanied by his daughter, Emiko, and her boyfriend, Ogata, a naval salvage officer, among others. On the island, they bear witness to the mighty Godzilla—a survivor from the Jurassic age according to Dr. Yamane who holds a press conference when they return to Japan. Meanwhile, Emiko visits Dr. Serizawa, a man she was intended to marry, to break the news to him that she is now betrothed to Ogata. She never gets a chance to tell him though as Serizawa shares the secret of his fearsome invention, the Oxygen Destroyer, with her and makes her vow not to tell anyone of its existence. Godzilla then surfaces

in Tokyo Bay and comes ashore to set the city ablaze. In the aftermath Emiko can't bear to keep Serizawa's secret, so she and Ogata go to convince him to use the weapon on the monster. A torn Serizawa burns his notes and then agrees the Oxygen Destroyer will be used, but only once. He and Ogata descend into Tokyo Bay where Serizawa activates the device. As Ogata surfaces, Serizawa remains below and cuts his life line so that he may die with his terrible creation and Godzilla, who dissolves into bones.

Background & Commentary

The film opens to the sound of thunderous footsteps, sounding not unlike the distant detonation of an H-Bomb to which Godzilla owes his birth both on the screen and behind the scenes. The gloomy film captured the Japanese imagination via the country's fears and anxieties, and is a very different affair compared to its light-hearted sequels. People are vaporized by the monster's atomic ray, a major character commits suicide, Tokyo becomes the new Hiroshima and the dead are the lucky ones with survivors slated to die a slow death from radiation poisoning. The fact that the first scene is of a boat being set aflame should clue one in to the story's origins in the Lucky Dragon No.5 incident. The families, notably the widows and young daughters asking about the missing ships whereabouts in particular are celluloid stand-ins for the real life families of the Lucky Dragon crew. A scene on a train between several Japanese citizens says it best when one laments, "First atomic tuna, and now this," while another complains about finding a new shelter in a reference to the WWII Tokyo air raids. These sequences lend the picture a sense of realism that likely would've been lost in the hands of other directors but Ishiro Honda, who had a background in documentaries, handles the proceedings exceptionally.

In the film Godzilla (or Gojira in the original Japanese) is named after an Oto Island legend, but behind the scenes the name came from the combination of the word gorilla and the Japanese word for whale: kujira. Supposedly Gojira was the nickname of a cumbersome Toho staff worker, though this has never been confirmed. On screen Godzilla makes his entrance via a well-executed puppet rearing his head over a hill, terrifying the Oto Islanders and allowing for an excellent close-up of a screaming Momoko Kochi in a signature shot of 1950s horror. The centerpiece of the film in terms of artistry and SPFX is the destruction of Tokyo, which goes on for 15 minutes from the time Godzilla emerges from Tokyo Bay to the instant he submerges again. And, this is on top of an earlier sequence where he comes ashore and attacks a train yard. The scenes are so well done in certain matte shots one doesn't even know the city is a miniature when it is mixed in with live extras. In a scene cut from the American version a widow and her two children choose not to run from the monster as he approaches. Instead they sit on the ground, the mother rocking her children as she says, "We'll be seeing father soon." All the while, Akira Ifukube's ponderous music evokes a sense of dread, slow but relentless like the monster itself.

As for the cast, this was lead actor Akira Takarada's third film. When Takarada introduced himself on set as the star of the film a studio employee retorted, "You aren't the star you fool! Gojira is." Takarada would go on to become "the Clark Gable of Japan" as a future co-star called him in America some years later. Momoko Kochi provides one of the strongest, if not the strongest, lead female roles in the series, though she never appeared in subsequent G-films until she reprised the character of Emiko in 1995's *Godzilla vs. Destroyah*. Akihiko Hirata's Dr. Serizawa is the piece's standout character, a reclusive scientist who lost his eye in the war and has created a new doomsday weapon on par with the H-Bomb: the Oxygen Destroyer. In a tragic scene between he, Emiko and Ogata, Hirata conveys the emotion that Serizawa knew he was doomed from the moment of his invention's inception. His moment of self-sacrifice at the picture's end makes for one of its most memorable moments, and the concept would be utilized by Honda again with many other characters in his monster films. *Seven Samurai* veteran Takashi Shimura's Dr. Yamane is likewise an intriguing character torn between studying Godzilla's ability to survive nuclear radiation and the realization that the monster must be destroyed. The film's last character shot is of Yamane, pondering the deaths of both Serizawa and Godzilla wondering if it was truly for the good of mankind in the long run before stating that there may be another Godzilla lurking in the depths.

Final Word

The film is the great granddaddy of 30 sequels (and counting), two American remakes, and a whole genre that the world would come to love. It also brought together the "four Godzilla fathers" of Honda, Tanaka, Tsuburaya and Ifukube who would go on to helm many of the sequels together.

Trivia

- Akira Takarada returned for five sequels in the G-series, including the final entry *Godzilla: Final Wars* (2004). He filmed a cameo for the 2014 *Godzilla* which was sadly left on the cutting room floor due to time restrictions.

- Akihiko Hirata would return to the series many times often playing scientists, and, in *Ebirah, Horror of the Deep* (1966), an eye patch wearing villain. Hirata was meant to appear in *The Return of Godzilla* (1984), but passed away before filming commenced.

- Momoko Kochi and Takashi Shimura both reprise their characters from this film (a rarity in Toho films outside of the Emi and Yumi Ito as the Shobijin) in sequels. Shimura returns as Dr. Yamane in *Godzilla Raids Again* (1955), and Koichi reprised her role as Emiko 41 years later in *Godzilla vs. Destroyah* (1995).

- Godzilla's first scene originally had him clutching a dead cow in his jaws. Had it not been cut, it would have been the only sequence to portray Godzilla eating anything in his entire film career (excluding the 1998 American *Godzilla*).

- Stills of Momoko Kochi as Emiko and Akihiko Hirata as Dr. Serizawa exist portraying the two characters before the war, but no footage to match the stills has ever surfaced leaving scholars to wonder if any such flashback scenes were ever actually filmed. For certain there were filmed a few additional sequences on Oto Island, including one of Ogata and Emiko glimpsing Godzilla's tail (which they mistake for a boulder) in the surf.

- Dr. Yamane makes mention of the Abominable Snowman of the Himalayas in his speech at the Diet Building. Perhaps not coincidentally, one of Toho's next monster movies was 1955's *Abominable Snowman* (better known as *Half Human* in America).

Godzilla Raids Again (1955)

Alternate Titles: *Godzilla's Counterattack* (Japan) *Gigantis the Fire Monster* (U.S.) *The King of the Monsters* (Spain) *The Return of Godzilla* (France) *Godzilla Returns* (Germany)
Release Date: April 24, 1955

Directed by: Motoyoshi Oda
Special Effects by: Eiji Tsuburaya
Screenplay by: Takeo Murata & Shigeaki Hidaka
Music by: Masaru Sato
Cast: Hiroshi Koizumi (Tsukioka) Minoru Chiaki (Kobayashi) Setsuko Wakayama (Hidemi) Yoshio Tsuchiya (Tajima) Sonosuke Sawamura (Shibeki) Yukio Kasama (Yamaji) Takashi Shimura (Dr. Yamane) **Suit Performers:** Haruo Nakajima (Godzilla) Katsumi Tezuka (Anguirus)

Academy Ratio, Black & White, 82 Minutes

Story
Two scout pilots, Tsukioka and Kobayashi, for a Japanese fishing fleet become stranded on a remote island where they discover a new Godzilla that is locked in battle with another prehistoric monster, Anguirus. The two pilots escape back to the mainland where they tell the authorities of their discovery and Tsukioka reunites with his sweetheart, Hidemi. The military makes preparations for the monsters'

landing, both of which come ashore in Osaka. Tsukioka and Hidemi escape to the countryside, but the cannery where they work is decimated by the two monsters in battle. Godzilla kills Anguirus and leaves Osaka burning in flames. Tsukioka, Hidemi and Kobayashi are transferred to another cannery in Hokkaido, and eventually the two pilots become enlisted in an aerial search for Godzilla at sea. Tsukioka tracks the monster to an icy island and alerts the authorities. An aerial attack commences on the monster which Kobayashi foolishly engages in and is shot down by Godzilla. The ensuing avalanche from Kobayashi's sacrifice gives the JSDAF an idea as how to defeat the monster, and so they begin bombing the icy mountains around Godzilla—who is then entombed in a massive avalanche.

Background & Commentary

During *Godzilla's* successful run at the Japanese Box Office, Toho President Iwao Mori was out of the country working on a production of *Madame Butterfly*, but once he returned he instructed Tomoyuki Tanaka to immediately begin work on a sequel. As Ishiro Honda was tied up on his new film, *Love Tide*, and Akira Ifukube was scoring another production, other than Eiji Tsuburaya, a new creative team had to be utilized. From their 1954 version of *The Invisible Man* Toho brought in that film's director Motoyoshi Oda, composer Masaru Sato (well known for his collaborations with Akira Kurosawa) and writer Shigeaki Hidaka to work on the next Godzilla film. Hidaka, along with the original's writers Takeo Murata and Shigeru Kayama, came up with a winning scenario pitting Godzilla against another monster. Also, as there was a strong demand for Godzilla to terrorize the Kansai area of Japan, Osaka was chosen to be the centerpiece of destruction. As such, extensive location scouting of Osaka was undertaken so that the miniature work would be as realistic as possible.

Filming commenced in the winter of 1955. In lead roles were Hiroshi Koizumi, a future staple of Toho's SPFX features, and Minoru Chiaki, a well-known member of Akira Kurosawa's stock company of actors. The duo fare well under Oda's direction along with Setsuko Wakayama, though one can't help but notice the trio participates in yet another love triangle which resolves in an act of self-sacrifice that can't measure up to the original's. That being said, among Oda's better directorial touches are a very palpable sense of dread before the attack on Osaka, in large part due to the aftermath of Tokyo as seen in the last film. And, at times, this picture has an even heavier sense of dread, as the citizens of Osaka fear that their city will become the new Tokyo. For that matter, the film's standout image in terms of symbolism is the burning Osaka from a great distance, which somewhat resembles a mushroom could. As for Sato's music, his themes lack the grand panache of Ifukube's, but the new composer comes up with some supremely eerie mood music for Godzilla—some of which he accomplished by playing the music backwards. On the SPFX end, a lighter more agile Godzilla suit inhabited by Haruo Nakajima was created rather than re-using the more cumbersome original. Katsumi Tezuka, who saw limited action as Godzilla in the previous film, dons the Anguirus costume, which he entered through two flaps in the back of the spiked portion of the suit. In the liveliest scene Godzilla and Anguirus tussle near an oil refinery which Godzilla sets ablaze as panicked extras run underfoot in some supreme chaos. Unfortunately, these exciting scenes are all overshadowed by a mistake made by one of the cameramen who didn't set his camera to film at 72 frames per second. While cameras A and B were set at the right speed, Camera C was set to only 18 frames per second. When Tsuburaya saw the difference he was quite surprised, but seemed to consider it a lucky accident and claimed that the sped up footage looked better for the monster fight. Whether or not Tsuburaya was just being kind to the cameraman is unknown, but the sped up footage from Camera C was used for all the battle footage edited into the film. As such, it gives the brutal battle a more animalistic quality. After this, Tsuburaya would often film SPFX sequences at different speeds to see if he captured any more lucky accidents.

Released just five months on the heels of the original, the film was another resounding success though it was considered a critical disappointment overall. Overseas the film was to have had an even more elaborate Americanization than *Godzilla, King of the Monsters! The Volcano Monsters,* as it was to be titled, would focus on a frozen T-Rex (Godzilla) and Ankylosaurus (Anguirus) transported to San Francisco where they would revive and wreak havoc in Chinatown (so as to utilize the Osaka battle). In addition to all new footage of American actors that would replace the Japanese cast entirely, Toho even constructed two new Godzilla and Anguirus suits for new footage that were lost, resulting in the abandonment of the film. When the film did eventually make it to American cinemas in 1959 via Warner Bros, it was merely a dubbed version of the original that inserted stock footage and music from a few other 1950s sci-fi films. Oddly, it still wasn't marketed as a Godzilla film, but rather *Gigantis the Fire Monster.* Apparently the distributers felt a "new" monster would fare better.

Final Word
Though sometimes forgotten in the wider pantheon of Toho SPFX films, at over 8 million admissions, this would be the third highest grossing Japanese Godzilla film if adjusted for inflation.

Trivia

- The ice used during the climax was real, some of which was made by Korakuen Amusement Park.

- As with the previous film, a radio drama and a novel were produced to tie in with the film.

- Though featured prominently in the film's poster, Takashi Shimura's reprisal of Dr. Yamane amounts to little more than a cameo.

- The centerpiece of the city destruction was an elaborate recreation of Osaka castle, which proved so sturdy it was difficult to collapse as planned. Reportedly Toho used this story as a mean's of boosting the film's PR.

- Setsuko Wakayama (Hidemi) was married to the well-known Toho director Senkichi Taniguchi who helmed the film (1965's *Key of Keys*) that later turned into *What's Up, Tiger Lilly?* by Woody Allen.

- The film's Japanese release saw the first licensed toy tie in for the series in the form of a gun and target game for children.

- Suggestions for the naming of the new monster were open to everyone on the Toho lot. Yoshio Tsuchiya thought the name should be "Gyottosu."

- Motoyoshi Oda had already helmed around a dozen films, his most notable being *Lady from Hell* (1949) based on a script by Akira Kurosawa, before he was given *Godzilla Raids Again.*

- The film's English voice cast features a who's who of Asian American actors including Keye Luke, Paul Frees and George Takei (Captain Sulu on *Star Trek*).

- *Gigantis the Fire Monster* was double-billed with *Teenagers from Outer Space.*

Abominable Snowman (1955)

Alternate Titles: *Half Human* (U.S.)
Release Date: August 14, 1955

Directed by: Ishiro Honda
Special Effects by: Eiji Tsuburaya
Screenplay by: Takeo Murata & Shigeru Kayama
Music by: Masaru Sato
Cast: Akira Takarada (Takeshi Ijima) Momoko Kochi (Machiko Takeno) Akemi Negishi (Chika) Nobuo Nakamura (Prof. Koizumi) Kenji Kasahara (Shinsuke Takeno) Sachio Sakai (Nakata) Kokuten Kodo (Village Elder) Yoshio

Kosugi (Oba) **Suit Performers:** Sanshiro Sagara
(Snowman) Takashi Ito (Snowman's son)

Academy Ratio, Black & White, 95 Minutes

Story
An expedition high in the Japanese Alps searches for the
abominable snowman and goes missing after a terrible
avalanche. A rescue party is sent looking for them. Among
their numbers are one of the missing men's siblings: Shinsuke
and Machiko—along with Machiko's boyfriend Takeshi.
They encounter a mountain tribe that worships the snowman
as well as hostile carnival workers intent on capturing the
beast. The carnival workers manage to capture the
benevolent snowman's son, and later the beast himself. When
the snowman's son is killed by the carnies as they escape, the
snowman flies into a rage and destroys the mountain village.
He then kidnaps Machiko and drags her back to his cave. On
the trail of Machiko and the snowman, the party discovers
that the snowman had in fact earlier saved Machiko and
Shinsuke's missing brother, who later died from
complications from his injuries. Chika, a girl from the village,
then sacrifices herself to save Machiko, and she and the
snowman tumble into a sulphur pit to their deaths.

Background & Commentary
In the original *Godzilla*, Dr. Yamane makes a passing
mention of the Abominable Snowman legend while speaking
to the Diet about Godzilla. Coincidence or not, Toho's next
planned monster film had always been about a giant
snowman (called "Project S"). However, the success of
Godzilla put the snowman on ice in favor of a quickie
Godzilla sequel. Therefore, Ishiro Honda and Eiji Tsuburaya
didn't get around to filming *Abominable Snowman* until May
of 1955. Returning with Tsuburaya and Honda from the
original *Godzilla* were many of that film's production crew
sans Akira Ifukube, with Masaru Sato providing this film's
score. Even the two romantic leads from the aforementioned
film were again portrayed by Akira Takarada and Momoko
Kochi—with Sachio Sakai again in a small supporting role.

The Snowman is the true star of the film of course, and actually comes away as the film's most sympathetic character after the death of his son at the hands of some circus men. During the climax it is revealed that the race of snowmen has been going extinct because they began eating a type of poisonous fungus growing in the caves and the last snowman only ventured down the mountain because he was becoming lonely. However, the benevolent Snowman becomes berserk at the death of his son and sets fire to a native village on the mountain and then kidnaps Kochi's character Machiko Takeno. Machiko is later saved by another female character, one of the Burukamin natives named Chika, and she and the monster tumble into a sulphur pit together. So, in this sense, one could argue that Chika pre-dates 1965's Miss Namikawa from *Invasion of Astro-Monster* as Honda's first self-sacrificing female hero. As for the Snowman himself, the beast was supposedly portrayed by Sanshiro Sagara, though other sources claim it was in fact forty year old suit designer Fuminori Ohashi himself! The suit, covered in goat hair, came with a soft rubber face mask capable of a surprisingly wide range of expression.

Though the film was received well enough upon release, it came into trouble due to complaints by the real Burakumin peoples, who didn't like the fact that they were portrayed as inbred, superstitious fools. Therefore, in 1986, when this film was gearing up for a VHS release via Toho Video, at the last minute Toho decided not to release the film along with 1974's *Great Prophecies of Nostradamus*. The last time the film was screened was at an Ishiro Honda film festival in 1997 and is today something of a lost film.

Final Word
Though relatively unseen outside of its butchered American version, *Abominable Snowman* is a well done and interesting "follow-up" of sorts to *Godzilla*.

Trivia

• Akemi Negishi (Chika) would again play a native girl in *King Kong vs. Godzilla* (1962).

- Fuminori Ohashi had previously designed and portrayed the ape in 1938's *King Kong Appears in Edo*.

- Haruo Nakajima has a cameo as a member of a search party.

- Tsuburaya fought to keep the snowman's design—which originally had fangs and was ten feet tall—from becoming too scary.

Warning from Space (1956)

Alternate Titles: *Spacemen Appear in Tokyo* (Japan) *The Mysterious Satellite* (U.S. Theatrical Release)
Release Date: January 29, 1956

Directed by: Koji Shima
Special Effects by: Toru Togi
Screenplay by: Hideo Oguni
Music by: Seitaro Omori
Cast: Keizo Kawasaki (Dr. Toru Itsobe) Toyomi Karita (Hikari Aozora/Ginko) Bin Yagisawa (No. 2 Pairan) Shozo Nanbu (the elder Dr. Itsobe) Isao Yamagata (Dr. Matsuda) Bontaro Miake (Dr. Kamura) **Suit Performers:** Uncredited

Academy Ratio, Daieicolor, 82 Minutes

Story

When a runaway planet threatens the earth, peaceful aliens from the planet Pyra come to warn mankind. But, due to their frightful starfish-like appearance, the aliens must assume a human form. A Pyran named Ginko assumes the form of famous singer Hikari Aozora and begins to warn earth's scientists of the impending danger from the approaching Planet R. She also warns one of the scientists, Dr. Matsuda, that the new weapon he is designing, Urium 101, is far too powerful and needs to be destroyed. Though initially the world doesn't believe the Pyrans, the appearance of Planet R in earth's orbit soon changes their minds. When all of the world's nuclear weapons are fired at Planet R to no effect, the Pyrans help Dr. Matsuda develop his Urium 101 and fire it at Planet R. The runaway planet is destroyed, and the earth is now rid of all nuclear weapons to boot.

Background & Commentary

Daiei's *Warning from Space*—the first Japanese sci-fi film to be shot in color in fact—was inspired by several sources, perhaps chief among them the recent success of Toho's *Godzilla* (1954). The storyline revolving around benevolent aliens came both from 1951's *The Day the Earth Stood Still* and also a Japanese novel by Gentaro Nakajima.

Warning from Space has an excellently plotted three act structure, with the first act (slow that it might be at times) setting up a swell mystery surrounding the starfish-like Pyrans. The fleeting glimpses of the Pyrans (mostly hidden in the shadows) as they try to approach humanity are well done, but unfortunately the silly looking aliens have already been glimpsed aboard their spacecraft at this point and would have fared better if their full on reveal came later in the film. The story doesn't really get off the ground until the second act when one of the aliens takes on the form of famous singer Hikari Aozora. This "starfish out of water" scenario is fun for a while, but sadly the character fades into the background at the onset of the third act which revolves around the appearance of Planet R. A sequence where the earth's populace looks to the skies in curiosity and dread as the planet approaches is exceptionally well handled. The runaway planet is an interesting precursor to Toho's 1962 *Gorath*, with its gravitational pull causing Tokyo to flood. These effects scenes are also quite well done when compared to the alien costume designs.

Overall, the film has a maturity to it that just almost exceeds that of its peers like the same year's *Rodan* and the next year's *The Mysterians*. The only thing going against the film's serious nature is the execution of the Pyrans—designed well by Taro Okamoto and executed somewhat poorly by Toru Togi (who would go on to work on TV's *Ultra Q*). As it is, the aliens look too much like what they really are: people in fabric suits. However, the U.S. dub makes mention of the Pyrans wearing "strange protective clothing", so perhaps that is what it was meant to be. The film was well received in Japan and it was released in Britain in 1957, but didn't hit the U.S. until 1963. Later, American International Pictures began airing it on TV where it received wider exposure.

Final Word
An excellent science fiction film marred only perhaps by its goofy looking aliens.

Trivia

- The sound effects used for the Pyrans are the same ones used for Gamera's flying saucer form in the Showa Gamera series.

- Supposedly, this film was held in high esteem by Stanley Kubrick.

- To cash in on the success of Toho's two Godzilla films, in promotional stills the Pyran aliens were depicted as giants despite only being human-sized in the film.

Godzilla, King of the Monsters! (1956)

Alternate Titles: *King Monster Godzilla* (Japan)
Release Date: April 27, 1956

Directed by: Terry Morse & Ishiro Honda
Special Effects by: Eiji Tsuburaya
Screenplay by: Terry Morse, Takeo Murata, Shigeru Kayama & Ishiro Honda
Music by: Akira Ifukube
Cast: Raymond Burr (Steve Martin) Frank Iwanagawa (Tomo) Akira Takarada (Ogata) Momoko Koichi (Emiko) Akihiko Hirata (Dr. Serizawa) Takashi Shimura (Dr. Yamane) **Suit Performers:** Haruo Nakajima/Katsumi Tezuka (Godzilla)

Academy Ratio, Black & White, 80 Minutes

Story

Reporter Steve Martin is in route to Cairo by plane, unaware that below him a ship has been mysteriously sunk. Martin, who has a layover in Japan, decides to stick around to visit an old friend, Serizawa, and also get in on the investigations into the ship disasters. As such, he joins a trip to Oto Island where he witnesses the monster Godzilla first hand. He also witnesses the monster's rampages through Tokyo and barely survives the second encounter as one of the wounded amidst the wreckage. Emiko Yamane tells Steve of his friend Serizawa's powerful new invention the Oxygen Destroyer and Steve persuades Emiko to convince Serizawa to use it on Godzilla. Serizawa agrees to use his weapon to kill the monster in Tokyo Bay, but he also takes his own life in the process.

Background & Commentary

While all Japanese monster films are inevitably dubbed into English and slightly re-edited for their American releases, they don't usually warrant themselves as being a totally different film. *Godzilla, King of the Monsters!* is one such exception, but it is by no means a complete bastardization of the Japanese version. Godzilla is still a dealer of graphic death and destruction and Serizawa is still the self-sacrificing hero, he now just also happens to be an old friend of reporter Steve Martin played by Raymond Burr. In the heavily re-edited film, the end is now the beginning with the picture starting in the ruins of Tokyo accompanied by the haunting words of Burr who calls Tokyo "a smoldering memorial to the unknown." Conversely, this version ends on a positive note with Martin concluding, "The whole world can wake up and live again." The Japanese version ended with a sorrowed Dr. Yamane speculating that there may be yet another Godzilla waiting to strike. The downside to the Americanized film is that the nuclear subtext was not surprisingly watered down for the U.S. audience.

The editing between the American and Japanese footage is excellent, and flaws are mostly visible only if one is looking for them and has seen the original version. Amazingly, Burr's footage in which he interacts with the original cast via body doubles was said to have been shot in only one day—though in some interviews Burr refutes this saying it was six days. All sets doubling for the Japanese locations (including Oto Island) were recreated on the same rented soundstage. Frank Iwanaga, the other new lead who plays Tomo, was only a part time actor who was predominantly an insurance salesman. Furthermore, the dubbed sequences took only one session to record over five hours. This is not entirely surprising though, as not all of the Japanese footage is dubbed into English and some of it remains in the original un-subtitled Japanese. This strange juxtaposition of Japanese and English meshes ironically well with Honda's original documentary style direction. Terry Morse, director of several small Warner Bros pictures in the past, was tapped to direct the American footage for only $10,000. For the same amount, Raymond Burr, not yet famous for *Perry Mason* and *Ironsides*, was signed to star. Unlike many actors ashamed of their parts in 50s sci-fi films, Burr always remained quite fond of his work on *Godzilla, King of the Monsters!* and even tried to gain part ownership of the picture. It was also for this reason that he agreed to star in the Americanized version of Toho's 1984 *Return of Godzilla*, released in America by Roger Corman's New World Pictures as *Godzilla 1985*. Again, Burr shot all of his footage in one day.

Godzilla, King of the Monsters! was a big hit in the U.S. grossing $2 million, a large sum for a Japanese film released through relatively small distributor Trans World. It was also the first Japanese picture to be a big hit worldwide and it was an even bigger hit on television, garnering huge ratings.

Final Word

Though the Japanese version is superior, Godzilla still owes much of his overseas success to this cleverly done Americanization which is a classic in its own right.

Trivia

- The film was re-released in Japan as *King Monster Godzilla* in 1957 so Japanese audiences could see the new footage with Raymond Burr.

- The movie has a French cousin released in 1957 that runs eight minutes longer and reshuffles some of the Burr footage. In addition to this is another variation of *Godzilla* released in Manila in 1957 as *Tokyo 1960* which inserted new footage of actors from the Philippines.

- Supposedly, rather than "King of the Monsters!", the original subtitle for this film would have made it *Godzilla, the Sea Monster.*

Rodan (1956)

Japanese Title: *Giant Monster of the Sky Radon*
Release Date: December 26, 1956

Directed by: Ishiro Honda
Special Effects by: Eiji Tsuburaya
Screenplay by: Kaoru Mabuchi, Takeo Murata
& Ken Kuronuma
Music by: Akira Ifukube
Cast: Kenji Sahara (Shigeru) Yumi Shirakawa (Kiyo)
Akihiko Hirata (Professor Kashiwagi) Akio Kobori (Chief
Nishimura) **Suit Performers:** Haruo Nakajima (Rodan)

Academy Ratio, Eastmancolor, 82 Minutes

Story
Workers are going missing one by one in the Kyushu mines. Eventually it is discovered the mines are home to prehistoric insects causing the deaths. Shigeru, a miner, becomes lost in a skirmish with the bugs. In the skies days later, a mysterious UFO is being sighted all over the world while people and livestock are going missing. Shigeru is finally found, but in a

catatonic state. Cared for by his lover Kio, Shigeru watches a pair of tiny bird eggs hatch which causes him to flashback to the cave. Surrounded by the giant bugs, he watches as a giant egg hatches a Pterodactyl-like creature which then proceeds to eat the tiny insects. He tells the authorities of the monster which they soon deduct is the UFO. Their suspicions are confirmed when not one, but two of the creatures dubbed Rodan attack Fukuoka. The military attacks the two creatures when they fly back to their lair inducing a volcanic eruption that kills both.

Background & Commentary

Said to have been birthed in a dream of producer Tomoyuki Tanaka, its possible *Rodan* actually has its origins in an unproduced third Godzilla film slated for 1956. Called *The Bride of Godzilla?*, the un-produced script was written by Hideo Unagami (future writer of 1958's *The H-Man*) who spins a wild tale about a doctor who builds a gigantic robot daughter who battles Godzilla, Anguirus and also a giant Archaeopteryx (a type of prehistoric bird). Perhaps not coincidentally, Rodan's early designs looked similar to an Archaeopteryx, and portions of *The Bride of Godzilla?* take place both in Kyushu and in a frightening hollow earth cavern. Whatever the case, horror writer Ken Kuronuma gets credited on the finished script along with Takeo Murata and Kaoru Mabuchi. Kuronuma was inspired to write his draft of *Rodan* from a real life incident in 1948 where a U.S. fighter pilot in pursuit of a UFO crashed and died, hence Rodan first being thought of as a UFO. Whatever *Rodan's* origins in the writing process, the finished film set itself apart from the previous year's *Godzilla Raids Again* as the first dai kaiju eiga filmed in color, and proved that Eiji Tsuburaya had nothing to hide in black and white.

Often thought of as children's films by the mainstream public today, *Rodan's* U.S. poster states: Not Suitable for Children. In this case, the sensational warning is correct. There is a sizeable amount of gore in the film which also has a few genuine moments of horror. Three mining inspectors tied together on a rope are pulled under waist-deep water one by one by an unseen force. The only escapee is tracked down by a giant shadow accompanied by a horrific ringing noise before he meets his inevitable fate. The culprits are later revealed as giant bugs called the Meganeuron, operated via three men in one costume. In long shots using marionettes the giant bugs dart across the screen in a startling manner much like real insects. During a time when *Them!* and other giant bug pictures were popular in the U.S., the Meganeuron easily outdo their American counterparts in viciousness tearing their victims apart in full color. And yet, they're just the opening act. The real star of the show is Rodan, whose first big reveal shows him eating the bugs. Honda's close up on Shigeru as he reacts in horror to Rodan's hatching is an iconic moment in 1950s sci-fi. This flashback sequence actually comes after Rodan's first mysterious appearances—similar to the bugs' in that he is never fully shown. At first he is thought to be a UFO flying at supersonic speeds which engages a jet fighter in a tense scene. Though we don't see the crash, the bloody helmet revealed later is perhaps more effective. Livestock begin mysteriously disappearing into thin air, and a honeymooning couple also vanishes. Only their camera is found which reveals a giant wing. Lacking large arms and legs to tackle buildings with, Rodan's wings are put to good use as he flies over cities catching cars and people in his massive wind streams, some of which produce sonic booms. The amount of detail during the city destruction centerpiece is stunning, as panicked extras can be seen running inside a building as debris falls outside and tiles peel from rooftops in the ensuing windstorms. The film also includes an aerial dogfight between Rodan and a fleet of jet fighters, another highlight of the miniature work Tsuburaya excelled at. At the film's end Rodan chooses to perish alongside his mate, who has been overcome by the smoke, during a volcanic eruption in a strangely touching scene. Actually, part of the scene's touching nature was due to a mistake when the female Rodan's wire broke and the marionette went plummeting to the volcano set. Tsuburaya kept the cameras rolling as the technicians tried to hoist the model up, thus inadvertently giving the impression that the female Rodan was struggling for its life in the fire. For his efforts, Tsuburaya received a Japanese Film Technique

Award for his work on this picture and the film was anpther huge hit in native Japan.

For *Rodan's* U.S. release the film was distributed by King Brothers, who added in a prologue of Atomic testing documentary footage. Otherwise, the film escaped the heavy alteration awarded to *Godzilla, King of the Monsters!* and no American actors are forced into the proceedings. The film was a massive success in America for a Japanese film at that time, receiving a much larger advertising campaign than normal and grossing $500,000 in the New York area alone on its opening weekend. Some trades even claimed it was the highest grossing science fiction film ever up to that time, while other sources say it actually didn't surpass the grosses of *Godzilla, King of the Monsters!* in 1956.

Final Word

While not a cultural cornerstone like the original *Godzilla*, *Rodan* nonetheless was a huge hit on both sides of the Pacific and ushered in a new era of color spectacle and possibilities. And, in spite of his "death," Rodan went on to become an integral part of the Godzilla series as a comical enemy/ally of Godzilla.

Trivia

- Like Godzilla, Rodan carries a different name in Japan: Radon—short for Pteranodon. American distributors feared the film would be associated with radon, so they switched the 'o' and the 'a' thus creating Rodan. Since then, the only two American dubs ever to call Rodan by the name Radon are 1965's *Invasion of Astro-Monster* (though only by Nick Adam's character) and *Godzilla vs. Mechagodzilla II* (1993).

- George Takei, who would go on to star in *Star Trek* as Captain Sulu did a lot of the dubbing for the film, reportedly his first acting job. Asian actor Keye Luke dubbed Shigeru.

- Rodan emits a strange vapor breath from his beak meant to be similar to Godzilla's atomic ray, however, this ability never returns in sequels.

- Ken Kuronuma also wrote a novelization of *Rodan* called "The Birth of Rodan" for *Boys* Magazine. The story mostly follows the film except for the climax, where Rodan is frozen and sinks to the bottom of the sea.

- After the film's release, tourism to Mt. Aso (where Rodan is entombed in the film) saw an increase.

- Famous director Akira Kurosawa, one of Ishiro Honda's friends, looked at the film's script and contributed some ideas involving Rodan and the Meganeuron according to *Toho Special Effects Movie Total History*. It was said it was Kurosawa's suggestion to display Rodan's power by having him eat the menacing Meganeuron, which themselves had been feasting upon humans.

- A 1973 episode of *Ultraman Taro* features a story revolving around a bird monster and prehistoric insects emerging from a volcano in tribute to *Rodan*.

Half Human (1957)

Release Date: May 17, 1957

Directed by: Kenneth G. Krane & Ishiro Honda
Special Effects by: Eiji Tsuburaya
Screenplay by: Takeo Murata & Shigeru Kayama
Music by: Uncredited
Cast: John Carradine (Dr. John Rayburn) Russell Thorson (Prof. Osborne) Robert Karnes (Prof. Templeton) Morris Ankrum (Dr. Johnson) Akira Takarada (Takeshi Ijima) Momoko Kochi (Machiko Takeno) **Suit Performers:** Sanshiro Sagara (Snowman) Takashi Ito (Snowman's son)

Academy Ratio, Black & White, 70 Minutes

Story

When the body of a deceased young snowman is brought back to America, it is autopsied by Dr. Carl Johnson while Dr. John Rayburn recounts the tale of the infant snowman and its father's death in Japan to two of his skeptical colleagues.

Background & Commentary

Unlike *Godzilla, King of the Monsters!*—but very much like 1962's *Varan the Unbelievable*—1957's *Half Human* is a half-baked Americanization of a good Toho monster movie, in this case *Abominable Snowman*. Toho's 1955 monster film was snatched up by Distributors Corp. of America, which ran from 1952 to 1959, and unleashed upon the world such turkeys as *Plan 9 from Outer Space* (1959).

In an attempt to make the film more appealing to American viewers, a new storyline with Caucasian actors was concocted. However, for those hoping to see screen veteran John Carradine (Aaron in *The Ten Commandments* among many other credits) in the Japanese Alps on the trail of the Snowman they will be sourly disappointed. As it turns out upon viewing, Carradine is little more than the film's narrator who sits behind a desk describing nearly every detail of the Japanese footage, presented in flashback form. Though this could have been an intent to mirror the story structure of the original version (which is told to a reporter after the adventure is over) to a degree, it is inferior. Carradine's scenes, which pop up frequently in between the Japanese narrative, eventually become comical for two reasons. For one, every single character smokes like a chimney and talks in the typical dumbed down "golly-gee" 1950s manner; and second, their scenes add absolutely nothing to the story. Furthermore, the Japanese footage is actually so sparsely seen that it was never even dubbed into English! Also, Masaru Sato's wonderful score has also been completely excised in favor of stock tracks.

It would almost seem an effort was made to have you believe this was not a Japanese film at all as far as the credits are concerned, as none of the Japanese cast or crew are credited at all except for Tomoyuki Tanaka at the opening. Only at the picture's end are the proper cast and crew actually credited and some text also reads, "The segments of this picture depicting Japanese people and locales were written and filmed in Japan. Special credit is due to the artists and technicians there who contributed much to the authenticity of this picture." Today, *Half Human's* 1996 VHS release from Rhino Home Video is sadly the only way for many Americans to see footage from Toho's *Abominable Snowman*.

Final Word

Of all the Americanized Toho films over the years, this one is undoubtedly the worst.

Trivia

- Toho shipped the young snowman suit to America for filming of additional scenes of the monster's corpse on an autopsy table surrounded by Carradine and the other new leads.

- The film was double billed with two alternating features: *Monster from Green Hell* and *The Man Without a Body*.

The Mysterians (1957)

Japanese Title: *Earth Defense Force*
Release Date: December 28, 1957

Directed by: Ishiro Honda
Special Effects by: Eiji Tsuburaya
Screenplay by: Kaoru Mabuchi
Music by: Akira Ifukube
Cast: Kenji Sahara (Joji) Yumi Shirakawa (Etsuko) Akihiko Hirata (Ryoichi) Takashi Shimura (Dr. Adachi) Yoshio Tsuchiya (Mysterian leader) **Suit Performers:** Haruo Nakajima/Katsumi Tezuka (Mogera)

Tohoscope, Eastmancolor, 88 Minutes

Story

A series of what appear to be natural disasters begin occurring around the Mt. Fuji area. However, when scientist Ryoichi Shiraishi goes missing his close friend and colleague Joji Atsumi goes looking for him. In the process Joji and his group are attacked by a gigantic robot, Mogera, which proceeds to destroy a local village before being stopped by the military. Soon after aliens called the Mysterians emerge from a dome under the ground and request that Japan give them a large tract of land along with permission to interbreed with Earth's women. An all-out war ensues in which the nations of the world band together to aid Japan in evicting their unwanted visitors. Joji manages to storm the base during the final attack where he is aided by Dr. Shiraishi in rescuing the captive earth women and destroying the base.

Background & Commentary

The Mysterians was a trendsetter for Toho in several ways. Notably it was the studio's first color widescreen SPFX production and it was filmed as a straight Sci-fi extravaganza rather than another dai kaiju eiga. However, Tomoyuki Tanaka insisted that the story feature a monster which initially started out as a subterranean reptile similar to Baragon, though Ishiro Honda insisted the monster be a burrowing robot to show the aliens' technical superiority. Thusly, Toho's first giant robot monster, Mogera, was born. *The Mysterians* also began Eiji Tsuburaya and Toho's love of futuristic weaponry showcased here as two zeppelin type rocket-ships and the Markalites which shoot heat beams. The SPFX are fantastic all around, particularly the final battle where the earth defense forces launch an all-out assault on the Mysterian dome. It offers up Toho's first use of optical ray effects in color, and primitive though they may be in comparison to future works are still a delight. For most the big "crowd pleaser" was still the giant monster Mogera, one of the best kaiju suits of the 1950s era.

Much of the principal cast of both *Godzilla* and *Rodan* reappear in similar roles, though some come with a twist. Again, Akihiko Hirata plays a tormented scientist who sacrifices himself to save the day. However, this scientist has a darker side than Dr. Serizawa and willingly serves the Mysterians for a time to gain scientific knowledge. Kenji Sahara again plays a hero, but has more to do here than Shigeru in *Rodan* as he singlehandedly storms the Mysterian base to rescue his sweetheart (once again Yumi Shirakawa from *Rodan*). Also lending a hand in the production was the Mt. Fuji division of the JSDF who participated in the filming with real tanks and equipment. As such, *The Mysterians* became a favorite film of Toho's to pilfer for realistic military footage in films such as *Godzilla vs. Megalon* (1973). Interestingly, even though the Mysterians are aliens, Honda still interjects a strong anti-nuclear theme through them when it is revealed the Mysterians' home world is destroyed in an atomic civil war. The aliens also mention that there is so much Strontium 90 in their bodies that most of their children are born with defects, hence their desire to breed with earth women.

The influence and success of *The Mysterians* was strong in Japanese cinema. Firstly, it spawned a semi-sequel *Battle in Outer Space* (1959), and many years later the robot Mogera was revamped to be included in *Godzilla vs. Space Godzilla* (1994). That film's SPFX director, Koichi Kawakita, championed *The Mysterians* as one of his favorite SPFX films and campaigned Toho to do a remake going so far as to write a script in 2001. Unfortunately it was never produced.

Final Word
A huge hit in Japan, *The Mysterians* showed that Toho could produce Sci-fi films that were just as enjoyable as their dai-kaiju eiga and guaranteed more Sci-fi SPFX epics would follow from the studio.

Trivia

- Originally the Mysterian dome was supposed to emerge from a lake.

- The film was successfully released in America via RKO in 1958. It was also one of the last films to be distributed theatrically through RKO Pictures.

- In America, Mogera only features in one scene. In the Japanese version there are actually two Mogeras, the second appearing during the film's climax burrowing underground.

- The Mogera suit was kept in storage at Toho until a fire during filming of *Great Prophecies of Nostradamus* in 1974 destroyed it.

- Yoshio Tsuchiya was originally offered the roles of one of the heroes but preferred to play the Mysterian leader.

- Eiji Tsuburaya received another Japanese Film Technique Award for his work on this film.

- *The Mysterians* was the final "main attraction" feature of the last Toho Champion Festival in 1978. It was the oldest film in Toho's library that they ever re-issued for the Champion Festival.

!!!!!!!!!!!!!!!!!!Bonus Review!!!!!!!!!!!!!!!!!!!!

The H-Man (1958)

Japanese Title: *Beauty and the Liquid Man*
Release Date: June 24, 1958

Directed by: Ishiro Honda
Special Effects by: Eiji Tsuburaya
Screenplay by: Kaoru Mabuchi & Hideo Unagami
Music by: Masaru Sato
Cast: Kenji Sahara (Masada) Yumi Shirakawa (Chikako) Eitaro Ozawa (Sgt. Miyashita) Koreya Senda (Dr. Maki) Akihiko Hirata (Tominaga) Yoshio Tsuchiya (Detective Taguchi) Makoto Sato (Uchida)

Tohoscope, Eastmancolor, 87 Minutes

Story

When the suspect in a drug deal gone wrong disappears from the scene leaving only his clothes behind, the police begin tailing the dead man's wife, Chikako, a nightclub singer. Soon a young scientist named Masada puts forth the theory that the man was killed by a new race of mutant humans, the H-Men, which can dissolve anything they touch. Though it takes some convincing, Masada convinces the police of his theory and it is eventually learned the H-Men can be defeated by means of evaporation. Soon several H-Men attack the nightclub where Chikako works, and in the chaos gangster boss Uchida kidnaps the beautiful singer. Taking her to the sewers where he has stashed stolen narcotics, the duo are attacked by the H-Men. Uchida is killed by the creatures though Masada rescues Chikako from the sewers just as they are set fire to in an effort to dissolve the H-Men.

Background & Commentary

In 1953, actor Hideo Unagami pitched a movie to Toho president Iwao Mori. Though Mori rejected the film, either he or Tomoyuki Tanaka liked Mori's pitch enough to task him with writing the third planned Godzilla film, 1955's aborted *Bride of Godzilla?* In 1958, Toho finally began lensing the one script of Mori's that they did accept, *The H-Man*, which he wrote in 1957. Unfortunately for Unagami, the writer/actor had already passed away in November of 1957 after appearing in a small role in the same year's *The Mysterians* as one of the title aliens.

The finished film, scripted by Kaoru Mabuchi and directed by Ishiro Honda, is more or less a yakuza movie with a sci-fi element. Unlike Toho's previous fantasy film, *The Mysterians*, *The H-Man* is a mature (for the time) horror film, complete with gruesome deaths and even dancing girls in skimpy costumes. As for the monstrous H-Men—and despite the singular title there are indeed several H-Men—they are presented as eerie, bluish green, ghost-like figures that dissolve their victims. Ingeniously, to create the dissolving effect of the human victims, Tsuburaya filmed life-sized deflating human blow-up dolls in fast motion, and then ran the shot footage at normal speed. And though not a suitmation performance, everyone's favorite monster Haruo Nakajima naturally portrays one of the H-Men.

The film was released in America in 1959 by Columbia Pictures on a double bill with *The Woman Eater*—a low budget British horror film about a flesh eating tree. The American version cut out eight minutes of footage, mostly to do with the gangster scenes, but was given positive reviews by critics from *Variety* which considered it superior to both *The Mysterians* and *Gigantis, the Fire Monster.*

Final Word
Thanks to its stellar cast of Toho greats, *The H-Man* ranks as one of the studio's better horror films.

Trivia

- Yoshio Tsuchiya claims that, "One of the actors who played [a] Mysterian died of stress from the material of the costume." It is believed he is referring to *The H-Man* writer Hideo Unagami.

- Yumi Shirakawa's singing voice was dubbed by famous Japanese jazz singer Martha Miyake.

Varan (1958)

Alternate Titles: *Giant Monster Varan* (Japan) *Varan the Unbelievable* (U.S.)
Release Date: October 14, 1958

Directed by: Ishiro Honda
Special Effects by: Eiji Tsuburaya
Screenplay by: Shinichi Sekizawa
Music by: Akira Ifukube
Cast: Kozo Nomura (Kenji) Ayumi Sonoda (Yuriko) Koreya Senda (Dr. Sugimoto) Akihiko Hirata (Dr. Fujimura) **Suit Performers:** Haruo Nakajima (Varan)

Tohoscope, Black & White, 87 Minutes

Story

High in the mountains of Japan a rare species of butterfly is found prompting scientists to explore the area. Two of the men are killed mysteriously, prompting a reporter, a photographer, and one of the dead men's sisters to investigate. There they find a small village hostile to outsiders that insist the nearby lake is home to the monster Varan. The creature soon emerges and crushes the small village. The government sends the military to attack the monster but it surprises them by jumping into the air and flying away. It attacks a fishing fleet at sea and later battles the navy but it is to no avail; the creature reaches Tokyo and begins laying an airport to waste. The military devises a plan to trick Varan into swallowing a new experimental type of explosive. The plan succeeds and the wounded monster retreats to the sea where it explodes.

Background & Commentary

Akira Ifukube's stirring violin chords that accompany the opening Tohoscope logo promise a wonderful film, but the proceedings never quite match the masterful music. Perhaps this is due in part to *Varan's* origins as an American TV movie. Due to the high ratings received by *Godzilla, King of the Monsters!* first TV Broadcast, AB-PT Pictures Corporation (a division of ABC) enlisted Toho to create a new monster film just for television. Unfortunately for Toho, who had begun to lens the picture, ABC backed out. Despite this fact, Tomoyuki Tanaka decided to go on with the production and turn it into a widescreen release. Ishiro Honda explained the film's switch to widescreen to David Milner like this, "After we had shot five or six scenes in the standard 35mm format required for television, Toho decided to show the movie in theaters as well as on television. We at first planned to simply re-shoot the scenes in the wider cinemascope format used in theaters, but we were in a rush. So, we just cropped the existing film to fit the cinemascope format." Had it not already begun filming in black and white, it probably would've been a color release as well. The fact that this was never scripted (or budgeted) to be a big feature shows in terms of the casting and the rather simple story that exists to set-up the monster's rampages and nothing else. For instance, Toho stalwart Akihiko Hirata only appears briefly in the third act as the inventor of the explosives that unimaginatively kill the monster who conveniently likes to swallow flares dropped from planes. That being said, the script's debut writer, Shinichi Sekizawa, would go on to pen most of Toho's future classics such as *Mothra* and *King Kong vs. Godzilla* even if his work here is somewhat lackluster.

The main standout of *Varan* is its musical score by Ifukube. Even though this is Ifukube's third kaiju film scored for Toho it raised the bar for what was to come. Many of the themes composed for *Varan* would be reused, tweaked, and perfected to become classic themes in the 1960s and even the 1990s Godzilla series. His work on *Varan* also precedes several well-known western composers. At one point Ifukube uses a simple but effective composition of cello strings similar to John William's *Jaws* theme as Varan approaches a small boat of unsuspecting fishermen. Ifukube precedes Williams again with a main title theme sung by a male chorus that evokes *Indiana Jones and the Temple of Doom*.

Despite the smaller budget, Varan is one of the best monster suits Eiji Tsuburaya ever produced. The arms and legs have the illusion of realistic muscles rather than the baggy, loose rubber that usually gives it away that it is a man in a suit walking about. The monster looks good in both its quadruped and bipedal stances, though the former is actually better. At one point Varan jumps into the sky and glides away on membranes between his forearms and hind legs (oddly, this well staged sequence was cut from the American version). Tsuburaya, whose early work involved miniatures for several WWII films, demonstrates his masterful skills during the navy attack on Varan with battleship models that are incredibly realistic for the time. Unfortunately the budget only allowed for a limited amount of city destruction scenes and the model set of Haneda Airport was the only Tokyo miniature built. These scenes are also intercut with stock footage from *Godzilla*. As in the case of *Godzilla, King of the Monsters!*, the film was heavily reedited for its release in the U.S. in 1962 by Crown International Pictures as *Varan the*

Unbelievable which inserted new footage of actor Myron Healey into the proceedings.

Final Word
On a technical level (aside from a few instances of stock footage) the film excels, but its script has no spirit and sadly doesn't go anywhere. Its monster star deserved much better, but Varan would only return for a brief cameo ten years later in *Destroy All Monsters*.

Trivia

- Once again the original story for *Varan* came from horror novelist Ken Kuronuma.

The Birth of Japan (1959)

Alternate Titles: *The Three Treasures* (U.S.)
Release Date: October 25, 1959

Directed by: Hiroshi Inagaki
Special Effects by: Eiji Tsuburaya
Screenplay by: Toshio Hachiju & Ryuzo Kikushima
Music by: Akira Ifukube
Cast: Toshiro Mifune (Yamato Takeru/Susanoo) Yoko Tsukasa (Princess Oto Tachibana) Akihiko Hirata (Kibino Takehiko) Kyoko Kagawa (Princess Miyazu) Takashi Shimura (Elder Kumaso) Akira Takarada (Prince Wakatarashi) Akira Kubo (Prince Iogi) Eijiro Tono (Ootomo) Kumi Mizuno (Azami) Misa Uehara (Princess Kushinada) Ganjiro Nakamura (Emperor) Haruko Sugimura (Narrator)

Tohoscope, Eastmancolor, 181 Minutes

Story
In fourth century Japan, Prince Ouso catches his brother having an affair with one of his father's palace girls, and sends him away. Ouso's enemies make it appear that he has killed

his own brother, and so his father sends the prince off to die on a suicide mission. Instead Prince Ouso returns victorious under the new name of Yamato Takeru—"the strongest man." However, his enemies still plot against him and in a final ambush by his enemies, Yamato Takeru and his men are all killed. However, in death Takeru's spirit transforms into a white bird and flies over Mt. Fuji causing it to erupt and swallow his enemies.

Background & Commentary

Though films like *Gorath*, *Atragon* and *The Mysterians* are often grouped in with Toho's monster films, *The Birth of Japan* oddly is not despite being a fantasy film featuring a monster which has as much screen time as Magma, Manda or Mogera. This is perhaps because the monster, Orochi the eight headed dragon, is eclipsed by the film's lavish production and leading man Toshiro Mifune. Produced as Toho's 1000th feature and budgeted at ¥250 million, the film has since become known as "*The Ten Commandments* of Japan" due to its epic running length and religious nature.

Though a historical drama of sorts, the film has a cornucopia of SPFX scenes and elaborate sets. And just as much as the monster, for SPFX fans the sets are some of the true stars of the film, notably Tsuburaya's interpretation of the Japanese equivalent of Mt. Olympus. As for Orochi, the eight headed sea snake is an inferior precursor to King Ghidorah, which pulsated with life in 1964. Here, Orochi's mouths are always agape and never move giving the heads an impression of lifelessness. The battle between it and Susanoo is more or less the Japanese marionette equivalent to the climax of 1963's *Jason and the Argonauts*. The scene is actually one of several mythological flashbacks/vignettes of which this film is frequently interspersed with. In fact, these segments at first seem only to be folktales which the main characters believe in. This is perhaps further emphasized due to the fact that Mifune himself plays dual roles as Yamato Takeru and the mythical Susanoo. That these fairy tales turn out to be "true" in the context of the film is only fully confirmed in the climax, when Yamato Takeru is killed and transforms into an animated white bid which causes the eruption of Mt. Fuji. This climax is quite similar to both the Hal Roach 1940 *One Million B.C.* and its 1966 remake's ending as people are swallowed up into the ground and overtaken by walls of lava.

The Birth of Japan was a sizeable hit grossing ¥344,320,000. The film was not surprisingly a little too Japanese for western audiences and saw only limited release as the 112 minute *The Three Treasures* via Toho International. The film was remade as the high budgeted but poorly received monster fest *Yamato Takeru* in 1994.

Final Word

Though a good film for those interested in Japanese history and mythology, western kaiju fans will find it of interest mostly for Orochi itself and Tsuburaya's eruption of Mt. Fuji.

Trivia

- In the "Japanese Mt. Olympus" can be glimpsed many familiar faces from Ichiro Arishima to Eisei Amamoto.

- 10 tons of water was used for the flood scene.

!!!!!!!!!!!!!!!!!!Bonus Review!!!!!!!!!!!!!!!!!!!!!

Battle in Outer Space (1959)

Japanese Title: *Great Space War*
Release Date: December 26, 1959

Directed by: Ishiro Honda
Special Effects by: Eiji Tsuburaya
Screenplay by: Shinichi Sekizawa
Music by: Akira Ifukube
Cast: Ryo Ikebe (Major Katsumiya) Kyoko Anzai (Etsuko) Koreya Senda (Dr. Adachi) Yoshio Tsuchiya (Iwamura) Minoru Takada (the Commander) Harold Conway (Dr. Immerman)

Tohoscope, Eastmancolor, 96 Minutes

Story

Aliens from the Planet Natal destroy an orbiting satellite above the earth which prompts the nations of the world to form a task force to deal with the aliens. Two rocket-ships head for the moon to take the fight to the aliens, but things take an unexpected turn when the aliens possess one of their own, Ikomura. While most of the team is away attacking the Natal Moon Base, Ikomura destroys one of the rocket-ships. However, when the Natal Moon Base is destroyed he returns to his senses and sacrifices himself so that his comrades can escape the remaining aliens. A dogfight between earth based rocket ships and the alien saucers commence in the earth's atmosphere and the aliens are eventually defeated.

Background & Commentary

While *Battle in Outer Space* is indeed a spiritual sequel to *The Mysterians* and inspired by that film's success, it is hotly debated whether or not this is indeed an in continuity sequel to the aforementioned film. "Returning" from *The Mysterians* are the characters of Dr. Adachi and Etsuko, now played by Koreya Senda and Kyoko Anzai respectively, while Harold Conway does return as Dr. Immerman. Japanese websites attest that Takashi Shimura and Yumi Shirakawa were unable to return to reprise the roles and so were recast. Tokusatsu historians Steve Ryfle and Ed Godziszewski argue that the film isn't actually a sequel to *The Mysterians*, though early drafts of the script were intended to be, and only when the script was later reworked the old character names were kept. In either case, it's hard to say whether or not this film surpasses *The Mysterians* in quality. On the one hand it is a much livelier affair with the second half of the whole film being one straight battle—including ray gun fights on the moon and spaceship dogfights above earth's atmosphere. On the other hand, there is less character development, particularly among the aliens, represented only by a mysterious disembodied voice. This specter would be more frightening if not for the aliens' lone physical appearance later in the film represented by a group of dwarf-like creatures in space suits which, creepy though they may be, are not the least bit physically intimidating.

Akira Ifukube composes some of his very best themes for this film. If the music sounds familiar to Godzilla fans, this is because when Ifukube declined to score 1972's *Godzilla vs. Gigan* Tomoyuki Tanaka lifted Ifukube tracks, notably the main theme from *Battle in Outer Space,* to score the film. Ifukube himself reworked a few of his *Battle in Outer Space* themes for future Toho SPFX films, including *Terror of Mechagodzilla* (1975). On the SPFX front Eiji Tsuburaya devises a new and spectacular way to destroy Tokyo when the aliens literally suck buildings into the air in a sort of gravity vortex. Nor is the destruction confined to Tokyo, but in a refreshing twist miniatures of New York and San Francisco are also destroyed by the aliens. This international appeal extends to the cast as well, which is made up of a fairly balanced group of Japanese and Caucasians. This wasn't exclusively a means of boosting the film's international appeal, but rather Ishiro Honda's wish to show the nations of the world uniting to battle a common foe.

Though this film was a big hit in Japan (and had a successful theatrical release in America from Columbia Pictures in July of 1960), strangely Toho didn't get around to doing another alien invasion film until 1965's Godzilla opus *Invasion of Astro-Monster.* Curiously, from that point on, the alien invaders would stick to the Godzilla series until 1977's *The War in Space*—initially called *Battle in Outer Space 2.*

Final Word
One of Toho's great SPFX films, it manages to stand on its own without any giant monsters to prop it up.

Trivia

- Another of the reasons fans assume this film to be a sequel to *The Mysterians* is the fact that Eiji Tsuburaya reused the Mysterian spaceships for the Natal aliens.

- The "futuristic" looking Science Center was actually the newly constructed Japan National Sports Center.

Mothra (1961)

Alternate Titles: *Mothra the Indestructible* (Mexico) *Mothra Threatens the World* (Germany)
Release Date: July 30, 1961

Directed by: Ishiro Honda
Special Effects by: Eiji Tsuburaya
Screenplay by: Shinichi Sekizawa, Shinichiro Nakamura, Takehiko Fukunaga & Yoshie Hotta
Music by: Yuji Koseki
Cast: Frankie Sakai (Senichiro) Kyoko Kagawa (Michi) Hiroshi Koizumi (Chujo) Jerry Ito (Nelson) Emi & Yumi Ito (the Shobijin) Masamitsu Tayama (Shinji) Takashi Shimura (Editor) **Suit Performers:** Haruo Nakajima/Hiroshi Sekida/Uncredited (Mothra Larva)

Tohoscope, Eastmancolor, 101 Minutes

Story

An expedition to Infant Island in the South Seas discovers a native population seemingly immune to radiation presided over by small twin fairies. Nelson, the smarmy expedition leader, kidnaps the girls and puts them on display in Japan making a fortune off of them. Two of the men from the expedition, Senichiro, a reporter, and Chujo, a linguist, team with photographer Michi to try and free the girls to no avail. Soon Mothra, a giant caterpillar which happens to be the fairies' guardian comes looking for them. It then demolishes Tokyo and spins a cocoon there. Later, it emerges as a giant butterfly which flies to Rolisica, Nelson's native country where he has taken refuge, and begins destroying New Kirk City. With help from Chujo, Senichiro, and Michi, the fairies are rescued from Nelson who is killed by the police. Mothra and the fairies are reunited at an airstrip and then fly back to Infant Island and the natives.

Background & Commentary

The opening widescreen color Toho-Scope logo that opens *Mothra* is a beautiful sight accompanied to melodic music. Unlike a similar ambitious opening to *Varan,* the proceedings are by no means a letdown and *Mothra* delivers on all levels. The film excels as both whimsical fantasy, with the many onstage musical numbers by the fairies, and adventure via the island exploration scenes and Mothra's destruction of both Tokyo and the fictional New Kirk City. As a fantasy *Mothra* veers away from Honda's typical documentary style direction with touches of humor and whimsy, yet still delves into the subject of nuclear fallout. In an early scene undercutting past fears of the Lucky Dragon incident, the crew of a boat caught in a typhoon are more worried about their proximity to Infant Island, the site of a recent nuclear test, than they are the storm. However, the island and its natives end up being the shipwrecked-survivors' saviors, providing them with a mysterious juice that prevents them from getting radiation poisoning. It should be noted that Mothra and her fairies are not the result of atomic mutation, but are implied to be divine figures, though their exact origins are never elaborated upon. These twin fairies, played by pop singers Emi and Yumi Ito (known as "the Peanuts"), are as much a focus in the film as Mothra is. The duo was contracted with Columbia Records, who insisted they be featured in *Mothra*. As *Mothra*'s original script actually featured four fairies, it's possible this casting decision nixed the other two. The Peanuts would reprise the roles in two films in the Godzilla series, and although many actresses have since portrayed Mothra's fairies, the Peanuts remain the definitive personages of the roles. Most people will be surprised to know Akira Ifukube did not provide the wonderful score for this, the most musical of all Toho's monster films. Instead, Yuji Koseki was chosen because he had already written songs for the Peanuts and was considered a better fit.

The film features a human villain, Clark Nelson, a first for a Toho monster film. As Nelson, Jerry Ito delivers his lines well in both Japanese and English, a rarity for gaijin actors. In addition to kidnapping the fairies, Nelson also murders many of the islanders. Dirty to the end, he even wrestles a cane away from an old man as he is shot by the police and, all in all, makes for a memorable villain from a Caucasian superpower. Knowing American villains would sour the film's chances for success stateside, Toho decided to have their cake and eat it too by simply renaming America

"Rolisica." The many Caucasian actors running about New Kirk City and its familiar landmarks can't hide the fact that it is a stand in for New York. Yet, this was ironically one of the earliest Toho pictures to be backed financially by an American studio, Columbia Pictures, which distributed it in the U.S. as well. Thanks to Columbia, the film was Toho's most epic production to date with the largest miniatures Tsuburaya had ever created. The Mothra larva suit was nearly forty feet long, though there also existed a much smaller marionette. Some of the best SPFX sequences are overhead shots of the Mothra larva representing POV shots from the jet fighters. The film also introduces what would later evolve into one of Tsuburaya's most famed creations: the Atomic Heat Ray (later called Maser Tanks) that attempts to roast Mothra in her cocoon. In the film's signature scene, Nelson begins to laugh at the news of Mothra's "demise" and taunts the fairies who begin to sing a melody just as the adult Mothra emerges from the cocoon and spreads her gossamer wings for the first time (the scene would be recreated in future entries of the Godzilla series, notably 1992's *Godzilla and Mothra: The Battle for Earth*). Mothra's following devastation of New Kirk City in a windstorm is a masterpiece of miniature work. This is again thanks to Columbia Pictures who provided the funding for the massive set, and also the fact that Tsuburaya had some practice with flying monsters thanks to *Rodan*. The film has a partially shot alternate ending in which Mothra was scripted to force Nelson's escaping plane to land in the Japanese mountains. She then intimidates Nelson off of a cliff where he falls to his death. Jerry Ito and the actors actually filmed the scenes, but the SPFX portion of the shoot was scrapped when Columbia allocated extra funds for the more elaborate destruction of New Kirk City instead.

An ambitious production for Toho Studios with a ¥200 million budget, *Mothra* had begun life as a story in *Weekly Asahi* called *Mothra and Her Luminous Fairies* by Shinichiro Nakamura, Takehiko Fukunaga and Yoshie Hotta. Iwao Mori and other Toho bigwigs hoped the new production could be Toho's "third big monster" after Godzilla and Rodan while also appealing to women. As hoped it was a hit in the U.S. and in native Japan, where it drew 9 million admissions, nearly as many as 1954's *Godzilla*. Mothra would go on to become a star player in the Godzilla sequels, and was Toho's go to monster whenever they felt the series needed a boost in attendance.

Final Word

Though the term classic is used loosely these days, *Mothra* fully deserves the distinction.

Trivia

- The fictional country of Rolisica is meant to represent both Russia and America, hence the name.

- Mothra was originally meant to spin her cocoon around the Diet Building (Japan's parliament building), an idea which is used in 1992's *Godzilla and Mothra: The Battle for Earth*.

- In the Toho cafeteria during filming "Mothra larva bread rolls" and "Mothra eggs" were served.

- Along with *Godzilla* and *Gorath*, Ishiro Honda considers *Mothra* one of his favorite films.

- For the alternate ending where Mothra blows Nelson off of a cliff with her wings, Honda and crew threw a dummy off the side of a mountain but never retrieved it. Later some climbers spotted it and called the police resulting in a rescue mission for the dummy!

- Twins were a rarity in Japan which made the Ito sisters superstars as the performing duo the Peanuts; recording many hit records in Japan. They even appeared on *The Ed Sullivan Show* in America in addition to hosting their own variety show in Japan.

- Kenji Sahara has a cameo as a helicopter pilot.

- This is the first Japanese kaiju eiga in which the monster isn't killed or defeated in some way and returns home peacefully.

- Mothra was the first Toho monster to spin onto the Godzilla series, and also the first (and only) monster to spin back off from the Godzilla series in *Rebrith of Mothra* (1996).

!!!!!!!!!!!!!!!!!!!!*Bonus Review!!!!!!!!!!!!!!!!!!!!!*

The Last War (1961)

Alternate Titles: *The Last War of the Apocalypse* (France) *Death Rays from Outer Space* (Germany)
Release Date: October 08, 1961

Directed by: Shue Matsubayasahi
Special Effects by: Eiji Tsuburaya
Screenplay by: Kaoru Mabuchi & Toshio Yasumi
Music by: Dan Ikuma
Cast: Frankie Sakai (Mokichi Tamura) Akira Takarada (Takano) Yuriko Hoshi (Saeko Tamura) Nobuko Otowa (Mother Tamura) Yumi Shirakawa (Sanae) Shu Ryuchi (Ehara) Jerry Ito (Watkins)

Tohoscope, Eastmancolor, 110 Minutes

Story
Mokichi Tamura is a simple but ambitious limo driver who works hard to provide for his family, and he has begrudgingly just given his daughter Saeko permission to marry her sweetheart, the naval officer Takano. All the while, the two world super powers, the Federation and the Alliance, stockpile nuclear weapons as Cold War tensions rise. When an accident starts World War III, Tokyo is one of the first cities slated to be destroyed. The Tamura family chooses not to evacuate and enjoys one last dinner together before the city is destroyed, while Takano helplessly watches Tokyo destroyed from the sea.

Background & Commentary

For fans of the military confrontations in the Godzilla films, in terms of SPFX, *The Last War* essentially amounts to a two hour version of one of those scenes, only instead of battling Godzilla, the miniature tanks and fighter jets of Tsuburaya battle each other. However, in terms of human drama it naturally far eclipses the Godzilla films. In fact, it is a very powerful film and has an even greater anti-nuclear message than *Godzilla* (1954).

The film's heart and soul is comedic actor Frankie Sakai, who works hard to provide for his wife and three children. Contrasting the dreams of this simple man are the escalating tensions of two world super powers, obvious stand-ins for the U.S. and the Soviets, named the Federation and the Alliance. Though some say Sakai was miscast, seeing a cheerful comedic actor in such a tragic film makes it all the more powerful. The best scene involves Sakai and his family in a deserted Tokyo, evacuated due to threats of nuclear war, having one last family dinner together. Sakai remains in a state of denial, reminding his sick wife to take her medicine even though it is pointless while his eldest daughter pines for her husband, played by Akira Takarada, who is out to sea. Finally Sakai has a breakdown feeling that all his hard work has been for nothing. And then the film pulls no punches, for when the nukes fly, it is for real—there is no epilogue revealing it all to be a dream or a "what if" scenario as in *Great Prophecies of Nostradamus* (1974). Sakai and his loveable family do in fact perish in Tokyo, and adding to the tragedy is the fact that Akira Takarada actually survives because he is out to sea, knowing full well his wife must be dead. Furthermore, he and his shipmates all decide to return to Tokyo even though they know it means a slow death due to radiation poisoning.

The SPFX in this film are somewhat hit and miss unless one is a diehard miniature enthusiast. There are a bevy of fantastic miniature sets, from nuclear missile bases in the North Pole to nearly every famous landmark imaginable—including the Kremlin, the Statue of Liberty, the Arc De Triumph and more—exploding spectacularly. In this sense, the film is like a much more poignant version of a Roland Emmerich disaster film, albeit set in the 1960s. This film was released just after a similar film from Toei, *The Final War* in 1960, though *The Last War* has the edge on its competitor due to being filmed in color along with Tsuburaya's effects work. *The Last War* played semi-frequently on American TV throughout the 1960s but never secured a theatrical release.

Final Word
A film that deserves to be recognized as more iconic than it is, and it ironically beats *Godzilla* (1954) as one of the greatest anti-nuke films of all time.

Trivia

- This film was loosely remade in 1974 as part of the inspiration for *Great Prophecies of Nostradamus.*

- Frankie Sakai reunites with his co-star from *Mothra*, Jerry Ito, in this film.

- Though many western fans think *Latitude Zero* (1969) was the first time Akira Takarada spoke English in a film, it was actually this picture in which he converses with Jerry Ito's reporter character in English for one scene.

- Yuriko Hoshi and Akira Takarada play sweethearts in this film, though they were later reteamed as a pair of bickering platonic co-workers in *Mothra vs. Godzilla* (1964).

Gorath (1962)

Japanese Title: *Gorath, the Monstrous Star*
Release Date: March 21, 1962

Directed by: Ishiro Honda
Special Effects by: Eiji Tsuburaya
Screenplay by: Kaoru Mabuchi
Music by: Akira Ifukube

Cast: Ryo Ikebe (Dr. Tazawa) Yumi Shirakawa (Tomoko) Akira Kubo (Kanai) Takashi Shimura (Kensuke) Kenji Sahara (Saiki) Kumi Mizuno (Takiko) Jun Tazaki (Capt. Sonoda) **Suit Performers:** Haruo Nakajima/Katsumi Tezuka (Magma)

Tohoscope, Eastmancolor, 88 Minutes

Story

A research ship, the JX-1, is sent to investigate a mysterious star, dubbed Gorath, hurtling towards the earth. Unfortunately Gorath's mass is so large the ship is unable to escape the star's gravity, but before it is destroyed the crew manages to warn earth of the star's trajectory. As nuclear weapons aren't enough to destroy the star, the nations of the world instead band together in the South Pole to build a large rocket propulsion system powerful enough to move the earth out of Gorath's path. The plan is a success and the earth is moved, but Gorath's gravitational pull still causes great damage as it passes by earth, but at least the planet will survive.

Background & Commentary

Hot off the 1961 successes of the big budget fantasy *Mothra* and the pessimistic disaster film *The Last War*, Toho concocted an interesting sort of fusion for their next picture: a downbeat disaster film with *Mothra's* fantasy element. Feeling confident in the production, Toho allocated an even bigger budget than the previous two films and a nearly yearlong production process for their new SPFX epic *Gorath*, about a colossal asteroid on a collision course with earth.

    Gorath is unusual for its time in that the film has a downbeat, apocalyptic atmosphere more akin to disaster films of the 1970s. This atmosphere is best exemplified through Akira Kubo's astronaut character, who starts the picture youthful and enthusiastic, but becomes stricken with amnesia once he gets too close to Gorath during a mission in space. Kubo then spends the rest of the picture detached and depressed until he regains his memory after Gorath passes earth. In addition to Kubo (whom Toho was grooming as an up and comer), *Gorath* boasts fellow newcomer Kumi Mizuno and Toho stalwarts Ryo Ikebe, Takashi Shimura, Yumi Shirakawa, Jun Tazaki and Kenji Sahara giving the film a top notch cast. Jun Tazaki is particularly good as the captain of the doomed JX-1, who knows his ship's final fate well before anyone else. As with *The Mysterians*, Tomoyuki Tanaka also requested a monster be present, though Honda was reluctant to include any kaiju in the story (and many years later in interviews indicated he still regretted the monster's inclusion). Honda was right to not want the kaiju in the film on the one hand, as the monster walrus Magma adds nothing to the story. In fact, in a surprise move, the American distributer removed all scenes featuring Magma (they reportedly called him "Wally the Walrus") and it didn't impact the story at all. The poorly executed kaiju walrus pops up out of nowhere in the film's final act, and is easily dispatched within ten minutes. On the other hand though, Magma's inclusion in the film has kept *Gorath* well known in kaiju circles. The real monster of the film is the titular giant asteroid Gorath, constantly pulsating with a menacing apocalyptic orange and red. The star doesn't truly get its chance to "shine" until the third act when it strips Saturn of its rings as it passes by and also obliterates the moon. Tsuburaya's best work in the film occurs when the star's massive gravitational pull causes Tokyo to be submerged in a massive flood.

Though *Gorath* isn't well known in the U.S., it was another hit in Japan for Toho. *Gorath* was also one of Ishiro Honda's favorite films alongside *Godzilla* and *Mothra*. The reason for this was that unlike the frightening *The Last War* (where the world is obliterated), *Gorath* carried a positive message of world peace where the nations of the world set aside their differences and join forces to move the earth out of harm's way.

Final Word

Though there have been numerous films about asteroids on a collision course with earth, perhaps it's only natural that when Toho made such a picture the asteroid would be a kaiju-sized equivalent!

Trivia

- Eiji Tsuburaya was so impressed with art staff member Tsugizo Murase's use of poly resin to make Magma's tusks he thought they were real ivory.

- *Gorath* was double-billed in the U.S. with another Toho SPFX film, *The Human Vapor*, in 1964.

- Magma was originally more reptilian and had scales. The monster was also scripted to return as part of the kaiju ensemble of 1968's *Destroy All Monsters* before being removed.

- Kenji Sahara had a broken leg during production, but Ishiro Honda insisted he play the character of Saiki and no one else rather than recast him.

The Whale God (1962)

Release Date: July 15, 1962

Directed by: Tokuzo Tanaka
Special Effects by: Chikara Komatsubara, Takesaburo Watanabe & Hiroshi Ishida
Screenplay by: Kaneto Shindo
Music by: Akira Ifukube
Cast: Katsu Shintaro (Kishu) Kojiro Hongo (Shaki) Kyoko Enami (Toyo) Fujimura Shiho (Ei) Takashi Shimura (Village Elder) Fujiwara Reiko (Okoma)

Daieiscope, Black & White, 100 Minutes

Story

Early in the Meiji era, on the coast of Kyushu, every year a huge whale appears that kills dozens of fishermen in its wake. The village elder offers up his title, his estate, and his daughter, Toyo, to the man who kills the whale god. Shaki, whose grandfather, father and older brother have all been killed by the beast, is the first to volunteer. However, Shaki is soon challenged by vulgar drifter Kishu, who says he will be the one to kill the whale. As winter sets in, the whale swims to other waters while the village both dreads and eagerly awaits its return. In the interim, Shaki's girlfriend Ei is raped by a stranger and gives birth to a baby who Shaki decides to raise even though he knows is not his. When the whale returns, Kishu is killed when he defies Shaki's claim to the whale and attacks it first. Shaki then swims for the whale, climbs atop its head, and stabs it until it dies from blood loss. Shaki awakens days later a hero, but he is dying. Laying next to the whale god in a coffin, Ei reveals to Shaki that Kishu was the man who raped her. Shaki beseeches her to forgive his dead rival, and as Shaki slips away into death he proclaims that he will come back as the next whale god.

Background & Commentary

Often described as the Japanese film adaptation of *Moby Dick*, this is only half right. Daiei's *The Whale God* (*Kujira Gami*) began life as a novel of the same name by Koichiro Uji published in July of 1961. The book won the 46th Akutagawa Award, garnering the attention of Daiei Studios which payed ¥1 million for the screen rights. Within a year, Daiei had adapted the book into film and released it in July of 1962.

Daiei's giant whale compares favorably with the one from the 1956 *Moby Dick*, and surprisingly appears in the very first scene. That the whale appears early on is for the best, because it doesn't resurface until the film's climax. Also, had the whale not yet appeared, the anticipation for the beast could have become so high as to be a letdown. The bulk of SPFX filming, naturally, took place in Daiei's big pool in Kyoto. Though Chikara Komatsubara is credited with the lion's share of effects work, supposedly it was director Tanaka himself who oversaw most of it. Fuminori Ohashi constructed a scale Kujira Gami prop said to be over 30 meters in length for filming which cost around ¥8 million. In addition to this was a smaller 5.5 meter model as well. Unfortunately, these large scale models suffered from very limited mobility, and so the bulk of filming was done with a small model created by Ryosaku Takayama. That being said, naturally the full scale model was used for scenes with the actors, and the 5.5 meter model was used for diving scenes.

In between whale scenes the film is carried well by its period human drama, mainly revolving around Shaki (Kojiro Hongo) and Kishu (Katsu Shintaro), who has raped and gotten Shaki's girlfriend Ei (Fujimura Shiho) pregnant. However, Shaki is unaware of this until the very final scene, after Kishu has been killed by the whale, and Shaki lays dying himself in a coffin next to the now decapitated whale god that he killed. The coffin, naturally, is a nod to Queequeg's coffin from *Moby Dick*. There is also an interesting moment where, before the final hunt, Shaki looks back on his wife and surrogate child as if to ask himself whether his vengeance is still worth it. But it is too late, and he must carry out his oath to kill the whale, and in the end it costs him his life. These scenes are complimented further by the black and white photography, and *The Whale God* arguably fares better in this medium than it would have in color. Overall, Akira Ifukube's moody score and the movie's dark color pallet combine to make a wonderfully atmospheric film.

Final Word
Though thought of more so as a straight forward drama than a kaiju film, this could still be considered one of the best dai kaiju eigas that westerners have yet to see.

Trivia

- Technically, Kujira Gami predates both Gamera and Nezura as the first kaiju created by Daiei.

- Internet rumors circulate of an unmade Daiei take on Toho's *Destroy All Monsters* which would have featured Kujira Gami and giant rat Nezura aiding Gamera in a battle to save earth from a combined Viran/Zigran invasion. Kujira Gami was to have battled a Zigran in the waters off of New York. However, this synopsis was dreamed up by the author of an official Gamera book, *You Are Strong, Gamera!*, but was not a Daiei script.

- Kojiro Hongo and Kyko Enami would reteam four years later for *Gamera vs. Barugon* (1966).

- Kujira Gami's roar was later adapted to become one of Guiron's roars for *Gamera vs. Guiron* (1969).

King Kong vs. Godzilla (1962)

Alternate Titles: *The Triumph of King Kong* (Italy) *The Return of King Kong* (Germany)
Release Date: August 11, 1962

Directed by: Ishiro Honda
Special Effects by: Eiji Tsuburaya
Screenplay by: Shinichi Sekizawa
Music by: Akira Ifukube
Cast: Tadao Takashima (Sakurai) Kenji Sahara (Fujita) Mie Hama (Fumiko) Yu Fujuki (Kinsaburo) Akiko Wakabayashi (Tamiye) Ichiro Arishima (Mr. Tako) Jun Tazaki (JSDF General) **Suit Performers:** Shoichi Hirose (King Kong) Haruo Nakajima/Katsumi Tezuka (Godzilla)

Tohoscope, Eastmancolor, 98 Minutes

Story

A pharmaceutical company sets off to distant Faero Island to harvest strange red berries with powerful medicinal properties. They get more than they bargained for when they discover the giant ape King Kong on the island as well. After he battles a giant octopus, the natives drug Kong with red berry juice and the monster falls asleep. The explorers use the opportunity to capture Kong, who they hope to use as a publicity stunt. At the same time, Godzilla breaks free of an iceberg and heads for Japan. Kong, also in route to Japan via ocean liner, escapes and heads for Japan on his own. The country isn't big enough for both monsters who cross paths, but Kong is intimidated by Godzilla's atomic ray. Kong heads for Tokyo and wreaks havoc until the pharmaceutical company uses the berries to put him to sleep. With Kong out cold, the military decides the best way to deal with both monsters is to put them together and let them fight it out. Kong is airlifted to Mt. Fuji where he battles Godzilla once more, this time emerging as the victor.

Background & Commentary

Godzilla's return to the big screen in 1962 would seem to revolve solely around King Kong. The giant ape's creator, Willis O'Brien, had just authored a potential King Kong sequel entitled *King Kong vs. Prometheus*. In the story, Kong would do battle with a Frankenstein-style monster (stitched together from various African animals) in San Francisco when both monsters are brought there for a boxing match! O'Brien's script was picked up by Universal-International Producer John Beck. Unable to find any studio interest in America, Beck was directed to Toho in Japan by RKO Pictures (the rights holder to Kong, and also the recent U.S. distributer of Toho's *The Mysterians*). Toho was more than happy to helm the production but tossed out Frankenstein's monster in favor of Godzilla. As Toho's 30th Anniversary was looming, they had hoped to resurrect Godzilla, and a bout with King Kong would make things even better. Bringing in Kong wasn't without its shortcomings. Beck convinced Toho to foot the entire bill for Kong's expensive license fee from RKO Pictures. As such, most of the film's budget ended up being eaten up by Kong's licensing fees which totaled over $220,000. The SPFX budget was drastically reduced and planned on location filming in Sri Lanka was scrapped. On the bright side though, finally returning to the director's chair would be Ishiro Honda and his composer of choice Akira Ifukube, after missing out on the chance to participate in *Godzilla Raids Again* (1955). The resulting film would end up being the first time that both Kong and Godzilla were filmed in widescreen and color. It was also the third film, and second sequel, for both beasts overall.

As for the resulting film's critical merits, it differs from its predecessors in that there is no nuclear subtext, just pure popcorn entertainment. Whereas the American version opens gravely to a fake spinning earth model presented with a quote from Hamlet, in the Japanese version the camera pans back from the same cheesy earth prop to reveal it is merely the opening logo for an equally cheesy television show making clear the film's satiric intentions. The switch to comedy likely happened after the film's budget was cut and thus screenwriter Shinichi Sekizawa, who had penned the successful light fantasy *Mothra* (1961), was instructed to write the new film with a light satiric tone. Also trying to repeat the success of *Mothra* which featured comedy star Frankie Sakai in the lead, and to further hit home that this film was intended as a comedy, Tadao Takashima and Yu Fujuki (a popular duo in Toho's "salary-man" comedies) were cast in lead roles along with Ichiro Arishima (the "Charlie Chaplin of Japan"). The funniest scene occurs when the pharmaceutical executives win the island natives over by giving them all cigarettes, including the children. Godzilla and Kong are surprisingly also played for laughs, but the two monsters actually fair better than the human cast in this respect at times. Kong blinking in amazement at the first time he sees Godzilla's atomic ray comes to mind. The miniature work and effects don't reach the heights of *Mothra*, but they are still well done, as is the new Godzilla suit which would remain one of the monster's more popular designs even though it never saw a repeat performance. It is the ugly Kong suit with its un-heroic face and stiff overlong arms that drag the film down at times, ironic given that Tsuburaya was inspired to go into the effects field by the original 1933 *King Kong*.

Despite any shortcomings the film was a resounding financial success that surpassed even the original *Godzilla*, a rarity in those days. It remains the highest attended Japanese G-film of all time at over 11 million admissions, and if adjusted for inflation it would still be the most profitable entry of the series to this day. The film was altered for American release by Universal Pictures which cut several scenes of the Japanese cast and inserted new ones with Michael Keith as reporter Eric Carter and Harry Holcombe ("grandpa" in Countrytime's Lemonade commercials) as paleontologist Dr. Arnold Johnson. A good deal of Akira Ifukube's wonderful score is also curiously replaced with stock tracks from *Creature from the Black Lagoon*. Though panned by the *New York Times*, the film was a huge hit in America grossing around $3 million.

Final Word
Though it is the follow-up to this film, *Mothra vs. Godzilla*, that set the gold standard for Godzilla sequels, *King Kong vs. Godzilla* set up the formula that would sustain the series for the next 50 plus years. It was a great success worldwide and represents one of the best crossover films of all time, and although the monsters are sometimes played for comedy, the end battle is by no means a letdown.

Trivia

- After filming sequences with the live octopus that battles King Kong, Eiji Tsuburaya reportedly ate it for lunch.

- While on his honeymoon in New York, Yu Fujuki was impressed to see billboards for this film's American release.

- Using the 1956 U.S. release of *Godzilla, King of the Monsters!* as a template, John Beck hired Hollywood screenwriters Paul Mason and Bruce Howard (future writer for TV sitcoms *Gilligan's Island* and *The Brady Bunch*) to watch the film and then insert a new American story into the proceedings.

- The Kong suit was covered in a rare type of yak fur. Some sources claim Fuminori Ohashi constructed the suit, which would be ironic since he constructed Kong suits 30 years earlier for *King Kong Appears in Edo*. More credible sources say the suits (there were two) were created by Akira Watanabe and Teizo Toshimitsu.

- Haruo Nakajima plays Godzilla in all but one scene where the monster emerges from an iceberg. For that sequence Katsumi Tezuka played Godzilla.

- The film was reissued in Japan no less than three times it was so popular.

- Yu Fujuki and Tadao Takashima thought this would be the duo's last film together as "salarymen" because they were getting "too old." Ironically, they were immediately reteamed for Toho's next big SPFX film *Atragon* (1963).

- Before this, *Emperor Meiji and the Russo-Japanese War* was the record holder for highest attended film in Japan.

- Toho's ¥80 million fee to RKO actually gave them the rights to King Kong for five years, not just one film. Toho didn't end up using Kong again until the last year the license was applicable, 1967's *King Kong Escapes*.

- The "King-goji" Godzilla suit as it is called, was recreated in the early 1980s for an elaborate fan film entitled *Godzilla vs. the Wolfman* by director Shizuo Nakajima.

- This film's two female leads, Mie Hama and Akiko Wakabayashi, both appeared as the primary Bond girls in *You Only Live Twice* (1967).

- The film wasn't released in some European countries until the huge wave of publicity that occurred because of the 1976 *King Kong* remake.

- Unfortunately, for a time, the original uncut Japanese version of *King Kong vs. Godzilla* was a lost film. During the days of Toho's Champion Festival for Children, Godzilla films were edited down for re-release in the 1970s. *King Kong vs. Godzilla* was one such film, edited down by Ishiro Honda himself to 73 minutes, only Honda used the original print of the film to do so. As such, when the film was released on video in Japan, Toho had to find another print with the cut footage, which was badly faded, and then spliced the two together to make a compete cut. Eventually, another uncut print of the film was found in good quality and utilized for future releases.

- *King Kong vs. Godzilla* has a notorious non-existent alternate ending. Rumors claimed that in the Japanese version Godzilla wins the bout, while it was only in America that Kong won. This is completely false, as Toho had no problem depicting Godzilla as the villain who loses the match.

Varan the Unbelievable (1962)

Release Date: December 07, 1962

Directed by: Jerry A. Baerwitz & Ishiro Honda
Special Effects by: Eiji Tsuburaya
Screenplay by: Sid Harris
Music by: Akira Ifukube
Cast: Myron Healey (Cmdr. James Bradley) Tsuruko Kobayashi (Anna) Clifford Kawada (Capt. Kishi) Derick Shimatsu (Matsu) Kozo Nomura (Paul) Ayumi Sonoda (Shidori) **Suit Performers:** Haruo Nakajima (Varan)

Tohoscope, Black & White, 70 Minutes

Story
On the island of Kunoshiroshima, a joint U.S.-Japanese military experiment is led by Commander James Bradley. The point of the experiment is to find a means of purifying a salt water lake on the island. Instead, the chemical experiments awaken the monster Varan sleeping at the lake's bottom. Varan attacks a fishing fleet at sea and later battles the navy but it is to no avail; the creature reaches Oneda, a modern city on the island, and begins laying an airport to waste. Commander Bradley advises the military to trick Varan into swallowing his experimental saline chemicals.

The plan succeeds and the wounded monster retreats to the sea where it is later presumed dead.

Background & Commentary

As was done with *Godzilla, King of the Monsters!* in 1956, an American distributor snatched up Toho's *Varan*, re-edited it, and added in extensive sequences with new American actors. In this case the distributor was Crown International Pictures and the American star Myron Healey. It's curious however why the studio even went to the trouble for an elaborate Americanization, as the original *Varan* was never a stand out piece to begin with.

While *Godzilla, King of the Monsters!* could be viewed as a companion piece to the original *Godzilla* which it coexists peacefully with (it's conceivable continuity-wise that reporter Steve Martin is hanging around just out of frame in the Japanese version), the same cannot be said for *Varan the Unbelievable*. This film actually retcons the original's plot, something *Godzilla, King of the Monsters!* never did. The original *Varan* is set in the mountains of Japan, while this film is set on a Japanese island. Also, Varan is awakened from the lake due to a desalinization experiment. Nor does Varan attack Tokyo, but "Oneda", the only modern city on the fictional island of Kuroshiroshima. Like *Half Human*, none of the Japanese footage was even dubbed into English it is used so sparingly. Nor do the original Japanese cast have roles of any substance in this version, though Kozo Nomura and Ayumi Sonoda's characters from the original version are mentioned to be old friends of Bradley's, just as Dr. Serizawa was an "old friend" of reporter Steve Martin in *Godzilla, King of the Monsters!*

Despite the title being *Varan the Unbelievable*, the U.S. version cuts out the monster's fantastic flying scene—a highlight of the original version—in an effort to make the monster more believable. Additionally, Varan's name is never even spoken in the American version and instead he is referred to as the "Obaki." Ifukube's wonderful score, the standout aspect of the original, is also tastelessly removed aside from a few short cues here and there. The film's lead, James Bradley as played by Myron Healey, is not nearly as likeable as Raymond Burr's Steve Martin, and spends most of the picture talking down to his wife and the other silly folk that question his methods. Healey was mostly a TV and Western star, though he had done a few jungle genre films such as *Panther Girl of the Congo* (1955), entries in the Johnny Sheffield *Bomba the Jungle Boy* series, and Johnny Weissmuller's *Jungle Jim* franchise. Healey continued to work steadily in TV after this and also landed a small role in the John Wayne classic *True Grit* (1969). His final film was 1977's *The Incredible Melting Man*.

Final Word

For retconning the original *Varan*'s plot and score, in addition to its less-likeable lead, *Varan the Unbelievable* truly is a bastardization of the original version.

Trivia

- Myron Healey coincidentally acted across from *Godzilla King of the Monsters!* American lead, Raymond Burr, in an episode of *Perry Mason*.

- The film's sensational tagline was, "From a world below, it came to terrorize—to destroy—to revenge!"

- Among Crown International's other genre releases were *The Beast of Yucca Flats* (1961) and *The Crater Lake Monster* (1977).

- Curiously the date in the American version is said to be October of 1959 in spoken dialogue, making it possible the film's release was delayed until 1962 for some reason.

The Little Prince and the Eight Headed Dragon (1963)

Japanese Title: *The Naughty Prince's Slaying of Orochi*
Release Date: March 24, 1963

Directed by: Yugo Serikawa
Animation by: Toei Animation
Screenplay by: Ichiro Ikeda & Takashi Iijima
Music by: Akira Ifukube
Voice Cast: Morio Kazama (Susanoo) Yukiko Okada
(Princess Kushinada) Chiharu Kuri (Akahana) Kiyoshi
Kawakubo (Titan-bô) Masato Yamanouchi (Wadatsumi)
Hideo Kinoshita (Tarô/Tsukuyomi)

Toeiscope, Color, 86 Minutes

Story

Prince Susanoo lives happily on Onogoro Island with his
parents Izanagi and Izanami until the tragic death of his
mother. Not able to come to grips with Izanami's death, the
young prince makes a boat and sets sail with his rabbit
pal Akahana to find the land where he thinks his mother has
gone. After being attacked by a giant fish monster, he is aided
by Wadatsumi and it is guided to the Night Country where
his brother Tsukuyomi rules. There Tsukuyomi gives him a
magical ice gift, and Susanoo sets out for the Fire Country
where he battles a vengeful fire god using his brother's gift.
Next, Susanoo goes to Takamagahara where his
sister Amaterasu rules, but he causes so much mischief there
that she is forced to banish him. In the country of Izumo,
Susanoo meets young Princess Kushinada—set to be eaten
by the evil eight headed dragon Orochi. Infatuated with her
because she reminds him of his mother, Susanoo defends her
and kills Orochi. The dragon's dead body turns into a
beautiful system of rivers that restores the land, and Susanoo
looks to the clouds where he can see his mother Izanami.

Background & Commentary

Toei's sixth animated feature film began life as *Japanese
Myths Rainbow Bridge* and was always modeled on a child's
take on Susanoo battling Orochi. The large production
employed 180 persons, cost ¥70,000,000, used 250,000
sheets of drawing paper, and 1 ton of paint. The climactic
battle between Susanoo and Orochi alone took half a year to
animate and is considered one of the best scenes in the annals
of Japanese animation. Unlike Toei's other efforts of the

period, the film's animation is distinctly modernist and slightly abstract.

Like any odyssey/journey film, the story is episodic to an extent but fun all the same—never staying in one place long enough to become boring. The Prince's journey takes him into the depths of the sea (where he battles a giant fish), to an ice land (called the Night Country), then to a fire ravaged land where he fights the fire god that lives in the volcano, then to the Land of Light, and finally to Izumo where he finds the young princess at risk of being eaten by Orochi, the eight headed dragon. Naturally, Susanoo's confrontation with the dragon is the highlight of the film, and actually, it is probably the best onscreen representation of the battle between Susanoo and Orochi—easily eclipsing Eiji Tsuburaya and Toshiro Mifune's stab at the scene in Toho's *The Birth of Japan* a few years earlier. The dragon's intro as 16 glowing eyes in the dark is beautifully animated, as is the whole film really. The little prince ducks and weaves between the dragon's heads on his flying pony, killing the beast one head at a time to Ifukube's wonderful score. The project was somewhat personal for Ifukube, whose family came from the region of the Hinokawa River. In the story this is where Orochi meets his defeat and then transforms into said river. Furthermore, Ifukube worked closely with director Serikawa in timing the length of the scenes as Ifukube began scoring during the storyboard process and finished the majority of scoring after the film was animated.

The film was well received in Japan, and today remains a classic of the genre. It was released in America through Columbia as *The Little Prince and the Eight-Headed Dragon* on New Year's Day in 1964. William Ross was billed as director of the English version and MagiColor and WonderScope were names created to replace Toei's color and Toeiscope for western audiences.

Final Word
One of the greatest animated Japanese films of all time, and one of the best remembered tellings of the legend of Susanoo and Orochi even if aimed at a juvenile audience.

Trivia

- Won the Children's Film Festival Bronze Award at the Venice International Film Festival.

- Was the first and only animated feature by Akira Ifukube outside of the posthumously released *Tetsujin Nijūhachi-gō* (2007).

Matango (1963)

Alternate Titles: *Attack of the Mushroom People* (U.S.)
Release Date: August 11, 1963

Directed by: Ishiro Honda
Special Effects by: Eiji Tsuburaya
Screenplay by: Kaoru Mabuchi
Music by: Akira Ifukube
Cast: Akira Kubo (Murai) Kumi Mizuno (Asami) Hiroshi Koizumi (Sakuta) Hiroshi Tachikawa (Yoshida) Miki Yashiro (Akiko) Yoshio Tsuchiya (Kasai) Kenji Sahara (Senzo) **Suit Performers:** Haruo Nakajima (Matango)

Tohoscope, Eastmancolor, 89 Minutes

Story

Seven socialites including a writer, a company president, a university professor, and a singer take sail on a luxury yacht in the ocean but are caught up in a storm. Their damaged boat drifts to a ghostly island where they take refuge in an old ship washed ashore on the beach. Inside they find a strange fungus, and in the night are even plagued by a ghostly mushroom-man. The group agrees not to eat the mushrooms, lest they turn into a mushroom-man themselves. Slowly the group's savage instincts take hold and they begin to turn on one another in addition to eating the mushrooms. In the end, all but one resists temptation and escapes back to Tokyo.

Background & Commentary

This film began life as a story by William Hope Hodgson (called "A Voice in the Night") which was adapted by Masami Fukushima (editor of *Sci-fi* Magazine in Japan) into *Matango*. This was then adapted into screenplay format by Kaoru Mabuchi. Filming took place over the course of several weeks on Hachijo and Oshima Islands, where the cast and crew were plagued by poisonous snakes and large centipedes. Production was so rushed that Toho was actually editing the film while it was still shooting, and production wrapped on July 28th with the editing continuing up until the release date.

Though something of a ghost story with supernatural elements, the cause of the mutated mushrooms is naturally the H-Bomb. The H-Bomb can't explain a ghost ship scene earlier in the film, in addition to one of the Mushroom Men vanishing into thin air. On the note of the monsters, one could argue the Mushroom People are essentially the zombies of the "Toho Cinematic Universe" and at one point Akira Kubo breaks off one of their moldy arms. The film has a surprise ending where it is revealed that despite escaping the island (and not once eating the Matango), Murai has become infected by the mushrooms anyways, possibly through spores. However, the English dubbed version makes the character state that he ate the mushrooms. In terms of casting, this film boasts nearly all of the Toho greats. Actually the characters bear a few similarities to those from *Gilligan's Island*, which it should be noted this film predates by one year. Kumi Mizuno's character is a starlet, while the other female character, Akiko, essentially amounts to Marry Anne and is even in love with the professor, Akira Kubo's Murai. In addition to this, Hiroshi Koizumi plays the skipper, and Kenji Sahara plays the slimy first mate, though he is certainly no Gilligan. Rounding out the rest of the castaways were Yoshio Tsuchiya as a company president and Hiroshi Tachikawa as a novelist.

Overall the film is well-loved in Japan amongst critics, filmmakers and kaiju otaku alike. Kumi Mizuno and Akira Kubo both claim that this is their favorite Toho SPFX film. Though Toho never revisited the horrific Mushroom Men in remakes or sequels, Toho did authorize a sequel to this film in the form of a novel by Tatsuya Yoshimura entitled *Matango Strikes Back*.

Final Word
Easily the greatest of all of Toho's horror films.

Trivia

- One of the Mushroom Men was portrayed by Eisei Amamoto while one of the giant Matango was portrayed by Haruo Nakajima.

- This was the first film in which Tsuburaya got to use his special Oxberry 1900 Optical Printer.

- Katto Productions in Japan made an independent sequel to this film entitled *Matango 2* (1989) wherein a corporation wishing to build a resort on the island takes a military escort to investigate the tales of the strange mushroom men.

!!!!!!!!!!!!!!!!!!!*Bonus Review!*!!!!!!!!!!!!!!!!!!!!

The Lost World of Sinbad (1963)

Japanese Title: *The Great Thief* (Japan) *Samurai Pirate* (Limited U.S.-Japanese Theatrical Release)
Release Date: October 26, 1963

Directed by: Senkichi Tamaguchi
Special Effects by: Eiji Tsuburaya
Screenplay by: Shinichi Sekizawa, Kaoru Mabuchi & Toshio Yasumi
Music by: Masaru Sato
Cast: Toshiro Mifune (Luzon Sukezaemon/"Sinbad") Mie Hama (Princess Yaya) Kumi Mizuno (Miwa) Jun Tazaki (Itaka Tsuzuka) Ichiro Arishima (Sennin) Eisei Amamoto (Granny) Tadao Nakamaru (the Chancellor)

Tohoscope, Eastmancolor, 97 Minutes

Story

When his ship, carrying a load of treasure, is sunk and stolen by the Black Pirate, famed pirate Luzon Sukezaemon finds himself shipwrecked in a strange land. He is taken under the wing of Sennin, an ancient third class wizard who helps Luzon battle a chancellor intent on marrying Princess Yaya and killing her father, the King. Aiding the premier is the witch Granny, though Sennin defeats her as Sinbad and a band of rebels, lead by Miwa, overtakes the castle from the chancellor. The next morning as the king is set to reward Luzon, he is nowhere to be found and has set sail for a new adventure.

Background & Commentary

Fans hoping for a Toho version of the Columbia Sinbad films (ala Toho's interpretations of Dracula and Frankenstein) are in for a sore disappointment. What was renamed *The Lost World of Sinbad* to capitalize on Columbia's profitable franchise in America was in fact filmed in Japan as *The Great Thief.* In the original film, Toshiro Mifune is not playing Sinbad, but a real life legendary trade merchant named Luzon Sukezaemon. When AIP got a hold of the film—which ran high on swashbuckling pirate adventure and fantasy—they decided to advertise it as a Sinbad film, in fact an ingenious move on their part. Had they not renamed the film it wouldn't have stood a chance in American markets and would likely be all but forgotten today.

Though Tomoyuki Tanaka had managed to shoehorn monsters into films that didn't originally have them (these being *The Mysterians, Gorath,* and *Atragon*), in *The Lost World of Sinbad* he either had no such luck or didn't even try. And if ever there was a Toho fantasy film crying out for a monster it was this one. Adding insult to injury is the fact that the American poster has "Sinbad" riding atop a monstrous magic carpet that looks as though it is alive. In the finished film though it is nothing but a giant kite. For that matter, it's entirely possible that the film lacked a monster due to the lead Toshiro Mifune, whose inclusion may have eaten up most of the budget. Likewise, what is advertised as a "giant" on the poster turns out to be a 6½ foot tall man. Instead, the fantastical elements of *The Lost World of Sinbad* are represented in the form of two sorcerers, an evil witch named Granny portrayed by Eisei Amamoto in drag, and comedic legend Ichiro Arishima (Mr. Tako in *King Kong vs. Godzilla*) as a decrepit wizard who literally swoons every time he sees a woman. Fortunately Arishima's scenes as the wizard are genuinely funny, and in one spectacular SPFX scene he turns himself into a fly to spy on the enemy, but instead lands himself on a buxom bosom. The great Eisei Amamoto looks like a Claymation Rankin/Bass character come to life as Granny in his overblown fright wig and a mouth with goofy looking fangs. The rest of the cast is a who's who of the Toho greats, and in fact features all three of Toho's top starlets of the era: Kumi Mizuno, Mie Hama, and Akiko Wakabayashi. Mizuno fares the best as Miwa, the female rebel leader, and as she always does comes away with one of the film's best characters in the process. Jun Tazaki is likewise great as a gruff Imperial Guard who humorously spars with Mifune in a Bud Spencer/Terence Hill type dynamic. Naturally, Mifune is great as the titular pirate, and had played similar roles many times before.

Due to its lavish production values and Mifune's lead, the film had respectable grosses in Japan with ¥230,000,000. In its native country it was double-billed with one of the Crazy Cats comedies, while in America it was double-billed in March of 1965 with *War of the Zombies*. The American dub by Titra Studios is top notch, and Mifune is indeed called Sinbad throughout the film. Naturally, American critics and audiences alike found the "Japanese version" of Sinbad to be incredibly inferior to Columbia's *The 7ᵗʰ Voyage of Sinbad*.

Final Word
Though it has a fantastic AIP concocted title, the concept of a Toho version of Sinbad it sadly is not. If one can get over this fact, they will nonetheless find it an enjoyable time killer from Toho.

Trivia

- AIP originally intended to call this film *The 7ᵗʰ*

Wonder of Sinbad ala *The 7ᵗʰ Voyage of Sinbad* but changed it to *The Lost World of Sinbad.*

- The dwarf is portrayed by Little Man Machan, who would one day portray Minilla starting in 1967's *Son of Godzilla.*

Atragon (1963)

Japanese Title: *Undersea Warship*
Release Date: December 22, 1963

Directed by: Ishiro Honda
Special Effects by: Eiji Tsuburaya
Screenplay by: Shinichi Sekizawa
Music by: Akira Ifukube
Cast: Tadao Takashima (Susumu) Yoko Fujiyama (Makoto Jinguji) Ken Uehara (Adm. Kusumi) Yu Fujuki (Yoshito) Jun Tazaki (Capt. Jinguji) Kenji Sahara (Mu Agent) Tetsuko Kobayashi (Mu Empress) Hiroshi Koizumi (Detective Ito) Akihiko Hirata (Agent 23) Eisei Amamoto (Mu Priest)

Tohoscope, Eastmancolor, 94 Minutes

Story
When denizens of the underwater civilization of Mu begin surfacing to attack Japan, a quest begins to find Captain Jinguji, who disappeared many years ago while building the only weapon capable of confronting the invaders: the super submarine Atragon. The expedition is headed by Jinguji's old commander Admiral Kusumi, his daughter Makoto, and a photographer named Susumu among others. The group reaches Jinguji's hidden base on a remote island, but are stunned when Jinguji refuses to help rid the world of the Mu Empire. However, when Makoto and Susumu are kidnapped by a Mu agent, Jinguji sets out in the Atragon to rescue her. After defeating Manda, the guardian serpent of Mu, the

Atragon bores into the underwater city where Jinguji rescues his daughter and defeats the evil empire once and for all.

Background & Commentary

Believe it or not, the story of this futuristic submarine was written back in 1900 by novelist Shunro Oshikawa, and was serialized to great popularity in boys' adventure magazines hence the film's eventual onscreen adaptation. When Shinichi Sekizawa was instructed to adapt the old story, he surprisingly didn't bother to reread it and instead based it upon his childhood impressions. In addition to this, he also merged it with Shigeru Komatsuzaki's short story *The Undersea Kingdom*, hence the inclusion of the Mu Empire. The screenplay was approved and set for filming in September of 1963, giving the usual quartet of Honda, Tsuburaya, Tanaka and Ifukube only three months to make the film. And due to the SPFX filming that went on previously for that same year's *Matango*, *Atragon* had a SPFX shoot of only two months.

The resulting film is a Toho classic, and unlike *The Mysterians* and *Gorath* strikes a better balance between the monster action and the rest of the film. As per usual, Tomoyuki Tanaka had requested a kaiju be written into the story as Oshikawa's original plot featured no fantastic beasts. Therefore Akira Watanabe conceived of a gigantic snake (which in pre-production art is curiously drawn as a rattlesnake) named Manda and made to look like a Chinese dragon. Ironically though, the somewhat goofy Manda marionette is one of the poorer aspects of the film in execution. However, all of the other effects are top notch notably the submarines Atragon and the Mu Empire's flagship vessel, which can fire a colorful optical ray. Atragon on the other hand is capped by a fantastic drill, allowing it to bore through the earth while rocket blasters allow the submarine to jet through air and water alike. Also spectacular is an earthquake which devastates Tokyo compliments of the Mu Empire. The cast is comprised of some of Toho's best including a reteaming of Tadao Takashima and Yu Fujuki along with their other *King Kong vs. Godzilla* co-stars Akihiko Hirata, Kenji Sahara and Jun

Tazaki. Of note in this case are the latter two, as this was the up-to-this-point heroic Kenji Sahara's first turn as an all-out villain and this was easily Jun Tazaki's best role. Almost always cast in supporting roles as military generals, scientists or gruff editors, here Tazaki is once again a military man, but his arc as the embittered Captain Jinguji is an interesting one. Even as the world burns he refuses to help battle the Mu Empire until finally his daughter manages to sway him in a scene beautifully backlit by a shimmering lake.

Atragon was very popular during its initial release playing for over a month in Japanese cinemas in addition to being the biggest of the "New Year's Blockbusters." It's actually something of a shock Toho never got around to producing a sequel to *Atragon*. Though a quasi-sequel of sorts in the 1960s was planned, it never materialized, and the closest Toho ever got was oddly 1977's *The War in Space*, a loose remake of *Atragon* wherein the vessel is a spaceship rather than a submarine. That being said, the super sub finally reappears as a submersible in 2004's *Godzilla: Final Wars*.

Final Word

Out of all of Toho's more favored non-Godzilla SPFX films, *Atragon* is likely the best known internationally and for good reason.

Trivia

- For a time *Latitude Zero* (1969) was known as *Undersea Warship 2* in its planning phases. This is curious as *Latitude Zero* was based upon stories created by Ted Sherman and had nothing to do with *Atragon* other than the concept of the undersea battleships.

- The main reason that the film doesn't take place in the same time period as the novel was that the studio wanted the film to be set post WWII.

- In total there were five different Atragon models of varying sizes constructed, the largest being 16 feet long. Ironically for Manda, who has far less screen time, Tsuburaya had ten different models of the monster constructed.

- There is a rumor that when Toho concocted the term Atragon for International markets this was meant as a name for Manda, being a combination of the words Atlantis and Dragon. However, the U.S. Distributor AIP chose to name the submarine Atragon instead. In Japan the ship is known as Gohtengo in this film, *The War in Space* (1977), and *Godzilla: Final Wars* (2004).

- *Atragon* was revived by Toho as secondary "support feature" in 1968 for the release of *Destroy All Monsters*.

- This film's unmade quasi-sequel, called *Super Noah*, about a flying battleship, eventually turned into the TV series *Mighty Jack* from Tsuburaya Productions in 1967.

- Toshiro Mifune was eyed for Captain Jinguji until it was decided he was too expensive.

- Katto Productions produced an independent feature length sequel, *Atragon 2* (1983), wherein the Mu Empire rises again in the 1980s to challenge the world.

- This version of the Gohtengo reappears piloted by a Captain Jinguji in Toho's 2005 *Super Fleet Sazer X the Movie* complete with its original theme music by Akira Ifukube.

Mothra vs. Godzilla (1964)

Alternate Titles: *Godzilla vs. the Thing* (U.S.) *Godzilla vs. Mothra* (U.S. Home Video title) *Godzilla vs. the Prehistoric Caterpillars* (Germany) *Mothra Meets Godzilla* (Sweden) *Watang! The Fabulous Empire of Monsters* (Italy) *Godzilla Confronts the Monsters* (Spain)
Release Date: April 29, 1964

Directed by: Ishiro Honda
Special Effects by: Eiji Tsuburaya
Screenplay by: Shinichi Sekizawa
Music by: Akira Ifukube
Cast: Akira Takarada (Sakurai) Yuriko Hoshi (Junko)
Hiroshi Koizumi (Professor Murai) Emi & Yumi Ito (the
Shobijin) Kenji Sahara (Torohata) Yoshifumi Tajima
(Kumayama) Yu Fujuki (Jiro) Jun Tazaki (Editor) **Suit
Performers:** Haruo Nakajima (Godzilla)

Tohoscope, Eastmancolor, 89 Minutes

Story

After a fierce typhoon, a gigantic egg washes ashore in Japan
and is quickly snatched up by a duo of evil entrepreneurs
from Happy Enterprises. A reporter, Sakai, his photographer,
Junko, and a scientist studying the egg, Professor Murai,
team up against Happy Enterprises to get the egg back. The
heroic trio crosses paths with none other than Mothra's
fairies, the Shobijin, who reveal that the egg is in fact
Mothra's. The girls warn the heroes that if the egg isn't
returned great calamity will befall Japan when it hatches
before flying back to Infant Island on Mothra. Godzilla soon
surfaces and begins attacking Japan. When the military is
powerless to stop the monster Junko, Murai and Sakai fly to
Infant Island to ask for Mothra's help. Initially rebuked,
Junko makes an impassioned plea, which is heard by Mothra.
Despite the fact that she is nearing the end of her life cycle,
the giant moth agrees to fly to the mainland to battle
Godzilla. Mothra intercepts Godzilla just as he is
approaching her egg and the two beasts fight to the death.
As Mothra lay dying next to her egg, Godzilla makes way
for a nearby island where a group of schoolchildren have been
stranded. The egg hatches two larva just in time, which swim
out and distract Godzilla on the island while Junko, Sakai and
Murai save the children. Godzilla is encased in a giant cocoon
and tumbles into the ocean, and the larva return to Infant
Island.

Background & Commentary

Mothra vs. Godzilla was a result of *King Kong vs. Godzilla's* massive success, and the first draft of the sequel was actually to be a rematch between the two beasts which was wisely discarded. Instead, Toho decided to pit Godzilla against one of their own creations, Mothra—who debuted in her 1961 successful solo feature. The original script was heavy on call backs to that film, and would've seen Godzilla attacking the fictional country of Rolisica. Another notable difference had Godzilla first battling a larva, and then the adult Mothra. While in the finished film Godzilla's battle with the adult Mothra is indeed the highlight, the final battle has an interesting David vs. Goliath-like charm to it with the two tiny outmatched caterpillars. All around, the film improves upon *King Kong vs. Godzilla* in all departments, notably the long military confrontation with Godzilla.

Overall the finished film is widely regarded as the best of the G-sequels in the original series bar none, and not without good reason. In addition to a heartfelt, well-balanced story on the human front about greed and corruption, the SPFX are near flawless and Akira Ifukube gives one of the best, if not the best, scores of the Showa Era. His themes are swelling and emotional, and he does a good job of writing songs for the Peanuts, who typically only collaborated with Yuji Koseki, composer of *Mothra*. Tsuburaya and Honda also do an even better job of conveying the tiny size of Mothra's fairies in this film. This was all thanks to a new (and very expensive) piece of equipment Tsuburaya had convinced the Toho brass to purchase: an Oxberry 1900 Optical Printer. Tsuburaya had seen one while visiting Hollywood and convinced Toho that it would be worthwhile that they purchase one for themselves. Reportedly this made Toho Studios the only movie producer to possess the device aside from Walt Disney Pictures in America.

Oddly this film didn't come near the grosses of the previous film despite Mothra's popularity and it sold only 3.5 million tickets. In America AIP picked up distribution rights to the film, which they retitled *Godzilla vs. the Thing*. Fearing that Mothra wouldn't be perceived as an intimidating enough opponent for Godzilla, and also wanting to cook up some mystery for the advertising, Mothra was rechristened "the

Thing" and Godzilla battles a giant question mark on the poster. The English dub by Titra Studios is one of the best of the original series, the only downside being that—to match the posters—Mothra is inexplicably called "the Thing" throughout the proceedings. The American version is also unique for having a sequence cut from the Japanese version, wherein the U.S. military attacks Godzilla with Frontier Missiles.

Final Word
For many fans, this entry represents the gold standard of the entire Godzilla series with good reason.

Trivia

- Another opponent discussed for the fourth Godzilla film before deciding on Mothra was Frankenstein.

- In the interim between this film and *Mothra*, the Peanuts starred in *Double Trouble* (1963) with Mie Hama and also had their own variety show on TV.

- This was the first Godzilla film acquired for distribution by Henry G. Saperstein, who would become Godzilla's Godfather of sorts in America.

- There are conflicting stories regarding the Frontier Missile sequence being filmed exclusively for American audiences. One source claims Ishiro Honda merely cut it from the Japanese version because he felt Japanese audiences didn't want to see the U.S. trying to solve Japan's problems. Teruyoshi Nakano on the other hand says it was filmed at the request of American International Pictures.

- Mothra actually had to be scaled down in size from the original film so as not to dwarf Godzilla.

- Akira Ifukube and Ishiro Honda had an argument over whether a sequence where Godzilla's head emerges over a mountain should be scored or not. Ifukube felt it more effective silent, while Honda felt Ifukube's score worked better and edited it in without the maestro's approval.

- As Haruo Nakajima had since earned some clout at Toho, he was given input into the design and construction of the new G-suit. It was also finally officially revealed to the public that Nakajima was the man playing Godzilla for the past ten years.

- *Mothra vs. Godzilla* grew in esteem in later years and garnered 2.8 million ticket sales during a 1982 re-release and helped spark a renaissance of the series that led to 1984's *The Return of Godzilla*.

Dogora the Space Monster (1964)

Japanese Title: *Giant Space Monster Dogora*
Release Date: August 11, 1964

Directed by: Ishiro Honda
Special Effects by: Eiji Tsuburaya
Screenplay by: Tami Yasushiryo & Shinichi Sekizawa
Music by: Akira Ifukube
Cast: Yosuke Natsuki (Det. Kommei) Yoko Fujiyama (Masayo) Robert Dunham (Mark Jackson) Hiroshi Koizumi (Kirino) Akiko Wakabayashi (Hamako) Seizaburo Kawazu (Gangster Boss) Nobuo Nakamura (Dr. Munakata)

Tohoscope, Eastmancolor, 81 Minutes

Story
At the same time that a group of notorious gangsters go on a diamond heist, a monster from space descends upon Japan with a voracious appetite for carbon which includes the precious jewels. On the trail of the gangsters is a policeman, Kommei, and Diamond G-man, Mark Jackson. The two rivals eventually join forces to take down the gangsters when the real diamond thief, the jellyfish-like monster Dogora,

appears wreaking havoc across Kyushu. Eventually the military attacks Dogora with a serum made out of wasp venom which the monster is allergic to. Dogora becomes sick and begins to dissolve, dropping large chunks of carbon everywhere. As Kommei and Jackson chase down the gangsters who have made off with a real load of diamonds, one of Dogora's carbon clumps lands on the gangsters killing them instantly.

Background & Commentary

Dogora the Space Monster is by no means a classic, but it does perfectly exemplify the weirdness of Japanese monster movies compared to American counterparts. Red Foxx reads a wholly accurate *TV Guide* description of the film in an episode of *Sanford and Son* which generates immediate audience laughter. "A giant coal sucking jellyfish from space runs afoul of gangsters and is defeated by wasp venom," makes for an appropriately surreal logline. During Toho's renewed success with the Godzilla series, *Dogora* was their first foray into experimenting with new monsters again. Although some of their sci-fi films such as *Gorath* (1962) and *Atragon* (1963) featured appearances by giant monsters they were not giant monster films per se, and in some respects neither is this picture. Contrary to the title, Dogora is not the star of the show. The monster plays second fiddle to the human cast, frankly, because it has to, being far too uninteresting to carry the film on its own. However, it should be noted that the movie is a mad-cap comedy caper satirizing both the yakuza (gangster) genre and that of the kaiju eiga, two of director Ishiro Honda's trademarks. Remarkably this combo works thanks to stellar screenwriting and a competent cast to back it up.

Though not the headlining star, Robert Dunham steals the show as Mark Jackson the "Diamond G-Man" (that's not a superhero nickname, the "G" stands for government). Popular action star Yosuke Natsuki (the picture's main advertising draw in fact) plays comically inept police inspector Kommei, constantly getting bested by Jackson and berated by the elderly Dr. Munakata while trying to court his lab assistant, Masayo. The gangsters led by Seizaburo

Kawazu are also played for laughs. At the end of the picture they are all betrayed by the conniving bombshell portrayed by beautiful Akiko Wakabayashi, a future Bond girl. Honda crafts a particularly memorable visual of her as she lay dying on a beach amongst the spilled diamonds in the sand after being shot by the gangsters.

As for Dogora itself, the creature represents a rare example of a Japanese monster that isn't portrayed by a man in suit, but existed solely as a marionette in addition to several animated effects. Although an "uchu kaiju," or space monster, Dogora is still the result of earth based nuclear pollution with Dr. Munakata stating that "space cells" became mutated as they drifted over the airspaces near Atomic testing sites. The standout effects sequence occurs when Dogora's luminous animated tentacles reach from the skies and uproot a large bridge in Kyushu. Tsuburaya's work here is somewhat uneven as is Ifukube's score, however, both were busy men distracted between several other projects that year with *Dogora* notably sandwiched between two large Godzilla sequels. As for the good, Dogora is a completely convincing marionette as it glides spectrally through the skies and Tsuburaya's miniature coal fields are so convincing one doesn't even know that they are miniatures until the monster appears overhead. In terms of the bad, the model trucks look like toys as do several of the military's ground based weapons. Otherwise it is a solid if not offbeat production all around.

Final Word
The only kaiju film where the human storyline can be recommended over the monster scenes, but in this case it is a compliment rather than a detriment.

Trivia

- Robert Dunham tried to get Toho to do a non-monster spin-off film with the Mark Jackson character to no avail. Some sources claim this lead to Toho producing *The Killing Bottle* (1967) starring Nick Adams, though the Mark Jackson character doesn't appear in the film.

- The script was written back in 1962 as "Space Monster" with Dogora as of yet unnamed.

Ghidorah, the Three Headed Monster (1964)

Japanese Title: *Three Giant Monsters: Greatest Battle on Earth!*
Release Date: December 20, 1964

Directed by: Ishiro Honda
Special Effects by: Eiji Tsuburaya,
Screenplay by: Shinichi Sekizawa
Music by: Akira Ifukube
Cast: Yosuke Natsuki (Shindo) Yuriko Hoshi (Naoko) Akiko Wakabayashi (Princess Salno) Hiroshi Koizumi (Prof. Murai) Emi & Yumi Ito (the Shobijin) Takashi Shimura (Prof. Tsukamoto) Hisaya Ito (Malness) **Suit Performers:** Haruo Nakajima (Godzilla) Masaki Shinohara (Rodan) Shoichi Hirose (King Ghidorah)

Tohoscope, Eastmancolor, 92 Minutes

Story
In route to Japan, Princess Salno's plane is bombed by assassins. Later a woman claiming to be a prophet from Venus that bears a striking resemblance to the princess begins to warn about a string of catastrophes. The first occurs when a meteor crashes in Kurobe Gorge. Later Rodan awakens from Mt. Aso and Godzilla rises from the sea and heads for Japan. The prophetess is taken under the wing of a reporter, Naoko, and her brother, Shindo, a policeman who saves her from assassins convinced she is the princess. Meanwhile, Godzilla and Rodan battle across the Japanese countryside. Shindo and Naoko take the prophetess to a clinic but they are unable to determine whether the young woman is a princess or a Venusian. There she warns that the monster that destroyed Venus has arrived on Earth. The meteorite cracks open unleashing the three headed menace King Ghidorah to the skies. The Shobijin, in Japan on a PR tour, call for Mothra who then tries to recruit Godzilla and Rodan

for help to no avail. The two monsters have a change of heart and rescue the little caterpillar from Ghidorah and drive the creature back into space. At the same time, Shindo saves the prophetess once more from the assassins who are killed in a rockslide caused by the monsters. The Princess then regains her senses, returning to her former self, before flying back to her home country, Shindo and Naoko forever in her debt.

Background & Commentary

When production on that years "New Year's blockbuster" (Akira Kurosawa's *Red Beard*) became prolonged, Toho decided to hastily rush another Godzilla film into development. While Toho could have merely cranked out a "Godzilla vs. Rodan" picture, they instead opted for an ambitious *House of Dracula*-style teaming of three of their most popular creations against a powerful new foe: King Ghidorah, a marvelous monster designed by Akira Watanabe. With golden scales and massive solar wings the creature is majestic and monstrous at the same time made even more so to Ifukube's accompanying compositions. Ghidorah's fiery birth, a combination of pyrotechnics and animation, is one of the most memorable SPFX images in Japanese cinema. The monster's ensuing whirlwind destruction of Tokyo was so impressive it would be reused as stock footage nearly half a dozen times in later films. Operating the suit's three heads, two wings, and twin tails took an entire wire works team and shots with all four monsters in frame are a testament to the hard work of Tsuburaya and his crew. The film is actually minus a few monsters. In the original *Rodan* there were two giant Pterodactyls, but only one awakens here. Similarly, there were two larvae hatched in *Mothra vs. Godzilla* and there was originally to be a Mothra larva and an Imago Mothra side by side in this film. However, this would have been a disservice to the story, as the helpless caterpillar needs to evoke the sympathies of Godzilla and Rodan. Plus, there is something poetic about three monsters battling a three headed monster.

As for the cast, Hiroshi Koizumi reprises his role from *Mothra vs. Godzilla*, while oddly enough Yuriko Hoshi, who appeared in that same film as a photographer, here plays a reporter with a different name. Yosuke Natsuki also plays a more suave version of the character he originated in *Dogora the Space Monster* here as Detective Shindo. Also returning from *Dogora* is Akiko Wakabayashi, who cements herself as one of the series most beautiful leading ladies. Emi and Yumi Ito even appear as the Shobijin one last time. Their best scene comes in a monster congress between Godzilla, Rodan and Mothra where they act as translators. At one point they mutter, "Oh Godzilla, what terrible language." Like the human characters, the kaiju too have moral dilemmas and character arcs for the first time and, in a landmark moment, Godzilla comes to the aid of tiny Mothra against King Ghidorah and Rodan soon follows. In an exemplary example of team work, Godzilla holds Ghidorah in place while Rodan airlifts Mothra who sprays the monster's three heads together with her webbing—all to Ifukube's swelling score. Godzilla was now a hero, and the series would never be the same again.

Despite being the second Godzilla picture of 1964, it ended up being the more financially popular of the two and also saw a successful theatrical release in the States in 1965. Like *Godzilla vs. the Thing* before it, the film was for the most part unmolested aside from reshuffling some footage that makes it appear Rodan is stalking Godzilla. In fact, many fans consider the U.S. version to be an improvement over the Japanese version aside from one song by the Ito sisters being cut out. Sadly, it would be the last Godzilla film to reach U.S. theaters for five years.

Final Word
The film that officially turned Godzilla into a hero, established his friendship/rivalries with Mothra and Rodan, and introduced the seminal Godzilla foe King Ghidorah. Although it wasn't the highest grossing G-film of the 1960s, this film best represents the apex of the era.

Trivia

- The last Godzilla film to sell over 4 million tickets until *Godzilla and Mothra: The Battle for Earth* (1992).

- Supposedly, the storyline of the Venusian Prophetess/Princess in Japan was inspired by *Roman Holiday* (1953) according to Shinichi Sekizawa.

- King Ghidorah went through many different color schemes, notably red scales, then solid green, then blue with rainbow colored wings before gold was decided upon. The idea was Teruyoshi Nakano's, who thought the monster should be colored gold because Venus was known in Japan as the golden planet.

- It would appear one draft of the script planned to have King Ghidorah attack New York, as pre-production art shows the monster flying over Manhattan and publicity stills feature the monster attacking the Statue of Liberty.

- This is Emi and Yumi Ito's last appearance as the Shobijin (presumably tired of or unable to play the roles again they were recast for *Ebirah, Horror of the Deep* two years later). Their final feature film was *Mexican Free For All* with the Crazy Cats, a Japanese comedy troupe, in 1968.

- Some sources claim Honda was annoyed with this film's numerous plot threads which led to him taking a break from the series after *Invasion of Astro-Monster* (1965).

- The character of Malness (the Selginan assassin played by Hisaya Ito) was originally meant to be played by Yoshio Tsuchiya but the actor was tied up on *Red Beard*.

- In the American dub, the Princess claims to be from Mars rather than Venus.

- Despite emerging from Mt. Aso, some Toho Encyclopedias claim the Rodan in this film is not either of the two Rodans from *Rodan*, but another Rodan in suspended animation in the same volcano. Other sources say this Rodan is the child of the two Rodans from the original. Most fans choose not to believe this unpopular theory and consider this Rodan to be the surviving male from the original film.

- Supposedly, Tomoyuki Tanaka got the ball rolling on the then unnamed, new enemy monster when he brought in a book on Greek mythology into the studio and pointed at a seven headed monster.

- A Mysterian saucer prop from *The Mysterians* can be glimpsed in the office of the UFO enthusiast character played by Someshō Matsumoto.

Frankenstein Conquers the World (1965)

Japanese Title: *Frankenstein vs. Underground Monster Baragon*
Release Date: August 08, 1965

Directed by: Ishiro Honda
Special Effects by: Eiji Tsuburaya
Screenplay by: Kaoru Mabuchi & Reuben Bercovitch
Music by: Akira Ifukube
Cast: Nick Adams (Dr. Bowen) Kumi Mizuno (Sueko) Tadao Takashima (Kawaji) Yoshi Tsuchiya (Kawai) Koji Furuhata (Frankenstein Monster) **Suit Performers:** Haruo Nakajima (Baragon)

Tohoscope, Eastmancolor, 95 Minutes

Story
During the waning days of WWII, the Frankenstein monster's still beating heart is captured by the Nazis in Germany and taken to Hiroshima shortly before the bomb is dropped. Flash-forward fifteen years later and American scientist Dr. James Bowen runs a radiation clinic with nurse Sueko and partner Kawaji. Reports begin to surface of a strange teenaged boy killing animals. They discover the boy is in fact the regenerated heart of the Frankenstein monster.

Growing at an astonishing rate, the boy soon grows too large to be contained and escapes to the wilderness. At the same time, an underground monster, called Baragon, begins attacking villages and eating the inhabitants. The military assumes Frankenstein is to blame and set out to destroy him. Bowen and Sueko don't want to believe the boy has turned violent and search for him near Mt. Fuji but are attacked by Baragon. Frankenstein shows up to save them and the two monsters battle amidst a forest fire and then sink into the ground during a tremor.

Background & Commentary

That Toho made a film about a giant Frankenstein is odd enough—odder still is that it's actually quite good. Not surprising, perhaps, is that the film began life as "Frankenstein vs. Godzilla." Toho hoped to cash in on *King Kong vs. Godzilla*'s success by pitting their monster against yet another western icon. Supposedly, the final film (a Toho-UPA co-production) was partly the brainchild of Reuben Bercovitch, but much like the classic Frankenstein monster itself stitched together from various donors, it's not clear who originated what between Toho and the Americans. What is known is that Henry G. Saperstein of UPA had garnered the distribution rights to Toho's monster films in 1964, in a sense becoming Godzilla's American agent. Because the films were playing so well in America, he pitched Toho the idea of utilizing American "stars" to make their releases more appealing internationally. Nick Adams, who appeared in such American classics as *Rebel Without a Cause*, *Mister Roberts* and the TV series *The Rebel*, signed to play the lead in the film. Curiously, many sources indicate Adams was already cast in the movie by Toho before Saperstein officially became involved, making Bercovitch's screenplay credit all the more mysterious. More likely it was penned by Kaoru Mabuchi, writer of classics like *Rodan*. Whatever the case, the screenplay and its monsters are quite entertaining.

Rather than a man in a suit, actor Koji Furuhata portrayed the Frankenstein monster via make-up effects with a slightly flattened head reminiscent of Universal's classic design. There are a few other tips of the hat to the Universal series, such as the distinctly Bavarian style musical chords that open the Japanese version, and credits that play over a laboratory set full of beakers and chemicals in both versions. Tsuburaya even constructs a miniature German graveyard for one of the film's early scenes. At one point, Kawaji interviews an old German scientist who seems to reference the Universal films when he mentions how the monster had been killed many times before, but always came back to life. The rest of the proceedings are distinctly Japanese and the highlight of the film is the monster Baragon, sporting a unique design amongst the pantheon of Toho kaiju. Because of the two monsters' smaller sizes, Tsuburaya was able to construct a bevy of larger scale miniature sets that convey a heightened sense of realism. The standout is a well-lit forest that becomes ablaze at dusk during the final battle between the monsters. This film is also famous for an elaborate alternate ending that appears in neither the Japanese or American versions. At UPA's behest, a scene was filmed where, after defeating Baragon, a giant octopus shows up— seemingly out of nowhere—to battle Frankenstein. The two beasts struggle about and then fall into a body of water. Although an exciting sequence, it throws the film for a loop and UPA wisely chose to go with the original Japanese ending. The "lost" sequence was edited into a special version of the film released onto Japanese laserdisc in the 1990s, and the octopus prop would be put to better use in the sequel *War of the Gargantuas*.

As for the film's American star, Nick Adams was much loved at Toho, frequently joking with his co-stars, all of which admired him. He was also rumored to be having an affair with Kumi Mizuno. According to interviews with Mizuno, Adams once even proposed to her. Adams also headlined a Godzilla film, *Invasion of Astro Monster* (better known as *Monster Zero*), during his time in Japan which also starred Mizuno and was able to squeeze one more picture in with her, the non-monster film, *The Killing Bottle*, released in 1967 before he left. Ishiro Honda even remarked to David Milner that, "There should have been two or three more films produced with Mr. Adams whether they were monster movies or not." *Frankenstein Conquers the World* managed to reach U.S. theaters in 1966 before the tragic death of Adams (some say it was a suicide but others claim it was murder) in 1968.

Final Word
Worth seeing based upon the concept alone. Whether it equals or surpasses one's expectations is all a matter of taste.

Trivia

- In the 1970s Toho would also take a crack at Dracula, but he stays human-sized throughout the proceedings.

- In America, this film was double-billed with *Tarzan and the Lost Valley of Gold*.

- The Baragon suit was later retrofitted by Tsuburaya Productions to become several different monsters on their TV series *Ultra Q* and *Ultraman*. The monsters were Pagos, Neronga, Magular and Gabora.

- Another giant kaiju version of the Frankenstein monster appears in Toei's Super Sentai series *Kyōryū Sentai Zyuranger* (1992) and, as such, also appears in an episode of Saban's first season of *Power Rangers* ("Life's a Masquerade").

- Baragon became one of the most popular monsters among Japanese children and toys of the monster sold well.

- Toho's first idea to use the Frankenstein monster began with *Frankenstein vs. the Human Vapor* which was developed (and subsequently dropped) shortly after the release of *King Kong v. Godzilla*.

Gamera (1965)

Alternate Titles: *Giant Monster Gamera* (Japan)
Gammera the Invincible (U.S.)
Release Date: November 27, 1965

Directed by: Noriaki Yuasa
Special Effects by: Yonesaburo Tsukiji & Noriaki Yuasa
Screenplay by: Niisan Takahashi
Music by: Tadashi Yamauchi
Cast: Eiji Funakoshi (Dr. Hidaka) Harumi Kiritachi
(Yamamoto) Junichiro Yamashiko (Aoyagi) Yoshiro Uchida
(Toshio) **Suit Performers:** Uncredited (Gamera)

Daieiscope, Black & White, 78 Minutes

Story
During a Cold War skirmish in the Arctic a jet crashes and
releases the giant turtle Gamera. In Japan, young boy Toshio
is commanded by his father to get rid of his pet turtle. After
setting it free, Gamera shows up and destroys the family's
lighthouse but saves Toshio from falling to his death,
creating a bond between the two. After destroying a
geothermal power plant, it becomes apparent Gamera draws
strength from heat sources so the military attacks Gamera
with a newly developed bomb that briefly freezes targets on
contact. Gamera is knocked on his back by the blasts, and
scientists deduct that, being a turtle, he will never get up
again. Amidst the celebrations Gamera retracts into his shell
and flies into the air like a flying saucer in a fiery spectacle.
He soon attacks Tokyo while a joint venture between the
nations of the world, called Plan Z, is under construction on
nearby Oshima Island. On the island Gamera is lured into the
cargo bay of a large rocket. A domed enclosure traps him
inside and it blasts off into space as Toshio looks on.

Background & Commentary
Ironically, the inception of Godzilla's soon to be competitor
was not unlike his own birth in the mind of Tomoyuki
Tanaka. Daiei Studios was at the time unsuccessfully trying
to film a story titled *Giant Horde Beast Nezura* about giant

rats running afoul of Tokyo which was cancelled due to the difficulty of using live rats. Now Daiei was left with miniature sets and no monsters to accompany them. On an airline flight to Tokyo, Masaichi Nagata, then president of Daiei Studios, looked out the window and saw a cloud formation that reminded him of a flying turtle. Seeing Toho's success with Godzilla, Nagata insisted his screenwriters cook up a story about a flying turtle monster, which Niisan Takahashi did in record time. Noriaki Yuasa, a young director with only one film under his belt, was assigned the project because no senior directors at Daiei wanted to touch the film due to the nightmare responsibility of directing a SPFX picture. Not having an extensive SPFX department like Toho, Daiei had to improvise. Because processing monochrome film was easier than color film, the picture was shot in black and white (the last kaiju eiga to do so) and the monster actually looks better within its less revealing confines compared to color sequels. Because Daiei also lacked an optical printer to animate a ray effect from Gamera's mouth, Yuasa and effects director Yonesaburo Tsukiji used an actual flame thrower. Tsukiji quickly left the project resulting in Yuasa directing most of the film's effects sequences, a responsibility he would also take on in all the sequels, making him unique among directors of kaiju eiga. Despite the many technical problems in bringing the turtle to life and being filmed in black and white, the film became a big hit, particularly among children who no doubt connected with young Toshio who forms a strange bond with the kaiju.

While monsters in American films were always defeated by western ingenuity, in Japanese films, particularly those of Ishiro Honda, problems were often solved by the nations of the world putting aside their differences to work towards a common goal. Yuasa shares these sentiments as the film begins in a bout of Cold War tension but ends with these prejudices set aside as the nations of the world work together to rid themselves of the monster. Another trait of kaiju eiga exemplified here is the military's rather creative ways of dealing with their monster problem, first attacking Gamera with freeze bombs, and later trapping him inside of a rocket. Themselves in competition with Toho's Godzilla sequels, it is apparent by this non-lethal ending that Daiei hoped they could turn Gamera into a series as well. However, the Gamera presented here is not the hero he would become in sequels. Although he rescues a boy from falling, he isn't necessarily the friend of all children and causes tremendous death and destruction. At one point he actually roasts some Japanese citizens alive with his flame breath on a rooftop. Furthermore, his flying form is animated in some sequences, something that would not be repeated in sequels. Nor would his ability to jam radio waves be emphasized much in the future either.

Although many people assume Gamera's connection to Atlantis was something cooked up for 1995's *Gamera Guardian of the Universe* by Shusuke Kaneko, this film claims Gamera is a prehistoric species of turtle that lived on the Atlantis continent. However, this theory is never elaborated upon in the script, nor is it ever mentioned in sequels. This tidbit of information was also cut from the American version, released theatrically as *Gammera the Invincible.* New scenes of American actors Brian Donlevy and Albert Dekker were inserted to make it more marketable. It was the only Showa era Gamera film to be released theatrically in the U.S.; the sequels would go straight to television.

Final Word
While this film has a hard time making up its mind as to what it wants to be (Daiei wanted a straight monster story, Yuasa wanted to make a children's picture), it is no less a landmark as the birth of the Gamera series.

Trivia

- To look for suit-performers to play Gamera, Daiei scoured gymnasiums for bodybuilders.

- When the crew ran into trouble they reportedly called Eiji Tsuburaya for advice.

- Gamera's roar was created by scratching glass and cement, and also animal cries.

- To differentiate Gamera from Godzilla, Yuasa wanted to film the monster in quadruped stance as often as possible.

- Yuasa deeply loved the films and expressed interest in doing another all the way up to his death in 2004.

Invasion of Astro-Monster (1965)

Alternate Titles: *The Great Monster War* (Japan) *Monster Zero* (U.S.) *Godzilla vs. Monster Zero* (U.S. Home Video) *Command from the Dark* (Germany) *Invasion of Planet X* (France) *Invasion from Space* (Yugoslavia) *Monsters of the Galaxy* (Mexico) *Monsters Invade Earth* (Spain)
Release Date: December 19, 1965

Directed by: Ishiro Honda
Special Effects by: Eiji Tsuburaya
Screenplay by: Shinichi Sekizawa
Music by: Akira Ifukube
Cast: Nick Adams (Glenn) Akira Takarada (Fuji) Kumi Mizuno (Namikawa) Yoshio Tsuchiya (Controller of Planet X) Akira Kubo (Tetsuo) Keiko Sawai (Haruno) Jun Tazaki (Dr. Sakurai) **Suit Performers:** Haruo Nakajima (Godzilla) Masaki Shinohara (Rodan) Shoichi Hirose (King Ghidorah)

Tohoscope, Eastmancolor, 96 Minutes

Story
Signals from newly discovered Planet X prompt an expedition from the World Space Authority which sends astronauts Glenn and Fuji in Rocketship P-1 to investigate. There they find a barren planet inhabited by peaceful aliens besieged by King Ghidorah. The controller requests the loan of Godzilla and Rodan to battle the monster, to which earth obliges. The Xians arrive on earth ahead of schedule, somewhat troubling the people of earth, and take Godzilla and Rodan to Planet X where they vanquish Ghidorah. The Xians then deliver to Earth a recording said to contain a cure for all disease, but when played at a government meeting it instead delivers an ultimatum that earth surrender or the

Xians will unleash Godzilla, Rodan and King Ghidorah on the cities of Earth. As the monsters ravage the countryside, Glenn discovers the way to defeat the aliens via a sonic sound. The sound wave is deployed on the aliens destroying them, while Godzilla and Rodan come to their senses and battle King Ghidorah.

Background & Commentary

Having birthed an amazingly popular new creation in the form of King Ghidorah, and also coming off a hit co-production with UPA in *Frankenstein Conquers the World*, perhaps it should have been no surprise that Toho's next Godzilla film would be a direct sequel to *Ghidorah, the Three Headed Monster* co-produced with UPA. For the storyline Toho and UPA (which put up about half of the film's budget) both agreed that injecting an alien invasion theme into the series would work well. Thusly was born a major staple of the Godzilla series and other kaiju eiga which would be overused for years to come in the form of invading aliens which use monsters to do their bidding.

Though it reuses three monsters of the previous film's four and lacks innovation in that department, *Invasion of Astro-Monster* may well be the apex of the 1960s Japanese monster film in some respects. It features several stand out set-pieces (notably the Xians kidnapping of Godzilla and Rodan), an engaging action packed human storyline, and its American lead Nick Adams, who makes for a constantly lively presence. Several pieces of his dialogue such as, "You stinkin' rats!" and "We're gonna fight to the last man, baby!" have become fan favorite quotes. Also fantastic are the rest of the cast, particularly the self-sacrificing Miss Namikawa. Though Honda loved the element of self-sacrifice in his films, this was the first time a woman had been placed in the role of tragic hero in a G-film. The film's shortcomings sadly lie in its climax. Firstly, a few of the city destruction sequences are actually stock-footage from *Rodan* and *Mothra*, the start of a sad trend that would expand in the 1970s. Already having witnessed the monster battle on Planet X hyped in all of the posters and trailers, the end battle between Godzilla, Rodan and King Ghidorah on a grassy plain leaves much to be desired. Having already seen Rodan and Godzilla kick Ghidorah's tails earlier on Planet X—not to mention the previous picture—there is little suspense when the rumble begins and it seems obligatory more than anything else. In addition to this there are only about three Xian saucers present during the climax, which have already been defeated by the time the monsters begin to fight. On the other end of the spectrum, Godzilla and Rodan's battle on the surface of Planet X with King Ghidorah is a stand out sequence amongst the entire series. And, the fact that Shinichi Sekizawa was able to concoct an off-world battle for the monsters—and that Eiji Tsuburaya was able to pull it off— is commendable to say the least. This stellar sequence ends on a love it or hate it moment for most fans when Godzilla engages in a victory jig nicknamed the "jumping shie." It was a popular move in a comic strip at the time, and several people take credit for suggesting the scene, among them the Controller of Planet X himself Yoshio Tsuchiya. Ishiro Honda was against this scene, and perhaps it's no coincidence that the tiring director didn't return for the sequel.

In Japan the film was another dai-hit, though admissions were not as high as they were for the previous picture. Despite being beat to theaters by the more ambitious *Destroy All Monsters* in 1969, *Monster Zero* (as it was called in America) was still a sizeable hit when released stateside in July of 1970 on a double bill with *War of the Gargantuas*, taking in $3 million for distributor Maron films. While most people assume the film's release was delayed because of the death of Nick Adams, Henry G. Saperstein claimed Toho was dragging their feet about releasing the film internationally. A more likely possibility for the delay was because of a falling out Saperstein had with Samuel Z. Arkoff of AIP. Had this not happened, the film reportedly would've seen release via AIP in 1967 as *Invasion of Astro-Monster*. Whatever the case, the delay certainly didn't hurt the film.

Final Word
If the last half of the film could've matched the first, this film could've been the best Godzilla picture of the 1960s.

Trivia

- Rodan's wingspan increases from 120 meters in the previous film to 150 meters for this film.

- It has never been confirmed nor denied whether Mothra and the Shobijin figured into this film's original script. Some say an appearance by an Imago Mothra was cut for budgetary reasons (though this doesn't make sense as the Mothra Imago marionette was still in useable condition as it appears in the sequel) and this author suspects working the Shobijin into the script proved too complicated.

- Nick Adams and Yoshio Tsuchiya (Controller of Planet X) loved to play practical jokes on one another. Tsuchiya "taught" Adams to say "Good morning" when in fact he taught him to say, "I'm starving." Adams later hung a framed autographed photo of Tsuchiya in his home in America.

- At the time of the film's production Henry G. Saperstein entered into an agreement to produce a total of five films with Toho including three giant monster films, a spy thriller, a war movie and a TV series.

- The Rodan prop became the bird monster Litra on *Ultra Q* after this.

- David Janssen, from TV's hit series *The Fugitive*, was the first choice for the role of Astronaut F. Glenn before it went to Nick Adams.

- *Command from the Dark* (this film's German title) was not coincidentally the name of a famous German Sci-fi novel by Hans Dominik, and this film was actually passed off as his work in a 1967 release in Germany.

- The King Ghidorah suit's necks were lengthened and a new coat of gold paint was applied to the beast's scales for this film.

- Akira Takarada was dubbed for this film by Marvin Miller, Robbie the Robot on the *Lost in Space* TV series.

Daimajin (1966)

Alternate Titles: *The Giant Majin* (U.S.)
Release Date: April 17, 1966

Directed by: Kimiyoshi Yasuda
Special Effects by: Yoshiyuki Kuroda
Screenplay by: Tetsuro Yoshida
Music by: Akira Ifukube
Cast: Jun Fujimaki (Kogenta) Miwa Takada (Kozasa) Yoshihiko Aoyoma (Tadafumi) Ryutaro Gomi (Samanosuke) Shosaku Sugiyama (Shinobu) Ryuzo Shimada (Take) **Suit Performers:** Riki Hashimoto (Majin)

Daieiscope, Eastmancolor, 84 Minutes

Story

Thunderous footsteps cause a 17th Century Japanese village to tremble in fear. The village priestess stages a ceremony to appease the giant in the mountain while at the same time an uprising led by the evil chamberlain Samanosuke overthrows the benevolent Lord Hanabusa and his clan. Kogenta, a palace servant, the Hanabusa children, Tadafumi and Kozasa, and the priestess, Shinobu, escape to the mountain where the statue of the Daimajin stands. Ten years pass and the village is in dire straits, enslaved by the cruel Samanosuke and his men. Kogenta sneaks into the village to see if he can garner support for an uprising but is captured. Tadafumi goes to rescue him and is himself captured. Shinobu confronts Samanosuke to release the two men or incur the wrath of the Majin. Instead, Samanosuke kills her and sends his men to destroy the statue. Along the way they capture Kozasa and a village boy, Take. The men try to destroy the statue to no avail, so they begin to drive a spike into its forehead. Blood begins to flow, lightning strikes and the ground swallows up the evil doers, but still the statue does not wake. Kozasa pleads with the statue to awaken until she sheds tears. Finally, the mountain trembles and the statue comes alive and makes way for the village. Majin arrives in time to save Tadafumi and Kogenta from execution and in the process kills the evildoers before reverting back to his original form and then crumbling into dust.

Background & Commentary

From the first shot to the last, the quality is evident in every aspect of *Daimajin's* ambitious production. The matte paintings are stunning, as is the miniature work and SPFX as a whole. The cinematography by Fujio Morita, who also had a part in the effects work, is top notch as is Kimiyoshi Yasuda's engaging direction of the human cast. Akira Ifukube's stirring music that opens the film is instantly recognizable, though it is strange to see it over the Daiei logo instead of Toho's. It's hard to believe that this film came from the same studio currently producing the Gamera series. Touted as "Japan's first full-scale SPFX Samurai Spectacular!" the film is more *Rashoman* than it is *Gamera*. A jidaigeki epic set during the Tokugawa period, it switches to dai-kaiju eiga only in the last act in a tradition reminiscent of Kabuki Theater. As for Majin's appearance late in the game, there is no need to worry as the film doesn't rest upon the shoulders of the giant statue alone. The story and its cast could carry itself without any monster scenes; they are simply what set the picture apart and make it special amongst jidaigeki and kaiju eiga alike. Although there are several prominent child actors the film is strictly adult fare with a main character being tortured with hot pokers and later strung up by his heels. During the climax Majin nails the villain to a makeshift cross with a giant spike in addition to crushing numerous evil doers under his feet. These scenes are not bloody exploitation by any means though. The deaths of the villains are justified, and that of sympathetic characters are treated with great care, particularly the death of the priestess midway through the story which is particularly poignant due to Masuda's direction and Ifukube's score.

As for the film's effects shots, they are not limited to the climax. The picture opens with a wonderful miniature forest set shrouded in fog. In the distance an animated wolf howls at the moon. If one didn't know better, they might think they were watching a well-made piece of Hammer horror. A supernatural earthquake that occurs when the statue is attacked causes the ground to open and swallow several of the men. To emphasize this is no ordinary earthquake unearthly greenish glows emanate from the cracks, which close back up once the men are swallowed. There is also a sequence wherein young Take is plagued by ghosts in the forest. With brief glimpses the ghosts are well done, even if their purpose in the story is never explained. As for the main event, there is much build up to the Majin's release and what follows does not disappoint. The giant statue plods along slowly and deliberately, his heavy footsteps evoking a deserving sense of dread from the heroes and the villains alike. Rather than facing tanks and maser canons as Godzilla and Rodan did, Majin appropriately shrugs off catapult and musket fire in accordance with the era. Overall there isn't a bad effects shot in the entire film and several of them are positively stunning, particularly a long shot of Majin behind a fire. To accomplish this, Daiei built a full sized prop which meshes incredibly well with the actor. Majin was no regular suitmation monster, the eyes of Riki Hashimoto (a large man and former professional baseball player) behind the stoic mask clearly express emotion, though mostly rage. As for the Majin's character, he is morally ambiguous at times. Although he is clearly the hero of the picture, when Majin rescues Tadafumi he does so with great disdain. Furthermore, after dispatching the villain, Majin then proceeds to the village where the innocent peasants live and begins to tear it apart. Both young Take and Tadafumi beg him to stop, but it is Kozasa whose pleading reaches the monster's ears. She offers to let the monster crush her if it would appease his rage. It was by her tears the monster came to life, and it is her tears that cause it to revert back to its original stone form. The statue then crumbles to dust. The monster is portrayed almost as a force of nature, constantly accompanied by a stormy rushing wind. Once Majin accomplishes his mission, the skies are clear again.

The film was a released on a hit double bill with *Gamera vs. Barugon* that spawned two sequels within the same year creating the Daimajin trilogy. This distinctly Japanese film even managed to score a brief theatrical release (in some cases subtitled and others dubbed) in the U.S. in 1968, before being sold to television under the title *The Giant Majin*.

Final Word
A near flawless film on a par with Toho's 1954 *Godzilla*.

Trivia

- The budget was set at a large ¥100,000,000.

- Riki Hashimoto never blinked when the camera was rolling on his face.

- Won a Japanese Cinematography Association Miura Award.

- For a time the full sized Daimajin prop was stored at the front entrance to Daiei Studios in Kyoto.

- Daimajin was inspired by the axed villain, a Jotun Frost Giant, from the unproduced *Gamera vs. the Ice Men*. Daiei executives were intrigued by the idea of an ice giant, and decided to develop a new story around a stone giant which led to the creation of Daimajin.

Gamera vs. Barugon (1966)

Alternate Titles: *Duel of the Monsters: Gamera vs. Barugon* (Japan) *War of the Monsters* (U.S.)
Release Date: April 17, 1966

Directed by: Shigeo Tanaka
Special Effects by: Noriaki Yuasa

Screenplay by: Niisan Takahashi
Music by: Tadashi Kinoshita
Cast: Kojiro Hongo (Keisuke) Kyoko Enami (Karen) Koji
Fujiyama (Onodera) Akira Natsuki (Ichiro) Yuzo Hayakawa
(Kawajiri) **Suit Performers:** Arakaki Teruo (Gamera)
Uncredited (Baragon)

Daieiscope, Eastmancolor, 101 Minutes

Story

Three men, Keisuke, Kawajiri, and Onodera, set off to New
Guinea in search of a cave of fabulous opals that a mutual
friend of theirs claimed to have found during WWII. Upon
finding the cave, Onodera betrays his friends by dynamiting
the entrance and running off with one of the opals.
Unbeknownst to him, he has found no opal, but instead a
monster egg which hatches the monster Barugon upon his
return to Japan. Ravaging through Kobe and Osaka, the
JSDF's attempts to subdue Barugon (who has the ability to
freeze objects with its tongue and also shoot a rainbow beam
out of its back) all prove unsuccessful. Gamera, having been
freed from the Plan Z rocket, returns to Japan where he faces
Barugon in Osaka and ends up frozen. Help arrives in the
form of Keisuke and Karen, a native girl who knows how to
defeat the monster via a large diamond. However, whilst
trying to lure Barugon into a lake with the diamond where it
will drown, Onodera shows up and steals it thwarting the
plan though he also ends up being eaten by the monster.
Eventually Gamera thaws and flies to Lake Biwa where he
drags Barugon into the depths and drowns him.

Background & Commentary

Pleased with the success of *Gamera*, Daiei president Masaichi
Nagata quickly set about production on a color sequel with
an "unprecedented" ¥80,000,000 budget—about twice the
cost of the first film. Sadly, *Gamera's* director Noriaki Yuasa
was downgraded to SPFX director only while Shigeo Tanaka
(maker of WWII propaganda films for Daiei) was given the
director's chair. Reportedly, during the production of the
first film, Daiei and Yuasa went back and forth as to whether
or not *Gamera* should be a children's picture, though there

seemed to be no debate when it came to the sequel which was a strictly adult affair.

Gamera vs. Barugon is something of an anomaly among the Showa Gamera films. A grim and moody tale of greed and revenge, there are no child characters or monster humor in sight. Instead, Gamera and his formidable foe gush blue Eastmancolor blood by the bucket, and several of the cast are murdered by Onodera, the film's human villain. Though it takes nearly an hour for the monster action to begin, Kojiro Hongo and the rest of the cast actually play out an engaging story. However, when the monster footage begins via a creepy scene of Barugon hatching from his egg (reportedly Yuasa's favorite scene) it never lets up again. From this point forwards tokusatsu fans are treated to spectacular miniature city destruction as Barugon destroys both Kobe and Osaka. One of the film's more entertaining aspects comes in the form of the JSDF's innovative attempts to attack the monster, notably trying to lure it into a lake where it will drown, and later by constructing a giant mirror which will reflect the kaiju's outlandish rainbow beam. In this sense Barugon is the true star of the film, with Gamera showing up so sparingly that it feels as though he is guest starring in his own movie.

Unlike Toho who killed Godzilla in his first feature, Daiei had enough foresight to merely seal Gamera up inside of a rocket, which conveniently collides with a meteor at the beginning of this film setting the terrible terrapin free once again. This wisely occurs in the first scene and is followed by Gamera destroying a huge dam, after which he is not seen again until his confrontation with Barugon in Osaka. Though *Gamera vs. Barugon* was a financial success, Daiei and Yuasa took note of the fact that children were bored during the "adult scenes" and were disappointed with the scarcity of which their hero appeared, a mistake they would rectify in the next sequel.

Final Word
Though a Gamera film, this is also ironically one of the best adult level kaiju films ever made.

Trivia

- The film's original story initially pitted Gamera against a group of "ice men" from space who plan to throw the earth into a second ice age. This is actually the reason that Barugon was given the strange ability to freeze objects with his tongue to keep the "fire and ice" theme going.

- The film was double-billed quite successfully with Daiei's *Daimajin*.

- Monster suits for this film were constructed by Ryusaku Takayama, who built monster suits for Tsuburaya Production's *Ultra Q* and *Ultraman* series.

- Since the Barugon suit was too buoyant to sink for the final scene, it was cut up into sections until they reached the head for the last shot.

- A scene was filmed wherein Barugon runs across a bridge rigged with explosives, only the SPFX technician rigged them in the wrong direction resulting in a few burns to the suit performer and an unusable scene.

- Some water damage occurred during the dam break sequence when the flooding waters caused wire damage to some of the filming equipment.

- Kojiro Hongo was so reluctant to participate in a monster film he faked an illness to the extent of taking a cold shot in hopes Daiei would recast his role. However, Daiei executives insisted they wait on Hongo to recover before filming began.

- The film was released only five months after the original *Gamera*.

- *Gamera vs. Barugon* didn't receive a theatrical release in America and went straight to television as *War of the Monsters*.

- This is the last film in which Gamera is portrayed primarily as a quadruped, as Noriaki Yuasa wanted his kaiju to be more animalistic than Toho's.

- The film's U.S. Home Video release touted Barugon as the "loser of a Godzilla look-alike contest." Ironically Daiei intended Barugon as a quadruped version of Godzilla.

- Publicity shots were taken of Kyoko Enami (Karen) in full native garb dancing, though no scenes of this occur in the film.

- Though Daiei claims this was the first Japanese monster film to show a kaiju (Barugon) eating someone, it was actually Toho's Baragon who ate victims (albeit off-screen) in 1965's *Frankenstein Conquers the World*.

!!!!!!!!!!!!!!!!!!Bonus Review!!!!!!!!!!!!!!!!!!!!

Terror Beneath the Sea (1966)

Japanese Title: *Battle Beneath the Sea*
Release Date: July 01, 1966

Directed by: Hajime Sato
Special Effects by: Nobuo Yajima
Screenplay by: Kohichi Ohtsu
Music by: Shunsuke Kikuchi
Cast: Sonny Chiba (Ken Abe) Peggy Neal (Jenny Gleason) Erik Neilson (Dr. Moore) Andrew Hughes (Prof. Howard)
Suit Performers: Uncredited

Cinemascope, Eastmancolor, 84 Minutes

Story

While covering a U.S. Navy submarine's newest torpedo test, reporters Ken and Jenny spy a strange amphibious creature lurking in the depths. When the duo take to the sea in scuba gear to investigate, the two are captured by a trio of the amphibious humanoids. They are then taken to the secret underwater base of madman Dr. Moore, who intends to create a whole race of the humanoids. When Ken fails to bend to his will, Dr. Moore begins to turn Ken and Jenny into the monsters. However, an attack on the underwater base by the U.S. Navy causes the humanoids to revolt and thus gives Ken, Jenny, and the kidnaped Professor Howard the chance to escape. Back on the surface, Dr. Howard reverses the mutation process on Ken and Jenny, turning them back to normal.

Background & Commentary

One of the absolute worst and most clichéd Japanese suitmation monster movies of all time, this film was made by William Ross, future producer of such films as *The Green Slime* (1968), and shot by Toei Studio's TV department. And sadly, the fact that this was lensed by Toei's TV department rather than their feature film division is painfully evident. For one, the poor conditions of the monster suits make the film's infamous *Creature from the Black Lagoon*-type kaiju more appropriate for the small screen where the creatures would have been better suited as the dispensable lackeys for a fiendish overlord on a corny TV series. The underwater submarine sequences are also of a TV show quality, though the villain's underwater lair comes across well enough.

As the film has a James Bond-like villain complete with a cool underwater lair, the story should have benefited from a James Bond type hero rather than pre-stardom Sonny Chiba's bland reporter (that being said, Chiba's character does get to deal out some fisticuffs in the climax). Along with Chiba is female reporter Jenny, played by Peggy Neil, then 19 at the time, who would go on to play the female lead in Shochiku's *The X From Outer Space* (1967). Also in the mix is Andrew Hughes, a familiar Caucasian face in many of Toho's tokusatsu films (notably *Destroy All Monsters*), who gets a much larger part than usual in this Toei production. As for the big bad, while some villains have mechanical hands, flippers, or some sort of intriguing birth defect, in this film the villain Dr. Moore merely wears black sunglasses. In essence, he is a dime store Bond villain with a dime store base (complete with crude hand painted lettering on the controls).

As for other production values, Shunsuke Kikuchi, future composer of the sequels in Daiei's Gamera series, composes an incredibly repetitive score for this film—elements of which would later turn up in *Gamera vs. Guiron* (1969). Hajime Sato's direction is likewise lackluster, though the director would go on to direct such classics as *Goke, Body Snatcher from Hell* (1968). However, it should be noted that this was never actually intended as a feature film, but a three-part TV mini-series meant for broadcast in the U.S. When the broadcast was shelved, it was edited into a feature film and released in Japan in the summer of 1966, and aired on American television many years later in 1971.

Final Word

For those that enjoy hilariously inept filmmaking, *Terror Beneath the Sea* is sure to delight. For anyone else, it's a waste of time.

Trivia

- Though nearly all of the cast filmed their lines in English, they were redubbed by other actors in post-production anyways.

- The fish-men in this film are actually called "water cyborgs"—a moniker that makes no sense as they are organic.

War of the Gargantuas (1966)

Japanese Title: *Frankenstein's Monsters: Sanda vs. Gaira*
Release Date: July 31, 1966

122 / フランケンシュタインの 怪獣
サンダ対ガイラ

Directed by: Ishiro Honda
Special Effects by: Eiji Tsuburaya
Screenplay by: Kaoru Mabuchi
Music by: Akira Ifukube
Cast: Russ Tamblyn (Dr. Stewart) Kumi Mizuno (Akami)
Kenji Sahara (Dr. Majida) Jun Tuzaki (Military
Commander) **Suit Performers:** Hiroshi Sekida (Sanda)
Haruo Nakajima (Gaira)

Tohoscope, Eastmancolor, 92 Minutes

Story

Dr. Stewart and his assistant Akami study and care for a young Gargantua in their lab which escapes to the mountains. Five years later a similar giant monster is attacking ships off the coast of Japan before finally venturing on land where he begins to devour people. Yet, Dr. Stewart and Akami remain certain this monster is not the gentle creature they had in captivity. Their theory is proven correct when, as the military is battling the Green Gargantua in the forest, a Brown Gargantua appears to save his brother. Dr. Stewart is then able to determine the Green Gargantua was formed from the Brown Gargantua's DNA long ago, the implication being that whenever a chunk of flesh is torn off it has the possibility to grow into a new monster. The Green Gargantua wreaks havoc again when he appears in a forest chasing some hikers that happen to include Akami and Dr. Stewart. When Akami falls off a cliff she is caught and saved by the gentle Brown Gargantua. Later, when the Brown Gargantua sees the grizzly remains of his brother's victims he shows the green monster his disgust by hitting him with a tree. This provokes a battle between the brothers that takes them all the way to Tokyo. Dr. Stewart and Akami try to convince the military to spare the Brown Gargantua in their attacks but they will hear none of it and both monsters are bombarded with weaponry. Eventually both perish in a volcanic eruption at sea.

123 / フランケンシュタインの怪獣
サンダ対ガイラ

Background & Commentary

A quasi-sequel to *Frankenstein Conquers the World* (a connection never explained aside from the monsters being referred to as "Frankensteins" in the Japanese version); *War of the Gargantuas* presents yet more humanoid monsters on the loose to decidedly better results. The film's fans include everyone from Brad Pitt to Tim Burton and it is Toho's best known dai kaiju eiga outside of the G-series, and deservedly so. The opening scenes set on a fishing boat during a stormy night feature one creepy surprise after another to superb direction and ominous music. First a lone tentacle sneaks up on an unsuspecting crewman and later a great long shot reveals Gaira, the Green Gargantua, battling a giant octopus. Typically in a Japanese monster film this would signal the entrance of the hero monster, but not so here. After Gaira kills the octopus he goes on to sink the boat and eat the crew. Gaira makes several surprise entrances during the first act, seeming to pop up out of nowhere when two fishermen discover him looking up at them from under the clear water. Later he sneaks up to a nightclub balcony and grabs American songstress Kipp Hamilton.

Still in a phase of co-productions with UPA, Russ Tamblyn was the American star imported to Japan for this entry. However, it's painfully obvious he isn't enjoying himself as Nick Adams was and mostly phones in his performance. In a sense recreating the trio of characters seen in *Frankenstein Conquers the World* in all but name, Kumi Mizuno returns as the romantic lead/assistant and Tadao Takashima is replaced by Kenji Sahara in the role of the Caucasian doctor's Japanese sidekick. In addition to a wonderful screenplay the film is rife with standout SPFX sequences, among them a lengthy confrontation between Gaira and the military in the countryside with futuristic weaponry known as the Maser Canon. Although introduced as far back as the original *Mothra*, and continued in the previous year's *Invasion of Astro-Monster*, it is in this film that they are given a definitive name and in the process become a permanent fixture of Toho monster movies. The footage of Gaira rummaging through the trees as he is being shot with the lasers would be notoriously recycled in several 1970s G-films. The end battle sequence in Tokyo between the brothers is an all-out masterpiece of miniature destruction, and at one point a boat is used as a battering ram. Due to the kaiju's smaller sizes than those in the G-series, filming allowed for larger scale miniatures. There are numerous instances where the kaiju collapse into buildings that equal their size and the detail is shockingly good, even on the insides of the models which display various floors and bits of detailed wreckage. The battle starts in a forest and from there spans into the heart of Tokyo before moving to the dockyards, into the bay, and finally far out to sea into the mouth of an erupting volcano. All the while the Japanese military are either shooting them with Maser Canons or dropping bombs on them from the air. *War of the Gargantuas* typifies the Japanese monster film in that its beasts are not mindless engines of destruction, but characters that have moral dilemmas and stakes in the story. Sanda, the Brown Gargantua, for instance finally finds his long lost sibling only to discover that he is evil. He must then decide to make an enemy out of his only brother to save humanity and the audience knows that a happy ending is not in the cards. The film also takes up the subject of Nature vs. Nurture. Sanda was raised by humanity. Gaira was left to his own devices and eats people. Surprisingly, not many kaiju are people eaters, which makes Gaira all the more frightening, especially given his human appearance. His surprise reveal to a group of hikers obscured by mist in the mountains is truly a shock and a testament to Honda's direction. The same goes for Ifukube's music and Tsuburaya's effects which are nearly flawless in every respect, from seamless matte shots to convincing miniatures and even an ocean volcano that climaxes the picture. Perhaps this is why this film succeeds where so many others fail as the serious tone is not marred by laughable effects.

The film was a hit in Japan, and is well remembered to this day. It was also a big hit in America, raking in $3 million on a double bill with *Monster Zero*. Outside of the usual Godzilla gang of Rodan and Mothra, this is Toho's best known monster film internationally.

Final Word

At its heart a Cain and Able story with giant monsters (perhaps it should've been called *East of Edo?*) the film features Honda, Tsuburaya and Ifukube at their best.

Trivia

* Though Henry G. Saperstein was keen on a sequel to *Frankenstein Conquers the World*, when he saw the finished film he felt the designs of the two "Frankenstein Brothers" were too far removed from the original and renamed them the Gargantuas.

* The Sanda and Gaira costumes were re-used six years later on the short Toho TV series *Go! Godman* (1972-1973) and *Go! Greenman* (1973-1974).

* This film's "Special Guest Star", Kipp Hamilton, who gets snatched up by Gaira while singing "The Words Get Stuck in my Throat", was a minor actress and songstress. Her best known role was a supporting part in Frank Sinatra's film *Never So Few*, and the actress had guest spots on numerous TV series such as *Perry Mason* and *Bewitched* to name a few. She was also comedian Carol Burnett's sister-in-law. As to her involvement in *War of the Gargantuas*, this was due to her allegedly being Henry G. Saperstein's girlfriend. In any case, it was her last feature film role.

* The aquatic Gaira was originally designed to vaguely resemble the Gilman from *The Creature from the Black Lagoon.*

Return of Daimajin (1966)

Japanese Title: *Majin Grows Angry*
Release Date: August 13, 1966

Directed by: Kenji Misumi

Special Effects by: Yoshiyuki Kuroda
Screenplay by: Tetsuro Yoshida
Music by: Akira Ifukube
Cast: Kojiro Hongo (Lord Juro) Shiho Fujimura (Lady Sayuri) Takashi Kanada (Danjo) **Suit Performers:** Riki Hashimoto (Majin)

Daieiscope, Eastmancolor, 79 Minutes

Story
Two Japanese clans, the Nagoshi and the Chigusa, coexist peacefully on either side of a large lake, in the middle of which lies an island containing the statue of Daimajin. The evil Mikoshiba tribe, led by Danjo, wishes to overtake both villages. He uses a festival being held in Nagoshi as an opportunity to sneak his men into the city by hiding them in rolls of hay. The men come out at night and open the gates of the city and the Mikoshiba warriors storm the village, but Lord Juro escapes and reunites with his love from Chicagusa, Lady Sayuri. Danjo's next move is to send men to the island to blow up the Daimajin statue which they do at Sayuri's protest. Juro, Sayuri and their allies are eventually captured by Danjo and are tied to stakes in preparation for execution. Danjo decides Sayuri will be the first to die, tying her to a cross and then setting a fire under it. The winds begin to blow water from the lake putting out the fire. Majin rises reformed from the water and treks to the village to save Sayuri after which he executes his wrath on Danjo killing him in the lake. Majin turns back to stone and then dissolves into water.

Background & Commentary
This story is not surprisingly a rehash of the last film, setting up a sort of Majin formula. But considering what a delight the first film was, this is not entirely disappointing, and even Godzilla and Gamera had their respective formulas to a degree. With this sequel Majin also joined an exclusive club belonging to Godzilla, Gamera, and King Kong as one of few giant monsters to headline their own franchise. Otherwise, monsters were typically "one and done" affairs after their

premiere film; or they were spun into the Godzilla series in the case of Toho productions.

To differentiate itself form the last film the story appears to be set during a different time period and most of the action revolves around a lake, giving the film a waterfront setting. Because Majin's remains lie beneath the lake's surface, it sets up plenty of spooky water sequences. In one scene the lake's surface glows red and boils. In another, the enemy clan's boat is dragged under, presumably by Majin's unseen hand. Later a smashed canoe floats by with one of the enemy clansmen lying dead, part of the broken statue jabbed into him. The lake also provides plenty of action for the heroes, for instance Juro escapes the occupied village by jumping down a well and swimming into the lake. As Juro, Kojiro Hongo provides a solid lead to see Majin off in his first sequel just as he did for Gamera's second outing, *Gamera vs. Barugon,* that same year. However, it is Shiho Fujimura as Lady Sayuri that anchors the film and provides its heart and soul. As in the last film, it is her tears that eventually awaken the Majin. Unfortunately, the characters are slightly less developed than in the first picture, but perhaps the shorter running time is to blame. As for the character of the Majin, there appears to be a softening of his image in this outing. In stark contrast to how he indifferently rescues the young lord in the last film he rescues Sayuri with great care. What *Daimajin* films lacked in suspense during the end battles which are somewhat one sided, they make up for in the satisfying manner in which the villains are punished for their cruelty. In this film Danjo is about to burn a child in front of his mother before the group is saved by Majin. Danjo is also brazen enough to threaten the monster when he puts his sword to Juro's throat and warns, "Don't come any closer!" which Majin promptly ignores. The villains even set up a dynamite trap for Majin, and for a moment after detonation it seems as if the statue has been blown up. Majin soon emerges from the dust to prove otherwise. Finally, the villain meets his end in an ingenious way. Appearing to have escaped via sail boat, Majin sends a fiery spark across the lake that catches it on fire. Danjo tries to climb the sail, but instead ends up crucifying himself in the tangled rope and suffers the very fiery fate he intended for

Sayuri. As in the last film the storm accompanying Majin dissipates, and this time, instead of crumbling into stone, he dissolves into water.

The only instance wherein this film outdoes the original is perhaps Daimajin's entrance. Rising from the steaming water, the waves soon part *Ten Commandments* style and Majin makes his way to the village surrounded by massive walls of water in an impressive effects shot. The full sized Majin prop is again put to good use, eliminating the need for constant back-screen projection and distracting matte lines. In instances where the process is used the results are stellar, and never distracting. Complementing Kenji Misumi's direction and Fujiro Morita's cinematography again is Akira Ifukube returning as composer, his themes now even more evocative of his Toho scores than in the last film, particularly *Invasion of Astro-Monster* and *War of the Gargantuas*. Released only four months after *Daimajin* in Japan; in America this film went straight to television via AIP-TV as *The Return of the Giant Majin* in 1968.

Final Word
Although it lacks the novelty of the first film, this sequel is still leagues ahead of other kaiju films of the time.

Trivia

- Was made for the same budget as the original and grossed the same amount at the box office as the original as well.

Daimajin Strikes Again (1966)

Japanese Title: *Great Majin's Counterattack*
Release Date: December 10, 1966

Directed by: Kazuo Mori
Special Effects by: Yoshiyuki Kuroda
Screenplay by: Tetsuro Yoshida
Music by: Akira Ifukube

Cast: Hideki Ninomiya (Tsurukichi) Shinji Horii (Daisaku) Masahide Iizuka (Kinta) Muneyuki Nagatomo (Sugi) Yuzo Hayakawa (Yoshibei) Toru Abe (Arakawa) **Suit Performers:** Riki Hashimoto (Majin)

Daieiscope, Eastmancolor, 87 Minutes

Story

Thrashing about in the mountains, Daimajin's anger causes a series of disasters including floods, earthquakes and snowstorms as villagers tremble in fear. At the same time the evil lord Arakawa is kidnapping logging men from a nearby village to produce gunpowder from his sulfur pits at a large fort. One of the men escapes taking a shortcut through Majin's mountain and tells his village where the fort is before he dies. The man's younger brother, Tsurukichi, decides to set out across Majin's mountain to rescue his father and the other men. He is joined by younger brother Sugi and friends Daisaku and Kinta. The four boys trek across the wilderness avoiding a party of enemy samurai. Before they can make it to the enemy camp a snowstorm hits. Fearing death, Tsurukichi beseeches the faraway Majin statue to awaken and jumps from a cliff. Majin comes to life and teleports to the boys' location, and saves Tsurukichi from the deep snow. From there he treks to the fortress and destroys the evil doers thus freeing the loggers. Majin turns to snow and blows away in the wind.

Background & Commentary

This film starts out somewhat like the first, only instead of mere sound reverberations, Majin's footsteps cause a cornucopia of SPFX disasters including snowstorms, floods, earthquakes and lightning in their wake. The film truly begins with a bang, and in a break from tradition Majin is seen in the first reel, or rather his arms and legs if not his face. The unseen narrator proclaims that the story takes place in a time when all disasters were blamed on the Majin in a fairy tale-like manner. Perhaps this is a fitting introduction, as the main characters of the film are all children. The short running time and large cast of the last film somewhat prevented the audience from bonding with its characters, but this is rectified here in the quartet of young boys that anchor the story. All four become quite endearing over the course of the film, notably little Sugi. Just because the movie stars children doesn't mean it pulls any punches either. Kinta is swept away in the river and drowns, Daisaku's older brother is thrown into a sulfur pit, and while characters in the previous two films offered their lives to awaken Majin, Tsurukichi actually jumps from a cliff to do so. Considering the harsh nature of the past two films, it is surprising when Majin comes to his aid in the deep snow. Although Majin starts the film in a spout of moral ambiguity, towards the children he is nothing but benevolent.

Majin gains several new abilities in the film, among them teleportation. He also has a hawk that an old woman calls his avatar, in other words his eyes and ears on the mountain. At one point the hawk rescues the boys from evil patrolmen, and it is its death, along with Tsurukichi's jump from the mountain, that awakens Majin. Fans hoping Majin would finally unsheathe his sword in this entry wouldn't be disappointed as he finally puts the weapon to use when he pins the villain to a rock with it before dropping him in the sulfur pit. Unfortunately, the villain in this piece is less developed, making his death scene slightly less satisfying than that of his predecessors. Also, during this climax, Majin's scenes are focused more on the destruction of the fort rather than punishment of the wicked. Effects wise this picture can't claim the flawlessness of the original or its sequel. Majin's giant hand prop isn't used sparingly enough, and as a result its wobbly rubber nature is revealed and there are a few errors in scale during a rear-projection scene. Otherwise it's a top notch production once again with the same crew from the last film returning with a new director, Kazuo Mori. Ifukube provides another memorable score to conclude the trilogy with; elements of which precede his score for next year's Toho release *King Kong Escapes*.

The picture was shot with a slightly reduced budget compared to its predecessors directly after *Return of Daimajin*'s August 1966 release throughout September and October and was released that December. Unlike the previous two films, it was never released to U.S. theaters or television. There is also some confusion as to this film's placing in the series, as it was released to VHS in America in the 1990s as *Wrath of Daimajin*, a title more appropriate for the second film, which in Japanese translates as *Majin Grows Angry*. It was also placed as the second entry in the series in the VHS box set, further confusing the matter. Furthermore, many fans and scholars alike claim this film's child characters were a result of Daiei's "success" with Gamera, when in fact Gamera was not yet a children's franchise and the current film, *Gamera vs. Barugon*, featured no child actors at all.

Final Word
Whether this can be considered the better of the two Majin sequels depends upon whether one judges for technical merit or screenwriting, but it's safe to say thanks to its touching human drama this film manages to be the more endearing of the two sequels.

Trivia

- Supposedly, when the Daimajin turns to snow, the snow is made of soft serve ice cream.

- TBS in Japan approached Noriaki Yuasa about doing a Daimajin TV series shortly after this film's release, but the project was abandoned within a week.

Ebirah, Horror of the Deep (1966)

Alternate Titles: *Godzilla, Mothra, Ebirah: Big Duel in the South Seas* (Japan) *Godzilla versus the Sea Monster* (U.S.) *Frankenstein and the Monster from the Ocean* (Germany) *The Return of Godzilla* (Italy) *Monsters from the Sea* (Spain) *Godzilla vs. the Terror of the Seas* (Mexico) *Ebirah, Monster of Magic* (Poland) *Mothra: The Flying Dracula Monster* (Holland)
Release Date: December 17, 1966

Directed by: Jun Fukuda
Special Effects by: Sadamasa Arikawa & Eiji Tsuburaya
Screenplay by: Shinichi Sekizawa
Music by: Masaru Sato

Cast: Akira Takarada (Yoshimura) Kumi Mizuno (Daiyo) Toru Watanabe (Ryota) Akihiko Hirata (Dragon Squad Commander) Hideo Sunazaki (Nita) Chotaro Togin (Ichino) Tohru Ibuki (Yata) Pair Bambi (the Shobijin) Jun Tazaki (Red Bamboo Leader) **Suit Performers:** Haruo Nakajima (Godzilla) Hiroshi Sekida (Ebirah)

Tohoscope, Eastmancolor, 87 Minutes

Story

Ryota, a rural youth in search of his shipwrecked brother, sets sail on a stolen yacht with two friends and a bank robber named Yoshimura. The men themselves become shipwrecked on desolate Letchi Island. There they find a terrorist group, the Red Bamboo, in possession of nuclear weapons, a giant mutated lobster that guards the island, a group of enslaved natives from Infant Island, and Godzilla slumbering in a cave. The men team up with beautiful slave girl Daiyo to overthrow the soldiers and save the kidnapped islanders. Ryota manages to escape to Infant Island via weather balloon where his brother was shipwrecked. Back on Letchi, Yoshimura devises a scheme to wake up Godzilla during a thunderstorm. The beast awakens and immediately sets off to battle Ebirah with the battle ending in a draw. Ryota and his brother return to Letchi via canoe with instructions from Mothra's fairies for the islanders (freed during an attack by Godzilla on the Red Bamboo base) to begin constructing a giant net. Evacuating by yacht the soldiers have set the island to self-destruct in a nuclear catastrophe. The soldiers' yacht is ironically destroyed by their monster Ebirah while escaping. Godzilla then lumbers into the water where he rips the sea monster's claws off sending it in retreat. Mothra then arrives and rescues the castaways grouped together in the giant net moments before the island explodes.

Background & Commentary

Ebirah, Horror of the Deep was the introduction of what some unfairly call Toho's B-Team: director Jun Fukuda, composer Masaru Sato, and SPFX director Sadamasa Arikawa. Though they are considered inferior to Honda, Ifukube and

Tsuburaya, this new team lends the series an undeniably fresh feel. Part of the new vibe is also due to the fact this was never intended to be a G-film at all, but a King Kong vehicle called *Operation Robinson Crusoe: King Kong vs. Ebirah*. When Toho submitted the script to RKO (who had the rights to Kong) for approval it was rejected. RKO then connected Toho to Rankin/Bass who had also submitted an idea to them based on their animated *The King Kong Show* TV series. Toho agreed to make the Kong feature in conjunction with Rankin/Bass that became *King Kong Escapes*, but they had already constructed the Ebirah suit and miniature sets for *Operation Robinson Crusoe*. Not wanting to waste their investment they simply substituted Godzilla for Kong and went on with the production. The results are surprisingly good. While the film doesn't excel on a technical level (there was severe water damage to the G-suit and the miniatures weren't quite up to par), it does succeed as a brisk action adventure. In a series where children often clamor for the monsters to come on screen when they're absent, *Ebirah, Horror of the Deep* offers an entertaining human storyline. Stuart Galbraith makes the comment in his book *Monsters Are Attacking Tokyo* that "you could literally remove the monsters and still have a pretty solid, entertaining picture."

The cast consists of a number of Toho veterans, all of which have good story arcs, notably Akira Takarada's bank robber Yoshimura. As an interesting aside, this film is also a spiritual sequel to a past Takarada/Fukuda collaboration, the spy film *100 Shot/100 Killed*. Elements of the film's scrapped sequel to be called "Big Duel in the South Seas" ended up in *Ebirah*'s screenplay, which in Japan was eventually titled *Godzilla, Mothra, Ebirah: Big Duel in the South Seas*. While Takarada obviously isn't playing the same character, Yoshimura makes for an interesting anti-hero to contrast with the purely good characters and the evil villains. Likewise, the monsters all operate from different points on the moral compass as well. Mothra, like the Infant islanders, is pure and good going out of her way to save others. Ebirah, similar to the Red Bamboo, is evil and greedy in his pursuit of human victims. Godzilla, the good guy only by coincidence, plays the anti-hero like Yoshimura, who sometimes does something contrary to his nature to "help the little guy." The previous two films had explored Godzilla's parameters as a hero, but this is the first film in which he is presented as being, for lack of a better word, "cool." He is never bested by any of the villains (human or monster) and at one point breaks the fourth wall when he scratches his nose in a nod to Yuzo Kayama, the star of Fukuda's popular *Young Guy* series. *Ebirah* also has an element of suspense in its climax its predecessor, *Invasion of Astro-Monster*, severely lacked. In this film the clock is ticking for the islanders to finish the giant net, Mothra to awaken, and Godzilla to defeat Ebirah before the nuclear explosion occurs. The music and editing all work together superbly well to make for an exciting climax. And while *Invasion of Astro-Monster* featured a battle set on an alien planet, *Ebirah* showcased battles actually filmed underwater, a dangerous job for the suit actors to say the least.

This was the first Godzilla film to bypass theaters for television in America as *Godzilla versus the Sea Monster*. Contrary to popular belief this doesn't mean the film bombed in Japan. It saw a less sharp decline in attendance than *Invasion of Astro-Monster* had from *Ghidorah, the Three Headed Monster* and, considering the lower budget of this picture, it's entirely possible that it was the more profitable of the two.

Final Word

Although it lacks the traditional destruction of a large metropolis, this film shows that Godzilla can still have an entertaining adventure without Honda's direction, Ifukube's music, and Tsuburaya's miniature cityscapes.

Trivia

- The role of Daiyo originally went to 19 year old Noriko Takahashi, but she had to drop out when she was stricken with appendicitis, thusly Kumi Mizuno took her place. Takahashi was likely originally cast because she played an island girl in an episode of *Ultra Q* the same year.

- Akihiko Hirata playing the Dragon Squad Commander is an intentional parody of Dr. Serizawa. To emphasize the switch from hero to villain, the eye-patch was placed over his left eye rather than his right eye.

- Toho's sudden urge to produce a King Kong film came about because their five year licensing agreement with RKO would come to an end in 1967. Had Toho produced *Operation Robinson Crusoe* and it had been a hit, its thought they planned to renew the licensing agreement with RKO and start their own series of King Kong films. Also, contrary to speculation, Mothra was not added into the film after Kong was replaced by Godzilla, but likely was also present in the *Operation Robinson Crusoe* script alongside the giant ape.

- This was the first year that tie-in toys were produced to coincide with a Godzilla movie in Japan by toymaker Marusan, which produced figures of Godzilla, Ebirah and Mothra.

- In 1965, Jun Fukuda directed Akira Takadara in *100 Shot/100 Killed*, a take on the James Bond series with Takarada playing a suave agent. The sequel, *Big Duel in the South Seas*, was mysteriously scrapped and combined with the *Operation Robinson Crusoe* script, and it's entirely possible the Red Bamboo were the villains of the *100 Shot/100 Killed* sequel. This could also be the reason Takarada and Fukuda were put to work on the new Godzilla picture, as were Chotaro Togin, Tohru Ibuki and Akihiko Hirata, all of who had co-starred in *100 Shot/100 Killed*. Eventually a sequel was produced in 1968 called *100 Shot/100 Killed: Goldeneye*.

- Tohru Ibuki (Yata) starred with Frank Sinatra in *None But the Brave*.

- This is the last Showa Era appearance and use of the Mothra Imago marionette. A Mothra Imago was scripted to return in 1974's unproduced Godzilla film *Monsters Converge on Okinawa: Showdown in Cape Zanpa*.

- Masaru Sato was brought in at the insistence of Jun Fukuda, though Fukuda told David Milner that Tomoyuki Tanaka didn't agree with the decision and wanted Ifukube to score the film.

- Hal Linden (*Barney Miller*) dubbed Yoshimura for the U.S. TV release.

- Oddly, both Teruyoshi Nakano and Jun Fukuda remarked to David Milner they had never heard of a draft of the screenplay containing King Kong. Furthermore, Nakano claims the "sea monster" was initially a giant octopus.

- Before the cancellation of *Operation Robinson Crusoe: King Kong vs. Ebirah*, the 1966 Godzilla film was likely a script entitled *Giant Monster Assault* by Ei Ogawa which later turned into *Space Amoeba* (1970).

The Magic Serpent (1966)

Alternate Titles: *The Mystic Dragons Decisive Battle* (Japan) *War of the Monsters* (Mexico)
Release Date: December 21, 1966

Directed by: Tetsuya Yamauchi
Special Effects by: Motoya Washio
Screenplay by: Masaru Igami
Music by: Toshiaki Tsushima
Cast: Matsukata Hiroki (Jiraiya/Ikazuchimaru) Ryutaro Otomo (Orochimaru) Tomoko Ogawa (Tsunade) Bin Amatsu (Daijo) Nobuo Kaneko (Dojin Hiki) **Suit Performers:** Uncredited

Toeiscope, Eastmancolor, 86 Minutes

Story

As a young boy, Ikazuchimaru is rescued by a giant bird from the evil Daijo, who has slain his family and taken over their kingdom. Ikazuchimaru is taken far away where he is taught the art of ninja magic by his teacher, Dojin Hiki, who is killed by a former pupil Orochimaru, Daijo's second in command. In adulthood Ikazuchimaru dubs himself Jiraiya and sets out to avenge both his parents and his mentor. Along the way he meets Tsunade, unbeknownst to all Orochimaru's daughter who also knows magic, and a family of poor farmers who Jiraiya saves from disaster. The father is killed by Daijo's men and the daughter is captured, though Jiraiya rescues the younger brother. Arriving at the castle, Tsunade learns of her father's true identity and Orochimaru commands her to kill Jiraiya, which she cannot bring herself to do. In a final showdown Jiraiya kills Daijo and Orochimaru turns into a dragon to battle the ninja warrior who transforms into a giant spiked toad. Tsunade intervenes with her spider magic and Orochimaru is defeated. Jiraiya puts the kingdom in the hands of the united brother and sister, and then the giant bird returns and takes he and Tsunade back to the mountains.

Background & Commentary

In 1921 the first suitmation based Japanese monsters burst on the screen in Nikkatsu-Mukojima's *Goketsu Jiraiya,* a period piece which features the ninja Jiraiya who can turn himself into a giant toad, and also his enemy that transforms into a giant snake. The silent film was based upon an old folktale and was itself a remake of several earlier pictures focusing on Jiraiya. In 1966 Toei studios had the inspired idea to film a version of the story with giant monsters. Though Toei was one of Japan's largest studios they had yet to contribute to the dai kaiju boom.

The film's special effects fall somewhat short when compared to the work of Tsuburaya and even Daiei, but the story is undeniably fun. It has even been compared to *Star Wars* because the young hero is raised by a wizard that also tutored a Darth Vader-like apprentice who is later revealed to be the father of the female protagonist. Daijo, one of the film's two villains, gets a superb entrance when he warns an unknowing lord of an invasion in progress. "By who?" the lord asks and Daijo replies, "Me," and promptly dispatches him. The true villain is the magnetic Orochimaru played by Ryutaro Otomo who gives the film's liveliest performance. As for the kaiju, the giant spiked toad actually fares better than the dragon, which can't hide what it is most of the time: a puppet. Part of the puppet's problem is in the lifeless eyes. On the rare occasion that Tsuburaya constructed a goofy looking suit, if nothing else, the eyes at least had life to them. The toad spews real fire Gamera-style rather than optical rays, and the dragon puts them out with real water as well. For the toad a full sized prop of the foot was also built to stomp on the villains. This is interesting as in the 1921 version the smaller Jiraiya toad swallows and eats his enemies. The film also contains two other monsters, a giant spider that drops from the sky and a giant bird seen only at the beginning and the end. It is never fully glimpsed in the film, but it is clearly visible wires and all in the film's trailer. Many people are under the false assumption that the monsters don't appear until the end battle, however, Orochimaru transforms into the giant serpent within five minutes into the story.

The film was released in countries outside of Japan theatrically, including Latin America, but in the U.S. it went straight to television via AIP where even the monsters were dubbed over with different voices, in this case those of Godzilla and Rodan.

Final Word

All in all the screenwriter's scenarios are a bit too ambitious for the SPFX department to keep up with, and there are many ghostly superimposed images throughout. With better effects work this could've been a classic rather than a camp classic.

Trivia

- Though Toei never really got into the giant monster game on the big screen much, they had a huge presence on television with their *Kamen Rider* series, and *Kyoryu*

Sentai Zyuranger which later aired on American television as *Mighty Morphin Power Rangers.*

- Tsunade was originally supposed to turn into a slug, but a spider was deemed more popular.

- The giant toad was reused as a monster on Toei's TV series *Kamen no Ninja Aka Kade,* also set in feudal times which preceded Toei's more popular *Kamen Rider* series of the 1970s.

- A remake of this film, 1970's *Young Flying Hero* (aka *Return of the Magic Serpent*), was produced in Taiwan and again features a brief battle between a dragon and a giant frog.

Gamera vs. Gyaos (1967)

Alternate Titles: *Giant Monster Midair Battle: Gamera vs. Gyaos* (Japan) *Return of the Giant Monsters* (U.S.)
Release Date: March 15, 1967

Directed by: Noriaki Yuasa
Special Effects by: Noriaki Yuasa
Screenplay by: Niisan Takahashi
Music by: Tadashi Yamauchi
Cast: Naoyuki Abe (Eiichi) Kojiro Hongo (Tsutsumi) Reiko Kasahara (Sumiko) Kichijiro Ueda (Grandfather) **Suit Performers:** Teruo Arakaki (Gamera) Uncredited (Gyaos)

Daieiscope, Eastmancolor, 87 Minutes

Story
After a spout of volcanic activity, strange events plague Japan. A helicopter surveying one of the hot spots mysteriously crashes and livestock are running away in fear. Eiichi, a rural boy, explores a large cave and is attacked by Gyaos, a prehistoric vampire bat. Gamera, the friend of all children, shows up to save him and takes the boy back to his

village. The military decides to attack Gyaos with jet planes, but they are easily cut in half by the monster's ray. Gyaos takes flight for Nagoya where he wreaks havoc and eats its citizens. Gamera shows up and chases him away, but is unable to kill him. A plan is concocted to lure Gyaos out of his cave using fake blood, but this plan also fails. At Eiichi's insistence the village starts a forest fire which lures Gamera to the area. He and Gyaos battle again, and this time he is victorious and drags Gyaos into a live volcano.

Background & Commentary

Noticing how children ran amuck in the theaters during *Gamera vs. Barugon* between monster scenes, Daiei finally agreed with Noriaki Yuasa that the Gamera series should be geared towards children. Therefore, the studio put him back in the director's chair, cast a young boy as the protagonist, and even recorded a Gamera theme song sung by a chorus of children. Though budgeted at ¥60,000,000 (¥20 million less than its predecessor), the results yielded the highest grossing Gamera film of the original series, an impressive feat considering the film's stiff competition in 1967.

As for the flying vampire monster Gyaos, Daiei had unknowingly birthed an enduring creation. Unlike Godzilla, Gamera never fought the same monster twice. Gyaos was the lone exception as a silver Space Gyaos appears in 1969's *Gamera vs. Guiron* and when Gamera was revived in 1995 Gyaos was brought back as the main villain. From then on the creatures were either mentioned or featured in every subsequent entry. Gyaos is no mere Rodan rip-off either. Being nocturnal with an appetite for blood, his inspiration is clearly the vampire bat rather than the Pterodactyl. He also gets an exceptional surprise introduction. Early in the film, an unlikeable reporter is standing in the forest when he is suddenly lifted high into the air. Gyaos has picked him up, and from the reporter's POV we see Gyaos's glistening, wet mouth ready to gobble him up, which he does. Gyaos also gets a delightful destruction scene when he annihilates Nagoya. Impressive shots include him shattering a large window and slicing Nagoya castle in half with his sonic ray, the animation of which cost around a thousand U.S. dollars every time it was fired. Gyaos skillfully uses the ray to slice off the tops of moving bullet train cars and then begins to feast upon the passengers. As for the title bout (in Japan the film was called *Giant Monster Midair Battle: Gamera vs. Gyaos*) the aerial dogfight between the kaiju over Nagoya is undeniably creative and the standout sequence of the movie. At one point Gyaos puts out Gamera's jets in mid-air causing him to fall into the bay where he nearly capsizes a boat. Gamera battles his nemesis no less than three times during the film on land, in the air, and in the water.

While there had been moderate bloodshed in *Gamera vs. Barugon*, this film takes things to the next level. Gamera's arm is nearly severed by Gyaos's ray, and later he bites off some of Gyaos's toes. All of this is merely in addition to rampant bloodshed, be it Gamera's green or Gyaos's pink, throughout the film. Despite being aimed at children, the battles were far more graphic than Godzilla's as Eiji Tsuburaya felt it was his duty to spare children such images. Each subsequent Gamera film would take the bloodshed up a notch, with monsters getting blown in half and even cut into pieces. Not yet a marketable name in the states, Gamera's signature sequel was released to television as *Return of the Giant Monsters* the same year it premiered in Japan.

Final Word
The third time is the charm for Gamera as he settles into his groove and cements his role as the friend to all children.

Trivia

- "The Song of Gamera" by Tadashi Yamauchi was successfully released as a 45 rpm single by Daiei Records.

- Because Toho had recently made films using giant versions of King Kong and Frankenstein, Daiei took this as inspiration to do a giant version of Dracula. As such, the film's working title was *Giant Monster Midair Battle: Gamera vs. Vampire*.

- A separate Gamera torso prop was made that could breathe fire much to the relief of the suit performer.

- The elaborate means with which the human cast combats Gyaos were inspired by the *Mission: Impossible* TV series according to the producers.

- This is the first Gamera film in which he only retracts his back legs to fly. This method cut down on the cost of gun-powder and was therefore more cost effective, meaning Gamera rarely fully retracts and spins in his shell in subsequent entries.

- Paper "Gyaos Gliders" were given to some theater attendees.

The X From Outer Space (1967)

Alternate Titles: *Giant Space Monster Guilala* (Japan) *Frankenstein's Devil Monster Guilala* (Germany)
Release Date: March 25, 1967

Directed by: Kazui Nihonmatsu
Special Effects by: Hiroshi Ikeda
Screenplay by: Kazui Nihonmatsu, Moriyoshi Ishida & Eibi Motomoshi
Music by: Taku Izumi
Cast: Peggy Neal (Lisa) Shunya Wazaki (Capt. Sano) Itoko Harada (Michiko) Shinichi Yanagisawa (Miyamoto) Keisuke Sonoi (Dr. Shioda) **Suit Performers:** Uncredited

Shochiku-GrandScope, Eastmancolor, 88 Minutes

Story
Atomic Astroboat AAB-Gama is launched from the FAFC (Fuji Astro Flight Center) to investigate the disappearance of ships in route to Mars. The crew, comprised of Captain Sano, Dr. Shioda, Signal Officer Miyamoto and beautiful blonde biologist Lisa, are warned that the interference may be due to a UFO. On the way, the AAB-Gama makes a stop at the moon base to get a replacement for Dr. Shioda who has become ill. There Captain Sano is reunited with a former love, Michiko, while at the moment he has a flirtatious

relationship with Lisa. Resuming their mission with a new doctor, the crew comes in contact with the mysterious UFO near Mars, which buzzes the AAB-Gama leaving the ship's hull covered in a series of spores which Lisa collects samples of. Back on Earth, the spore reacts to the planet's atmosphere and hatches Guilala, which quickly grows to giant size. The monster marches on Tokyo un-phased by manmade weapons, while the crew of AAB-Gama deduct the means to defeat Guilala can be synthesized on the moon. Guilalalium is created by Lisa and brought back to earth along with Michiko. Finally, Guilala is cornered by the Japanese Air Force and sprayed with Guilalalium. The monster shrinks back to its tiny embryo form and is launched back into space. Lisa lets go of Sano who happily reunites with Michiko.

Background & Commentary
Shochiku was one of the oldest and most respected studios in Japan, but one would never know it from this film. It is one of the worst, most uninspired giant monster pictures of all time. Had the story been played as a comedy all could be forgiven, but one is expected to take the silly plot and even sillier looking monster seriously.

One would be correct in saying Shochiku made the film simply because everyone else was making dai kaiju pictures, and the results speak for themselves. The lion's share of the blame must go to the screenwriters Moriyoshi Ishida, Eibi Motomoshi and Kazui Nihonmatsu, who also directed. Even a film with bad SPFX can be saved by a good story, but not this one. The nonsensical script has several odd plot devices. The doctor, it would seem, suddenly becomes ill just so the crew has an excuse to stop by the moon base, show off some expensive sets, and introduce some new characters (none of which add anything to the story aside from Michiko). The mysterious UFO, which the AAB-Gama's mission revolves around, is never explained either. Its precise relation to the monster and what its intentions are towards the crew are never resolved. It pops back up in the third act to buzz the ship, but it would seem this is only to make use of the prop once more before the film ends. Actually, the outer space portions of the film are some of its most bland and uninteresting sequences. The direction improves once the story returns to earth. However, the film has by now dragged on for fifty minutes by the time the monster makes his entrance. And, what a turkey the creature is, or more accurately a "space chicken/lizard" hybrid. Guilala is the silliest Japanese monster ever designed for a feature film, and should've been confined to a TV screen fighting Ultraman and his brethren. That's not to say the SPFX are bad, some of them, the space sequences in particular, are quite good. The miniature buildings and sets are well done, but the miniature vehicles can't hold a candle to Tsuburaya's. At one point SPFX director Ikeda even rips off Tsuburaya's signature Maser Canons when similar creations attack Guilala.

Some critics claim Guilala is an analogy for interracial romance which at the time was taboo in Japan. The film's human element focuses on the love triangle between Lisa, Captain Sano, and Michiko, although it is never clear exactly what the relationship is, or has been, between Sano and the two women. In any case, at the film's conclusion Lisa comments Guilala taught her that, "Someone else cares for Sano as much as I do." Cut away to reveal Sano and Michiko walking together, happily holding hands. All is right in the world, and off of it, as Guilala (in embryo form) soars back into space where he belongs. Judging by the fact Guilala survives the proceedings it is conceivable Shochiku was leaving the door open for a sequel. Had they truly hoped this was a possibility then they should've put more effort into the film's screenplay and monster design. However, the monster would return in a sequel forty years later with *Monster X Strikes Back: Guilala Attacks the G8 Summit* (2008). This time, the monster is correctly played for laughs.

Final Word
Shochiku's entry in the dai kaiju eiga is undeniable weird, if not the weirdest dai kaiju eiga ever made.

Trivia

- Guilala has a cameo in the titular character's dream in *Tora-San's Forbidden Love* (1984).

- The production was loaned money by the Japanese Government to produce the film in light of the monster boom.

- Initially, Guilala was known as "bizarre insect" in the script and later, Demora. On January 28, 1967, many children were invited to a party were the monster's name was finally revealed. They also got to look at several of the SPFX props.

- The film began pre-production in May of 1966 and Shochiku claimed the film's final budget was ¥150,000,000.

Gappa the Triphibean Monster (1967)

Alternate Titles: *Giant Beast Gappa* (Japan)
Monster from a Prehistoric Planet (U.S.)
Release Date: April 22, 1967

Directed by: Haruyasu Noguchi
Special Effects by: Akira Watanabe
Screenplay by: Iwao Yamakazi & Ryuzo Nakanishi
Music by: Seitaro Omori
Cast: Tamio Kawaji (Kurosaki) Yoko Yamamoto (Itoko) Yuji Okada (Tonooka) Keisuke Inoue (President Funazu)
Suit Performers: Atami Hiroshiita/Takashi Konagai (Male Gappa) Misugi Ken/Tonami Shiro (Female Gappa) Uncredited (Baby Gappa)

Nikkatsuscope, Eastmancolor, 84 Minutes

Story
An expedition sets sail for the South Seas in order to collect exotic animals for a Japanese Island resort. On a tropical isle complete with an active volcano and various obelisks, they also find what appears to be a dinosaur egg which hatches a creature the natives call Gappa. The expedition takes the creature to Japan despite the natives' warnings. Soon after,

the parents show up and destroy the native village before heading to Japan where various scientific tests are being performed on their rapidly growing offspring. The parents make landfall in Japan and destroy a city before taking refuge in a lake. The military uses sound waves to force the creatures to the surface where they bombard them with artillery, but the indestructible monsters fly away and begin resuming their destruction elsewhere. Members of the expedition begin to feel guilty about what they have done and have the baby Gappa transported to Haneda Airport. They lure the parents to the location with recordings of the baby played over a megaphone. Infant and parents happily reunite and peacefully take to the skies.

Background & Commentary

Gappa the Triphibean Monster was released smack-dab in the middle of the 1967 dai kaiju-boom, in which nearly every major Japanese Studio produced a piece of kaiju eiga. The film followed on the heels of Daiei's second Gamera sequel, Shochiku's *The X From Outer Space* and preceded Toho's two offerings for that year. *Gappa* is somewhat of an amalgam of the many kaiju films to come before it, though this may be the writers' intent as the film was also a satire on the genre. The film borrows most heavily from *King Kong vs. Godzilla*, itself a parody involving Japanese executives greedily exploiting a creature from the South Seas. At one point the baby Gappa is airlifted by balloon while the main characters follow it by car, specifically aping the aforementioned film. The Gappas themselves could be considered crosses between Godzilla and Rodan, standing upright with arms and legs while also possessing wings and beak-like mouths. Even their fiery rays are carbon copies of Godzilla's. Gamera's contribution seems to be two prominent child characters and a rock-style theme song for the monsters. It would be remiss not to reveal *Gappa*'s connection to the *Ultraman* franchise as well in that its design had its genesis at Tsuburaya Productions. It began as the first design for the then monster-hero of what would evolve into the humanoid *Ultraman*. The design was scrapped and sold to Nikkatsu, who adapted it into Gappa.

The story that went on during *Gappa*'s pre-production was slightly more interesting than what played out on screen. In an interview by Stuart Galbraith in *Monsters Are Attacking Tokyo*, *Gappa*'s two screenwriters, Gan Yamazaki and Ryuzo Nakanishi, revealed the film was produced solely to procure government funding. The film's plot ironically revolves around real estate development of an island, while Nikkatsu was coincidentally using this film's budget to pay off debts on real estate property that they owned. The scheme worked like this: the government put up funding for the film's budget, which Nikkatsu would repay after the film was released. Instead, Nikkatsu used the funds to pay off their real-estate debts, and used what was left over on the film. The results turned out surprisingly well, and it was one of the better kaiju films released that year. Nikkatsu used an A-List cast and the satirical elements, lost in the American dub, work well in the Japanese version. For instance, in the aftermath of the first round of city stomping, the publishing magnate couldn't be happier as he makes a fortune off of magazine sales. Noguchi's direction is top notch during the climax where the parents are reunited with their hatchling at sunrise to Seitaro Omori's poignant flute based themes, evoking great sympathy for the monsters. In the same scene the greedy publisher also reconnects with his young daughter who takes his hand. On the technical front, the studio built some impressive sets, particularly the island cave beneath the volcano. When it came to SPFX work Nikkatsu didn't have a large scale effects department, so they hired Akira Watanabe, currently Eiji Tsuburaya's SPFX Art Director and the designer of such creatures as King Ghidorah. Watanabe's work on the film's suits and city miniatures are well done. His work is innovative in instances where the monsters are filmed at different angles with close-ups of the eyes and mouths as they fire their rays. There is also a large scale foot prop that crashes down on various panicked extras inside a building at one point. It is only in the department of model ships and submarines where Watanabe's work is sub-par. This film also offered more elaborate city destruction sequences compared to Toho's two releases that year, *King Kong Escapes* and *Son of Godzilla*, which were heavier on island action than urban warfare.

The film never did get a big theatrical release in America as hoped; instead it went straight to television as *Monster From a Prehistoric Planet*. Nikkatsu eventually went bankrupt in the 1970s and began producing soft-core porno films. Overall, even though no sequels were made, the film is fondly remembered in native Japan.

Final Word

In a story where the monsters are wronged by humans and not the other way around, the film provides yet another stellar example of the difference between Western and Japanese monster films.

Trivia

- Before production began on this picture, Nikkatsu played with several different concepts including the idea of a giant flying squirrel monster called *Momonra*; a film where a giant squid battles WWII Nazis in *Giant Squid Monster Arkitius*; a giant alien spider in *Giant Monster Gigant*, and a story wherein a giant iguana battles a huge Manta Ray for *Reigon: Devil of the Seabed*.

- In the mid-1990s, Shochiku considered doing a film wherein Gappa battles Guilala.

- While many sources call this Nikkatsu's only kaiju eiga, that isn't entirely correct. Nikkatsu ironically produced the very first Japanese suitmation monster film in 1921, *Goketsu Jiraiya*, featuring a giant toad and snake (although the monsters aren't dai kaiju sized per se and only matched that of their human counterparts).

King Kong Escapes (1967)

Alternate Titles: *King Kong's Counterattack* (Japan) *The Return of King Kong* (South America) *King Kong: Frankenstein's Son* (Germany)
Release Date: July 22, 1967

Directed by: Ishiro Honda
Special Effects by: Eiji Tsuburaya
Screenplay by: Kaoru Mabuchi
Music by: Akira Ifukube
Cast: Rhodes Reason (Cmdr. Nelson) Akira Takarada (Lt. Namura) Linda Miller (Susan) Eisei Amamoto (Dr. Who) Mie Hama (Madame Piranha) **Suit Performers:** Haruo Nakajima (King Kong) Hiroshi Sekida (Gorosaurus/Mechanikong)

Tohoscope, Eastmancolor, 104 Minutes

Story

In the Arctic, evil Dr. Who is using his robot Mechanikong to dig for Element X for his benefactor, Madame Piranha. Element X proves too powerful for the robot which short circuits. Elsewhere, UN submarine Explorer stops for repairs near Mondo Island, home of the mythical King Kong. Commander Carl Nelson, Lt. Susan Watson, and Lt. Jiro Namura venture to the island to explore. There Kong rescues Susan from a giant dinosaur and becomes infatuated with her. Holding her in the palm of his hand, Kong reluctantly returns her to the submarine and the trio heads for New York to report on their fantastic adventure. Dr. Who and his henchmen then kidnap Kong to dig for Element X. When submarine Explorer returns the trio finds Kong missing and suspects foul play. Soon the three are kidnapped by Dr. Who's minions and taken to the Arctic. Kong eventually grows angry digging for Element X and escapes the base. Dr. Who and crew board his ocean tanker and pursue Kong to Tokyo where he has come ashore. Madame Piranha becomes sympathetic to the prisoners and releases them. The trio goes to warn the military not to hurt the benign Kong while Dr. Who unleashes Mechanikong to take on the real thing. The robot abducts Susan and climbs Tokyo Tower with Kong in pursuit. Kong saves Susan and destroys his mechanical nemesis. Dr. Who shoots Madame Piranha for her betrayal and Kong shows up and sinks the ocean liner, after which he heads for Mondo Island leaving behind a tearful Susan.

Background & Commentary

This fantastic feature has its genesis in RKO's rejection of Toho's script for *Operation Robinson Crusoe: King Kong vs. Ebirah* which became the Godzilla vehicle *Ebirah, Horror of the Deep* (1966). RKO connected Toho with Rankin/Bass, looking to produce a live action version of their animated *The King Kong Show*, and a beautiful partnership was born. As a result, *King Kong Escapes* has an undoubtedly American flavor with the story moving along briskly, never stopping for long debate sequences or military strategies as seen in Toho's strictly Japanese productions.

It also strongly benefits from its cast, notably Eisei Amamoto's Dr. Who, a villain from the animated *King Kong Show*. The scenes between he and Mie Hama's Madame Piranha give the film a sense of James Bond-like grandeur, and Hama herself was a Bond girl in *You Only Live Twice* the same year. The humans also relate well to the monsters, and often times their action scenes work in tandem. For instance, Namura rescues Susan from Tokyo Tower at the same time Kong and his double do battle above them. In contrast to the interracial love affairs that ended badly in *Invasion of Astro-Monster* and *The X From Outer Space*, the relationship between Akira Takarada's Namura and Linda Miller's Susan is presented in a positive light, perhaps due to the film's American influence. Rhodes Reason, the younger brother of Rex Reason (*This Island Earth, The Creature Walks Among Us*) provides a solid lead and a strong presence that keeps the comic book story from descending into heavy camp territory, not an easy feat with the goofy Kong suit running about. While this suit is an improvement over the *King Kong vs. Godzilla* suit, it is none the less subpar when compared to other creations of the time. Mechanikong, on the other hand, is a fantastic suit, and being a robot doesn't need to appear lifelike (the robot was so popular Toho considered him as a Godzilla foe in the 1990s when they couldn't secure the rights for Kong). The dinosaur Gorosaurus also ended up becoming a popular creation that went on to become a staple of the Monster Island gang when he was spun into *Destroy All Monsters* and also cameos in *All Monsters Attack* and *Godzilla vs. Gigan*. Unfortunately, this was the last time

Kong would be seen in a Toho Production; an appearance in *Destroy All Monsters* certainly would've been welcome.

Interestingly, Toho put this film in the hands of Tsuburaya, Honda and Ifukube even though Toho had a G-film in production the same year. It would seem Kong's picture took priority, and some reports say Rankin/Bass insisted Honda and Tsuburaya work on the project. The film was successful in Japan where it was put on a double bill with *Ultraman*, a compilation film made up of episodes of the TV series edited together into one feature. In America it was released to theaters by Universal (a large distributer for Toho whose films were often distributed by UPA or AIP at the time) and double billed with Don Knott's *The Shakiest Gun in the West*. This would also be one of Toho's last international co-productions with American producers and stars, the final shebang being 1969's *Latitude Zero*.

Final Word

The excellent screenplay is marred only by the sub-par Kong suit, which is lovable in its own strange way. Of all the 1967 monster films, this was still the best.

Trivia

- On *The King Kong Show*, Dr. Who is a short, midget-sized bald man with a bulbous head and thick glasses. In addition to Mechanikong he also created a Mecha-Sphynx.

- This was celebrated as Toho's 35th Anniversary Film.

- Mechanikong's wreckage is made up of pieces of a TV circuit board, Atomic Heat Ray guns from *Mothra* and Maser Canons from *War of the Gargantuas*.

- Linda Miller was dating Yosuke Natsuki (*Dogora, the Space Monster; Ghidorah, the Three Headed Monster*) during her time in Japan.

- Haruo Nakajima studied gorillas at the zoo to better portray Kong.

- *The King Kong Show* was ironically produced by Toei Animation Studios for America, even though their competitor Toho ended up making the live action version in Japan through Rankin/Bass.

- The American producers wanted Gorosaurus to bleed when Kong snaps his jaws. Tsuburaya refused and had the monster foam at the mouth instead.

- Unlike *Operation Robinson Crusoe: King Kong vs. Ebirah* (which featured Mothra), *King Kong Escapes* was never meant to tie into the Godzilla series as the Kong in this film is only 35 meters high compared to the 50 meter Kong from *King Kong vs. Godzilla.* However, supplementary books in Japan have since denoted this version of Kong as a "Second Generation King Kong" to explain his difference in height to the other Kong.

- Both the Kong and Gorosaurus suits from this film were later reused for Toho's TV series *Go! Greenman* in 1973, with Kong rechristened "Giant Ape."

!!!!!!!!!!!!!!!!!!!!!Bonus Review!!!!!!!!!!!!!!!!!!!!!

Yongary, Monster from the Deep (1967)

Alternate Titles: *Godzilla, Monster of Destruction* (Germany) *Great Monster Yongary* (South Korea)
Release Date: August 13, 1967

Directed by: Ki-duk Kim
Special Effects by: Kenichi Nakagawa
Screenplay by: Ki-duk Kim & Seo Yun-sung
Music by: Jeong-geun Jeon
Cast: Kwang Ho Li (Eicho) Yeong-il Oh (Ilo) Jeong-im Nam (Suna) Sun-jae Lee (Yoo Kwang-nam) Moon Kang

(Kim Yu-ri) **Suit Performers:** Cho Kyoung-min (Yongary)

Cinemascope, Color, 92 Minutes

Story
A nuclear test in the Middle East in the Goma Desert awakens the ancient monster Yongary. At first thought be a series of earthquakes, the monster reveals itself when it bursts from the ground and begins attacking Seoul. Officials debate how to kill the monster but fear destroying their own landmarks in the process. A young boy named Eicho becomes sympathetic to the monster and beseeches the government not to kill the kaiju. However, his efforts are in vain and Yongary eventually succumbs to the military via an ammonia compound created by scientists.

Background & Commentary
Detailing the peak year of the "Japanese Giant Monster Boom" would not be complete without an overview of the Korean made *Yongary, Monster from the Deep*. Wanting to get in on the action, Keukdong Entertainment (meaning Far East Entertainment) imported Japanese SPFX technician Kenichi Nakagawa to Korea to bring their monster to life. Masao Yagi, designer of the Gamera suit, built the Yongary suit in Japan and then had it shipped to South Korea. Though director Ki-duk Kim was reportedly disappointed with what he got—he wanted a scarier looking monster—the suit had a nice design and came complete with light up eyes and nasal horn. Shooting began April 3rd 1967 with SPFX filming starting three days later and lasting three months. Two studios were used to shoot the SPFX, and reportedly there were 280 SPFX cuts in all, with the whole film being brought to life on a large (for South Korean standards) budget that amounted to $117,000.

The finished film's storyline is boring for the most part when the human characters are on screen—and to some degree when the monster shows up as well. Of all the characters, only the young boy Eicho—who starts off the film rather amusingly but grates on the audiences' nerves towards the end—makes much of an impression. As for the SPFX, the earthquake scenes are fantastic while the miniature buildings and monster suit are only passable. Yongary is an interesting amalgam of the dai kaiju to come before it. Although this description has also been used to describe Godzilla, notably by Harry Holcombe in the American version of *King Kong vs. Godzilla,* Yongary really does look like a T-Rex (or perhaps, Ceratosaurus due to the nasal horn) crossed with a Stegosaurus. From Gamera he inherited two tusks, some real flame breath and a child who champions him despite his destructive ways. It's also possible that his spiked tail was inspred by Anguirus and his glowing nasal horn by Baragon. Later, said nasal horn spontaneously develops the ability to fire a Gyaos-like optical ray that can slice things in half. The film takes its strangest turn in the third act when the monster abruptly gets up and begins to dance due to Eicho pointing an itching gun at him. At that point young Eicho, who for the past hour has been gung-ho along with everyone else about killing the monster, becomes sympathetic to the beast. Even stranger is the monster's death later on in the film. When the creature abruptly falls down into the water after being sprayed with an ammonia compound, a pool of blood begins to spread from between the monster's legs and it dies. Or so we are lead to believe in the American version. As it turns out in the original Korean scripted dialogue, Yongary doesn't actually succumb to his wounds and die. During the epilogue where Eicho speaks to some reporters, he mentions that he hopes the scientists of the world can construct a rocket and send Yongary off to another planet.

Great Monster Yongary (the film's real title) was received positively by audiences and critics alike in its native country where it drew an admission total reported to be between 110,000 to 150,000 tickets sold. It was distributed internationally with the help of Toei Studios from Japan, and saw theatrical release in a surprising amount of countries. In America it went straight to television via AIP-TV in 1969 as *Yongary, Monster from the Deep.* In 1999, in part due to the publicity surrounding the 1998 American *Godzilla,* Yongary even spawned a big budget remake, *Yonggary* (titled *Reptilian* in America).

Final Word

Of all the 1967 dai kaiju films, *Yongary, Monster from the Deep* is easily the most forgettable on an entertainment scale, with most of its merits coming from historical value as an interesting Korean curiosity.

Trivia

- In Germany Godzilla films were often retitled as Frankenstein films. However, in Yongary's case, the monster was advertised as Godzilla in Germany and Frankenstein's name is nowhere to be found in the title.

- The original Korean print was lost, and today all that remains of it is a 35mm 48 minute version.

- Yongary is only 35 meters tall like Gorosaurus in *King Kong Escapes*.

- The scriptwriter claims Yongary was originally a single celled organism from outer space that became mutated by earth's nuclear testing.

- Yongary had competition in its home country from Seki Production's *Space Monster, Wangmagwi* released on June 30, 1967. Far East tried to stop the release with a lawsuit.

- The name Yongary is derived from the Korean word for dragon, Yon, combined with the Korean folk monster Pulgasari, hence Yongary.

Son of Godzilla (1967)

Alternate Titles: *Monster Island's Decisive Battle: Son of Godzilla* (Japan) *Frankenstein's Monster Hunts Godzilla's Son* (Germany) *The Return of Gorgo* (Italy) *The Planet of Monsters* (France)
Release Date: December 16, 1967

Directed by: Jun Fukuda

Special Effects by: Sadamasa Arikawa
Screenplay by: Shinichi Sekizawa & Shiba Ichie
Music by: Masaru Sato
Cast: Akira Kubo (Goro) Beverly Maeda (Reiko) Tadao Takashima (Dr. Kusumi) Akihiko Hirata (Fujisaki) Yoshio Tsuchiya (Furukawa) Kenji Sahara (Morio) **Suit Performers:** Koji Onaka/Hiroshi Sekida/Haruo Nakajima (Godzilla) Little Man Machan (Minilla)

Tohoscope, Eastmancolor, 87 Minutes

Story

A reporter crashes a secret experiment by the United Nations on a tropical island. The island, where scientists are conducting experiments to control the weather, is also home to a mysterious native girl Reiko and a giant egg which hatches a baby Godzilla. Father Godzilla comes ashore and does battle with several insects mutated by the weather experiments to save his son. Goro meets with Reiko and discovers her father was a scientist studying a giant spider monster, Kumonga, on the island. Godzilla's infant son, Minilla, eventually awakens the spider and is caught in its web. At the same time the scientists attempt one last freezing experiment and Godzilla rescues his son. Together the monsters roast the spider as snow begins to fall. The scientists, Goro, and Reiko escape the island just as it begins to freeze.

Background & Commentary

From King Kong and Dracula to Tarzan and Lassie, it seems a cinematic rite of passage to center a film on a movie icon's heir. Unlike other famous characters, it took Godzilla 13 years and seven sequels to finally produce a son. The results are overall fun and comical, lightening an even lighter mood that began in the previous film. Again set on an island devoid of intricate miniatures, Toho seemed to focus more of their attention on the same year's *King Kong Escapes* (helmed by Honda, Tsuburaya and Ifukube) which did include a set of Tokyo. Instead the trio of the previous film returned for another island adventure (filmed on location in Guam) while a wonderfully realized tropical set played home to the monsters. However, there does exists a miniature set of a scientific outpost which conducts weather experiments for the monster to trash. This element of the story actually had its origins in the film's first draft: *Two Godzillas: Japan S.O.S.!* In the story, Reiko and her father both appear, and the weather control device is used to save Japan when Godzilla and his son attack Tokyo in tandem.

The title character, Minilla (as in Mini-godzilla), is still a fiercely debated subject amongst G-fans. Most despise him and some love him, but all agree that he looks nothing like his father. Most often described as a cross between the Pillsbury Doughboy and a dinosaur, the tike was actually fairly popular in Japan and more or less anchored 1969's *All Monsters Attack* (*Godzilla's Revenge*). The short statured monster was portrayed by pro-midget wrestler Little Man Machan, a sometimes Toho actor who had appeared in such productions as *The Lost World of Sinbad* (1963) with Toshiro Mifune. The Godzilla suit in this entry could more or less be considered the George Lazenby of the series as it made only one major appearance, and nor did Haruo Nakajima wear it exclusively. Instead, it was mostly worn by baseball player Koji Onaka and Nakajima's opponent, Hiroshi Sekida. Like the previous film's somewhat simplistic giant lobster, for this story Sekizawa concocted a group of giant insects consisting of a trio of giant praying mantises (called Kamacuras) and a giant spider Kumonga (Spiega in the American dub). The Kamacuras oddly begin the picture man-sized, and then grow larger after the weather experiment goes awry. Kumonga on the other hand is implied to have always been gigantic in size and serves as the main antagonist which Godzilla only overcomes with the help of his son. The end battle between the three is notable for taking place during a snow storm. Masaru Sato composes a particularly poignant final melody as Godzilla and son huddle together in the snow. "Godzilla can't act right? Therefore I had to express his feelings through music," Sato said in *Monsters Are Attacking Tokyo*. He also admitted in interviews that while Ifukube loved Godzilla and treated the monster as a tragedy, Sato tried to humanize the monster, particularly in this outing as Godzilla now had a son.

Marketed to the "date crowd" of young men and women, the film dropped by one million admissions in Japan which startled Tomoyuki Tanaka enough that he decided that Godzilla's next adventure would be his last. In America, this film was again snatched up by Walter Reade Organization which again sent it straight to television in 1969. Ironically at the same time AIP was releasing Tanaka's "last Godzilla film", *Destroy All Monsters*, in theaters, meaning American G-fans could catch new Godzilla flicks on both the big and small screens simultaneously.

Final Word
Though disliked by many fans, still an undeniably heartwarming film and a unique chapter in the history of Godzilla.

Trivia

- Tomoyuki Tanaka had said the idea of giving Godzilla a son came about out of desperation.

- Some sources claim Tadao Takashima refused to go to Guam (due to a fear of flying) to shoot his scenes, so a double was hired while Takashima filmed his scenes at Toho in Japan.

- Godzilla was played by three different actors over the course of filming. Haruo Nakajima plays Godzilla in the 1965 *Invasion of Astro-Monster* suit in water scenes, Koji Onaka played the part until he broke his finger, and finally Hiroshi Sekida took over the part for the remainder of filming.

- The spider Kumonga was even more of a hassle to operate than King Ghidorah, as it took more than 20 puppeteers, three for each leg in some cases, working from the rafters to bring the monster to life.

- A deleted scene was filmed showing Godzilla planning to escape the freezing island before he decides to go back for Minilla. Footage from this sequence can be glimpsed in the film's Japanese trailer.

- The Filipino version of this film opens with footage from *King Kong vs. Godzilla* wherein the two title monsters dive into the ocean, implying *Son of Godzilla* takes place directly after this film (it was also a legitimate excuse to showcase King Kong on the film's poster).

- The Godzilla suit and its frog-like appearance was very unpopular so, despite being in good condition, a new G-suit was built for the next year's *Destroy All Monsters*, though the suit does make a cameo in a long shot during the Tokyo scene. It also served as a water-double in the 1970s, appearing in *Godzilla vs. Gigan* and came close to being loaned out to Tsuburaya Productions for the aborted *Godzilla vs. Redmoon* in 1972.

- According to an interview with Jun Fukuda, he considered Beverly Maeda difficult to work with.

- When the film finished production, SPFX Director Arikawa gifted Machan with an electric razor.

!!!!!!!!!!!!!!!!!!!*Bonus Review*!!!!!!!!!!!!!!!!!!!!

Agon the Atomic Dragon (1968)

Japanese Title: *Giant Phantom Monster Agon*
Broadcast Date: January 2-5, 1968

Directed by: Norio Mine & Fuminori Ohashi
Special Effects by: Fuminori Ohashi
Screenplay by: Shinichi Sekizawa & Kozo Uchida
Music by: Wataru Saito
Cast: Shinji Hirota (Goro) Asao Matsumoto (Det. Yamato) Akemi Sawa (Satsuki) Yoshihiro Kobayashi (Monta)

Nobuhiku Shima (Prof. Ukyo) **Suit Performers:** Etsuji Higashi (Agon)

Academy Ratio, Black & White, 96 Minutes

Story

Goro, a reporter, teams with Detective Yamato to research strange occurrences along the Japanese coast. A giant monster dubbed Agon (for Atomic Dragon) emerges and attacks an atomic power plant. After learning that uranium can appease the monster, it is used to keep the beast sated underwater. However, two criminals disturb the monster's peace and it surfaces again and grabs a fishing boat in its jaws holding a small boy, Monta. Using a uranium lure on the end of a rope attached to a helicopter, Agon finally drops the boat and Monta is able to be rescued. Agon is then poisoned by narcotics and staggers off into the ocean, his fate uncertain.

Background & Commentary

Produced in February of 1964 (and some say even earlier than that) by Nippon Denpa Eiga (Japan Radio Pictures) for Fuji Television, this four part mini-series was prevented from airing until four years later. There are two conflicting stories as to why, the simpler of the two being that Fuji TV couldn't find a sponsor to air the program. The other more prominent story is that Toho felt the monster was too similar to Godzilla and put a stop to the broadcast. However, once Toho found out it was written by Shinichi Sekizawa and also was partially directed by their old pal Fuminori Ohashi (the man who built the original Godzilla suit) they decided to let the program be broadcast. While the monster is indeed evocative of Godzilla in its design, hunger for atomic energy, and other aspects, it's hard to believe Toho would be unaware of Sekizawa and Ohashi's involvement in the project until several years later. More likely the program was shelved until the giant monster boom of 1967 when *Ultraman* became a huge hit on TV, thus this special's airing in January of 1968.

For a TV miniseries filmed in 1964, *Agon the Atomic Dragon* isn't awful, but it's not terribly good either. Sekizawa uses his usual character types for the script with a reporter in the lead role (Sekizawa even recycles a gag from his

Mothra script where the lead reporter is nicknamed "snapping turtle" because he never lets go of a story) who romances a female laboratory assistant. Said lab assistant's elderly scientist boss also features in the story along with a policeman. Sekizawa's writing features the same crime aspect he incorporated into *Dogora, the Space Monster* and *Ghidorah, the Three Headed Monster* that same year when he includes a subplot involving a couple of criminals smuggling drugs who are eventually caught by Detective Yamato. As for the project's titular star, Agon sports a very Godzilla-like design, only with longer arms, more subdued dorsal plates, and a head more liken to an Iguanodon. Agon's mouth also cuts too far back into his head, giving him the look of a cheaply designed plastic dinosaur toy. Though the suit is poor in this regard, it does have one interesting feature that the Godzilla suits lacked as viewers were able to see Agon breathe. The mini-series was innovative in other ways as well. Had it been broadcast in the fall of 1964 as originally planned it would have been the first kaiju TV series, pre-dating *Ultra Q* in 1966. *Agon the Atomic Dragon* was also the first dai-kaiju eiga to feature a small child in a lead role beating out Daiei's *Gamera* from 1965. Ironically, Agon predates Godzilla's origin as an irradiated dinosaur as explained in 1991's *Godzilla vs. King Ghidorah* (in the original *Godzilla* Dr. Yamane postulates that the H-Bomb only awakened Godzilla from his slumber). It's interesting that Shinichi Sekizawa had the same idea as that film's eventual screenwriter Kazuki Omori and that it originated here.

Agon the Atomic Dragon finally aired over the course of four consecutive nights from January 2nd to the 5th in 1968. In the 1980s Toho Video actually released the film on VHS and, later in the 2000s, onto DVD. As for the Agon suit, the monster returned to TV as a dinosaur in an episode of the *Space Giants* TV show.

Final Word
Worth viewing mostly as a curiosity, otherwise there isn't much to recommend in this watered down TV rehash of Godzilla.

Gamera vs. Viras (1968)

Alternate Titles: *Gamera vs. Space Monster Viras* (Japan) *Destroy All Planets* (U.S.)
Release Date: March 20, 1968

Directed by: Noriaki Yuasa
Special Effects by: Noriaki Yuasa
Screenplay by: Niisan Takahashi
Music by: Kenjiro Hirose
Cast: Toru Takatsuka (Masao) Carl Craig Jr. (Jim) Kojiro Hongo (Shimada) Atsumi Mari (Junko) Michiko Yaegaki (Mariko) **Suit Performers:** Teruo Arakaki (Gamera) Uncredited (Viras)

Daieiscope, Eastmancolor, 72 Minutes

Story

Two mischievous boys, Masao and Jim, in the Japanese Boy Scouts take a new experimental sub for a joy ride into the ocean depths. There they are attacked by a strange alien spacecraft and rescued by Gamera. But, while the boys escape, Gamera is placed under mind control by the aliens. Later Jim and Masao are abducted by the aliens, called Virans, who hold the boys hostage on their ship, telling the world to surrender or the boys will be killed. Instead, the boys manage to free Gamera—who the Virans are using to attack Tokyo—from the mind control device and escape the ship. All the aliens combine into a giant squid monster, Viras, which battles Gamera. As always, the giant turtle emerges victorious over the evil aliens.

Background & Commentary

Coming off of their biggest success yet in *Gamera vs. Gyaos*, one would think Daei would have put more effort into Gamera #4, and perhaps the studio would have had it not found itself in financial trouble at the onset of 1968. As a result, the next Gamera film's budget was cut to that of a non-special effects feature at only ¥20 million (about $56,000). Yuasa and screenwriter Takahashi had to take drastic measures to get by, namely utilizing stock footage from past films in addition to scripting all the new monster footage in beachfront areas so as to be devoid of elaborate miniatures. Some of the stock footage is well integrated, as it appears in the form of "flashbacks" as the aliens study Gamera. Other footage is not, such as when the aliens take control of Gamera and use him to attack Tokyo in the form of black and white footage from the original *Gamera*.

On the other end of the spectrum, screenwriter Takahashi hits a home run in the form of his handling of the child characters. Gone is the helpless Eiji of the previous film, who is replaced by the more competent Masao and his pal Jim (adult star Kojiro Hongo is likewise given a less prominent role signaling the handover to children is complete). Masao and Jim provide solid avatars for the target audience, as they explore the sea in their miniature submarine and also run afoul of alien invaders on their ship. Having entered into an agreement with AIP-TV to distribute their kaiju films in the U.S., Daiei was instructed to cast an American boy in the role of Masao's compatriot to boost international appeal. As no actors could be found in Japan that understood Japanese, Carl Craig, the child of a U.S. army man stationed in Japan, was cast though he had no acting experience. On the technical end, limited though they may be, the new SPFX sequences still prove amusing, especially the yellow and black bumblebee-like design of the alien spacecraft. The new monster, the alien squid Viras, is something of a trendsetter as well. Introduced to the audience as a human-sized mindless beast in a cage, it is eventually revealed that Viras is the mastermind behind the whole invasion, and the humanoid aliens on the ship are actually his peons. When it comes time to battle Gamera, Viras beheads his subjects with one swipe of his tentacle and absorbs their life force to grow to Gamera's size. The ensuing battle on the beach is one of the more far-out Gamera battles in the series, and ends with Viras impaling Gamera (which children in theaters screamed in fear at the sight of). Gamera then flies so high into the air with Viras (still stabbed into Gamera's torso) that the squid freezes and breaks apart.

In spite of the oversaturation of the dai-kaiju eiga at the time and the film's over reliance on stock footage, *Gamera vs. Viras* still managed to be such a big success in Japan that

Daiei asked Yuasa if he could produce two Gamera films per year. Ironically, Yuasa had assumed that this would be the final Gamera film, and though Yuasa said that two a year would be impossible, he was still pleased to know that his series would continue into the future.

Final Word

In terms of character utilization and script, *Gamera vs. Viras* could be the film where it all came together. But, in terms of budget and SPFX, it was the film where it all started to fall apart.

Trivia

* Carl Craig grew up to become a fighter pilot in the U.S. Air Force in the 1980s. He also appeared several times at G-Fest.

* AIP released Toho's *Charge of the Monsters* in 1969 as *Destroy All Monsters* and released *Gamera vs. Viras* to TV as *Destroy All Planets*.

* Though the actual film features no new city destruction, the poster showcases an exciting image of Gamera crashing Viras's pointy head into a skyscraper.

* The film was shot in only 25 days.

* Masakazu Nagata, Daiei President, was also an advisor to the Boy Scouts Association of Japan at the time, hence their involvement.

* Starting with this film, Daiei offered a contest with *World WE Magazine* to name the new film's monster, a tradition that continued on with subsequent sequels.

* One of the Virans (in human form) is Riki Hashimoto, the actor who played Daimajin.

Yokai Monsters: 100 Monsters (1968)

Japanese Title: *One Hundred Yokai Tales*
Release Date: March 20, 1968

Directed by: Kimiyoshi Yasuda
Special Effects by: Yoshiyuki Kuroda
Screenplay by: Tetsurô Yoshida
Music by: Michiaki Watanabe
Cast: Jun Fujimaki (Yasutaro Oki) Takashi Kanda (Tajima)
Ryûtarô Gomi (Yutaka) Jun Hamamura (Gohei) Masaru
Hiraizumi (Takichi) Keiko Koyanagi (Okubi) Shozo
Hayashiya (Storyteller) Shinobu Araki (Old Priest)

Daieiscope, Eastmancolor, 78 Minutes

Story
In Edo, when an ancient shrine is torn down to make way for
a brothel by the greedy lord Tajima, strange events plague
the area. In town undercover is a magistrate, Yasutaro, who
does his best to help the locals wronged by Tajima, but in the
end Tajima is driven insane by a group of Yokai spooks
disturbed when the shrine was demolished.

Background & Commentary
Much like Daiei's Daimajin trilogy from two years previous,
this first installment of what would eventually become a
trilogy itself is of very fine quality. The film was
atmospherically directed by *Zatoichi, the Blind Swordsman* and
Daimajin alum Kimiyoshi Yasuda, and not surprisingly like
Daimajin is essentially a period samurai film with monsters
and supernatural elements thrown in intermittently. Also
like the Daimajin trilogy, entries in the Yokai Monsters
trilogy were only loosely connected, with each entry focusing
on the Yokai Monsters haunting evil doers in Feudal Japan.
Of all three films, the first is arguably the darkest.

The SPFX, directed by the same man who did the effects
on the Daimajin trilogy, are innovative, particularly a long
necked woman, the effects for which are created with clever
trick lighting and a long necked prop of the character.
Animation is also used to good extent when one of the

characters draws one of the monsters on the wall, after which the drawing comes to life and jumps off of the wall *Roger Rabbit* style. The scares towards the end are genuine, and the many Yokai are indeed quite creepy as intended. There are no traditional giant monsters per say, but one of the Yokai appears as a giant disembodied head. The music is well done, though some of it sounds more like something one would hear in a late 1960s spy film, not necessarily a bad thing, just an oddity in a horror film such as this.

It is presumable that this film's large budget, evident on the screen, resulted in budget cuts for *Gamera vs. Viras*, which *Yokai Monsters: 100 Monsters* was double billed with. The double bill was a hit, and due to *Yokai Monsters: 100 Monsters* surprise popularity, Daiei immediately began plans for a sequel as quickly as possible, which was released in December of that same year.

Final Word

As this film was followed by a more light-hearted sequel, for those that like their Yokai played straight, then this first entry is the best.

Trivia

- The idea for this film came about because of the success of the Toei Animation TV series *Gegege No Kitaro*.

Destroy All Monsters (1968)

Alternate Titles: *Charge of the Monsters* (Japan) *The Heirs of King Kong* (Italy) *Frankenstein and the Space Monster* (Germany) *Extraterrestrial Invasion* (Spain)
Release Date: August 1, 1968

Directed by: Ishiro Honda
Special Effects by: Sadamasa Arikawa & Eiji Tsuburaya
Screenplay by: Kaoru Mabuchi & Ishiro Honda
Music by: Akira Ifukube

Cast: Akira Kubo (Capt. Yamabe) Yukiko Kobayashi
(Kyoko) Jun Tazaki (Dr. Yoshida) Kyoko Ai (Kilaak Queen)
Yoshio Tsuchiya (Dr. Otani) **Suit Performers:** Haruo
Nakajima (Godzilla/Baragon) Susumi Utsumi (King
Ghidorah) Teruo Nigaki (Rodan) Tadaaki Watanabe/
Hiroshi Sekida (Anguirus/Gorosaurus) Little Man Machan
(Minilla)

Cinemascope, Eastmancolor, 89 Minutes

Story
In the distant future of 1999, earth's monsters have been
sequestered on Ogasawara Island aka Monsterland. Man has
also mastered space travel with rocket ship Moonlight SY-3
and has a Moon base. All is peaceful until the monsters
inexplicably disappear. Soon after, the world watches in
horror as Godzilla attacks New York; Rodan Moscow;
Mothra Beijing; and Gorosaurus Paris. Captain Yamabe flies
his SY-3 crew to Monsterland to investigate and finds that
aliens called the Kilaaks have taken over the island and
brainwashed the staff, including his girlfriend Kyoko.
Yamabe and his crew escape but are unable to rescue Kyoko.
Soon after Godzilla, Mothra, Rodan and Manda devastate
Tokyo. In the rubble Kyoko offers an ultimatum on behalf of
the Kilaaks. Yamabe will hear none of it and brutally rips off
the earrings that the aliens are using to control her. Yamabe
and his team then scour Mt. Fuji for the Kilaak base and learn
that the monster controller is in a secret base inside the
moon. The SY-3 crew storms the base and disconnects the
controller which they bring to earth. There scientists use it
to lead the monsters to the Mt. Fuji base, but the Kilaaks
have a secret weapon. King Ghidorah materializes to defend
them but is killed by the monsters who also destroy the base.
The monsters then peacefully return to Ogasawara.

Background & Commentary
This large scale crossover film out does Universal's *House of
Frankenstein* and also pre-dates *Marvel's the Avengers*. The
former film represented the combination of three different
series and the later a combination of four franchises. *Destroy
All Monsters* is the culmination of a process that began in

Mothra vs. Godzilla and continued in *Ghidorah, the Three Headed Monster* which spun Rodan and Mothra into the Godzilla universe. Including *Mothra, Rodan,* the G-series itself, and now *Varan* (1958), Baragon from *Frankenstein Conquers the World* (1965), Manda from *Atragon* (1963), and Gorosaurus from *King Kong Escapes (1967), Destroy All Monsters* (affectionately abbreviated as *DAM*) unifies seven total films into one massive movie. The crossover's emphasis is not on continuity, as the numerous originating films don't actually mesh, but rather on available monster suits. For instance, Gorosaurus (a last minute replacement for another monster) was portrayed as 35 meters tall in *King Kong Escapes* due to the miniature scale in that film, but here he is head to head with the 50 meter Godzilla and the same is true for some of the other monsters. A feast of diverse monster suits, *DAM* also features the return of Minilla (Godzilla's son) and Kumonga from *Son of Godzilla*, in addition to a new Anguirus suit, a monster not seen since *Godzilla Raids Again* (1955). As a last minute surprise—for someone who never saw a trailer or poster for the film that is—King Ghidorah also reappears. Due to Godzilla's unpopular design in *Son of Godzilla*, Toho built a new G-suit for what was at the time intended to be the "final Godzilla film" due to declining box-office grosses.

The film's story is a fun, whiz-bang extravaganza, even if it never quite allows one to connect with the characters. Captain Yamabe is given many exciting missions from storming Monsterland to raiding the Kilaak base on the moon. But, without any character depth, it is hard to feel any suspense for him and his men. On the other hand, children are never left waiting long to see a SPFX shot of some sort, be it a monster suit or a flying saucer. The kaiju assault on Tokyo is a monster movie lover's paradise. In one shot Manda coils around an expressway in the foreground while in the background Godzilla sets off a pyrotechnic fury. The real tour de force is the film's climax in which Ghidorah battles seven monsters at once. Due to its many participants, the final battle is one of the shorter ones of the series. Coordinating so many suit actors at once with the many wires it took to operate King Ghidorah was difficult to say the least. Each monster gets a unique moment to shine during the battle, particularly new comers Anguirus, who famously becomes airborne thanks to King Ghidorah, and Gorosaurus who delivers a kangaroo kick to the monster in a fan favorite moment. Rodan, having already battled Ghidorah twice before, is kept somewhat at a distance, while marionettes Kumonga and Mothra do little more than spray webbing on the monster after it is defeated. Manda and Varan sit the battle out as their props were limited in what they could do. As for Baragon, the kaiju was scripted to have a big part in the film but due to the fact that the suit was loaned out to Tsuburaya Productions most of the time the kaiju makes only a cameo during the film's epilogue. Somewhat misplaced is an aerial dogfight that occurs after the monster rumble where the SY-3 battles a flaming Kilaak saucer in a sequence that goes on a bit too long. For once it is the monsters that serve as spectators as the humans engage in their own battle. The scene might have fared better if it took place simultaneously to the monster battle cutting back and forth between the two.

Contrary to popular belief *DAM* (budgeted at a healthy ¥200,000,000) was not a dai-hit in Japan. Its attendance actually only increased from *Son of Godzilla* by 100,000 admissions. However, the jump in attendance was still enough to inspire Toho to forgo cancellation of the series and they quickly followed *DAM* with *All Monsters Attack* (better known as *Godzilla's Revenge*) in 1969. *DAM* was, however, the last collaborative effort between Honda, Ifukube, Tanaka, and Tsuburaya. The film was also one of Godzilla's last big hurrahs in America seeing theatrical release as *Destroy All Monsters*, a title Toho liked so much they kept it as the official International title.

Final Word

Although *DAM* lacks depth, the entertainment factor cannot be denied as it features set-piece after set-piece. Worth seeing alone for the final battle, the film is a fan favorite and a must see for any monster lover.

Trivia

- The story began life as a take on the classic Japanese story 47 Ronin called *Kaiju Chushingura*. The Kilaaks in the story are named after the Kirakozukenosuke of 47 Ronin, thus in Japan were named the Kiraku which in America became the Kilaaks.

- A Toho encyclopedia states that the Mothra larva in this film is the second Mothra larva from *Mothra vs. Godzilla* that was presumed dead. Instead it chose not to enter into its Imago stage and stay a larva. Newer Toho encyclopedias have since retconned this idea.

- The *Son of Godzilla* suit appears in a long shot during the Tokyo scene, and the *Invasion of Astro-Monster* suit is used for a waterfront scene where Godzilla blasts New York.

- Toho had hopes of reusing the *King Kong Escapes* Kong suit to have the famous gorilla appear in the film as well, but unfortunately their five year license to use the character from RKO had expired by the time the film went before cameras.

- Toho planned on utilizing Ebirah and the giant walrus Magma (from *Gorath*) as they appear in the first script draft but for whatever reason didn't make the final cut. Not much is known of Ebirah's role, but Magma would have been guardian to the underground Kilaak base along with Baragon. Sanda and Gaira were in an early story treatment as well, and Sanda was for a time scripted to be hanging around Monsterland after Gaira was axed.

- In America for many years this was the "lost Godzilla film" as it wasn't broadcast on television anymore and lacked a VHS release throughout the 1980s and 1990s.

- A Japanese book entitled *Everything About Godzilla Movies* (1993) implies that the new smaller Baragon from this film was born on Mount Shirane in Japan. After it was taken to Monsterland it was raised by none other than Rodan! This info was translated from the book by Toho Kingdom's Nicholas Driscoll.

- The futuristic guns used by both the Kilaaks and the Moonlight SY3 crew were recycled and reused as the alien guns in *Godzilla vs. Gigan* (1972), *Godzilla vs. Megalon* (1973) and *Godzilla vs. Mechagodzilla* (1974).

!!!!!!!!!!!!!!!!!!Bonus Review!!!!!!!!!!!!!!!!!!!

Goke, Body Snatcher from Hell (1968)

Alternate Titles: *Vampire Goke* (Japan) *Body Snatcher from Hell* (U.S.)
Release Date: August 14, 1968

Directed by: Hajime Sato
Special Effects by: Shosuke Kojima
Screenplay by: Susumu Takaku & Kyuzo Kobayashi
Music by: Shunsuke Kikuchi
Cast: Teruo Yoshida (Sugisaka) Tomomi Sato (Asakura) Eizo Kitamura (Senator Mano) Masaya Takahasi (Toshiyuki) Kazuo Kato (Dr. Momotake) Yuko Kusunoki (Noriko) Kathy Horan (Mrs. Neal) Nobuo Kaneko (Tokuyasu) Hideo Ko (Assassin/Goke) Kei'ichi Noda (voice of Goke)

Shochiku-GrandScope, Eastmancolor, 84 Minutes

Story
A Japan Air plane is hijacked by an assassin while bound for Osaka. When a luminescent, orange UFO buzzes the plane, its instruments go haywire and the plane crashes in an isolated wasteland. The assassin survives and is possessed by one of the beings from the UFO, which has landed nearby. As the vampiric alien picks off the survivors one by one tensions reach a fever pitch until finally the alien is set fire to

and killed. When only the co-pilot, Sugisaka, and a stewardess, Asakura, manage to escape alive back to society they find the world already overtaken by the same alien species that terrified them in the wasteland.

Background & Commentary

Strangely enough, *Goke, Body Snatcher from Hell* started life as a TV series from P-Productions (the future producers of *Spectreman*) planned for 1967. A test pilot featuring stuffed animals to play the aliens was shot and not surprisingly abandoned. The concept was somehow acquired by Shochiku, which teamed with P-Productions (who would handle the SPFX) to turn the concept into a much more serious horror film. Writer Susumu Takaku suggested Toei's Hajime Sato as director and off the film went. Initially Sato came up with an idea wherein invisible alien monsters ran amuck in a mental ward until he came up with the idea of instead opening the film on an airliner that crashes

From the very first shot, wherein a plane flies through a blood red sky, *Goke, Body Snatcher from Hell* is filled with striking imagery. Birds fly smack dab into the windows where they become bloody pulps, men walk into glowing orange spacecraft, and people are drained of their blood by the title character until they become a ghastly grey. Actually, though singer Hideo Ko portrayed Goke for most of the film, eventually the performer had a scheduling problem and had to leave, hence the script was changed during shooting and his character is killed off early and the alien vampire has to find a new host. In spite of this setback, the film still comes to a rousing climax thanks to its twist ending. In it, after surviving a series of horrific attacks by Goke, the two main characters finally make it back to civilization. There they find a strange traffic jam, and upon closer inspection find all the cars' occupants to be drained of their blood. The film then ends by panning back from a grey colored earth which is being beset upon by a bevy of flying saucers.

As it turned out, *Goke, Body Snatcher from Hell* ended up being the final directorial effort of Hajime Sato, and as such, the director managed to end his career on a high note. The film was finally released in the U.S. in 1979 as *Body Snatcher from Hell* with an R rating to boot.

Final Word
Overall atmospheric and chilling, the film's ranking as a cult classic is well deserved—especially for that grim twist ending.

Trivia

- After the film was released, Hideo Ko recalled many children he encountered feared him due to recognizing him from the movie.

- Quentin Tarantino is among the film's fans. In tribute to this film, a red sky can be seen outside of an airliner in *Kill Bill Vol. 1*.

- This film's UFO was later made into Dr. Gori's spaceship for P-Productions *Spectreman* TV series years later.

- Though this was Hajime Sato's last film, the director was approached to helm Toei's *Space Monster Devil Manta* in 1976 before production was cancelled.

Genocide (1968)

Japanese Title: *War of the Insects*
Release Date: November 08, 1968

Directed by: Kazui Nihonmatsu
Special Effects by: Keiji Kawakami & Shun Suganuma
Screenplay by: Susumu Takaku
Music by: Shunsuke Kikuchi
Cast: Yusuke Kawazu (Joji) Keisuke Sonoi (Yoshito) Emi Shindo (Yukari) Reiko Hitomi (Junko) Kathy Horan (Annabelle) Chico Roland (Charlie)

Shochiku-GrandScope, Eastmancolor, 84 Minutes

Story

A USAF plane carrying a hydrogen bomb on the way to Vietnam is attacked by a swarm of poisonous insects and crashes in the waters near Japan's southern islands. As the U.S. military searches for the missing bomb, and mysterious insect attacks mount, it is learned the killer bees are being controlled by a woman named Annabel. A biologist who survived the Nazi holocaust, Annabel is using the insects to inflict genocide on the world. When this plot is uncovered by scientist Joji he kills Annabel by trapping her in a room with her deadly bees which sting her to death. As the insects overtake the islands, the USAF decides the best way to solve all of their problems is to detonate the H-Bomb, in effect killing the insects and also ensuring the H-Bomb doesn't fall into enemy hands.

Background & Commentary

Directed by the same man that gave the world the awful *The X From Outer Space* the previous year, Kazui Nihonmatsu does a much better job on this insect themed horror film written by Susumu Takaku of *Goke, Body Snatcher from Hell.* The film was shot on location on Hachijo Island often using real insects. In fact, in one scene, a real bee even bites lead actor Yusuke Kawazu.

Scenes of the insects in action brought to life via animated swarms (and in the case of close-ups, real bees) aren't terribly interesting from a SPFX perspective. The first occurs when a swarm chokes the engines of the USAF plane carrying the H-Bomb. More interesting than the film's insects is its use of apocalyptic imagery as the film both opens and closes with the detonation of hydrogen bombs. In the case of the film's opening the bomb is just stock footage, but in the case of the ending the bomb is remotely detonated by the USAF to destroy both the insects and the bomb. One of the US airmen tries to stop the detonation aboard a military aircraft, but when his attempt proves futile and the bomb detonates anyways, he shoots himself in the head. Moments later, another swarm of insect descends upon the plane, choking the engines and destroying it while at the same time showing the bomb didn't take care of the bugs after all.

Released on a double bill with *The Living Skeleton* in Japan, *Genocide* ended up being the last of Shochiku's horror films as the studio switched gears to begin producing the family friendly (and very long running) *Tora-san* series. *Genocide* also saw limited release in America under the title *War of the Insects* through Shochiku Films of America in 1969.

Final Word

Though not on the level of *Goke, Body Snatcher from Hell,* as the last horror film from Shochiku—not to mention the last film of director Nihonmatsu—*Genocide* is still a solid effort.

Trivia

- Chico Roland, who plays Charlie, was one of the better known African American actors in Japan throughout the 1960s and 1970s and has a memorable encounter with Sonny Chiba in the first *Street Fighter*.

- Actor Yusuke Kawazu agreed to do the film the minute he found out that Kazui Nihonmatsu was directing.

- In this film's Japanese trailer, the UFO from *Goke, Body Snatcher from Hell* mysteriously appears.

!!!!!!!!!!!!!!!!!!!Bonus Review!!!!!!!!!!!!!!!!!!!!

The Green Slime (1968)

Japanese Title: *Gamma No.3 Space Division*
Release Date: December 01, 1968

Directed by: Kenji Fukasaku
Special Effects by: Akira Watanabe
Screenplay by: William Finger, Tom Rowe & Charles Sinclair
Music by: Toshiaki Tsushima & Charles Fox

Cast: Robert Horton (Cmdr. Jack Rankin) Richard Jaeckel (Cmdr. Vince Elliott) Luciana Paluzzi (Dr. Lisa Benson) Robert Dunham (Capt. Martin) **Suit Performers:** Uncredited

Toeiscope, Eastmancolor, 90 Minutes

Story

When a huge asteroid is discovered hurtling towards earth, Commander Jack Rankin is sent to rendezvous with Gamma No.3 Space Station on his way to plant explosives on the asteroid. There, an estranged friend, Commander Vince Elliot, now engaged to Rankin's ex flame, Dr. Lisa Benson, insists upon tagging along. While on the asteroid, a doctor from Gamma 3 picks up a specimen of strange green slime. Commander Rankin and his men escape back to Gamma 3 after the asteroid explodes. However, the green slime taken back by the doctor mutates and takes over the space station in the form of a swarm of deadly creatures. Only by evacuating Gamma No.3 and then setting the station to self-destruct are the monsters destroyed and in the process Commander Elliot is killed.

Background & Commentary

If one didn't know better, they might think that this was an American monster film if the distinctly Japanese SPFX (and names on the credits) didn't give it away. The film was a co-production between MGM and Toei. How it worked was MGM provided the stars and the script, while the story was shot at Toei Studios in Japan which also handled the SPFX. Among the American stars are Richard Jaeckel, one of the leads in *The Dirty Dozen* and the future star of Toho's *Latitude Zero* (1969). And, from the world of James Bond, comes Luciana Paluzzi (*Thunderball*).

    The Green Slime is actually much better than its detractors give it credit for and it actually plays like a tamer, kitschier precursor to 1979's *Alien*. That's not to say that the titular Green Slime doesn't leave quite a body count, and even gore, in its wake—campy though its design and execution may be. The SPFX were handled by the former

The Big Book of Japanese
Giant Monster Movies

Toho Art Director (and SPFX Director of Nikkatsu's *Gappa, the Triphibean Monster*) Akira Watanabe. So while the effects more or less sink the film, it is up to the human dynamic to carry the picture, and it actually does so fairly well. The film's best scene occurs when Richard Jaeckel leads a party of astronauts to the hull of the space station and engages in a laser battle with the monsters in zero gravity. When his gun malfunctions he throws it through one of the creature's eyes. Jaeckel's death during the climax is somewhat predictable though as he is part of a love triangle including Horton and Paluzzi. Said climax where Jaeckel bites the dust has quite an exciting moment when Horton bails with Jaeckel's body from the space station as it hurtles from orbit to self-destruct. The scene is so good that even the terrible SPFX don't ruin it completely.

The film premiered in America on December 1, 1968, but didn't see a formal wide release until May 21st the following year. The film also saw release in Japan in December of 1968 as well, albeit in a truncated 77 minute version which removes most of the arguing between Horton and Jaeckel along with the love triangle involving Paluzzi. The film was received negatively by critics in America at the time, though many baby boomers have fond memories of it— most notably the jazzy opening theme song.

Final Word
With better executed SPFX and creature designs, this film could have been a serious classic of science fiction rather than the camp classic it is regarded as today.

Trivia

- Linda Miller (*King Kong Escapes*) has a small part as a nurse.

- This was the first film to be featured on *Mystery Science Theater 3000*.

- Is the unofficial fifth film in a series beginning with *Wild, Wild Planet; War of the Planets; War Between the*

Planets and *Snow Devils* (all 1966) all of which featured Space Station Gamma 1, while this film features a similarly designed space station called Gamma 3.

Yokai Monsters: Great Yokai War (1968)

Japanese Title: *Great Yokai War*
Release Date: December 14, 1968

Directed by: Yoshiyuki Kuroda
Special Effects by: Yoshiyuki Kuroda
Screenplay by: Tetsurô Yoshida
Music by: Nari Ikuno
Cast: Yoshihiko Aoyama (Shinkansen) Akane Kawasaki (Chie) Osamu Okawa (Odate Iori) Takashi Kanda (Isobe Hyogo) Uchida Aso (Dainichiro) **Suit Performers:** Chikara Hashimoto (Daimon) Gen Kuroki (Kappa)

Daieiscope, Eastmancolor, 79 Minutes

Story

Explorers in the ancient city of Ur in Babylon awaken the ancient monster Daimon which flies to Japan upon its release. A shapeshifting vampire, the monster takes on the form of a local Samurai, Lord Hyogo Isobe, after drinking his blood. The local water Kappa is able to see past the monster's disguise and rounds up his fellow Yokai to drive away Daimon. In an effort to confront the numerous Yokai, Daimon makes doubles of himself until he matches their numbers. A battle ensues, and after taking Daimon's eye, the evil beast is finally defeated by the Yokai.

Background & Commentary

After the success of the hit double bill that was *Gamera vs. Viras* and *Yokai Monsters: 100 Monsters*, Daiei had asked Gamera director Noriaki Yuasa if he could put out two Gamera features per year. While Yuasa declined, Daiei apparently made the same request of the Yokai team, which did manage to turn out this sequel by December of the same year. The film was produced by the same team as the first film minus music composer Michiaki Watanabe and director Kimiyoshi Yasuda. In light of Yasuda's departure, Daiei wisely promoted SPFX director Yoshiyuki Kuroda to direct the first Yokai sequel, much like they had done with Noriaki Yuasa in the past.

Unlike the first sequel to Daiei's *Daimajin,* which more or less repeated the first film's formula, *Great Yokai War* is a completely different animal from its predecessor in many respects. The story begins intriguingly in the ruins of Babylon, where two plunderers open a tableau old tomb said to house a monster. Said monster turns out to be real, kills the men, and flies for Japan where it takes on the form of a village elder. This catches the attention of a local Kappa, a Japanese water nymph, who takes it upon himself to rid the area of this unwanted monster. In the form of this new character, the lead of the film in some respects, humor and satire (absent in the last film) are introduced to the series for the first time. However, that being said, this humor is at odds with many of the film's scares and horror scenes.

Of all the Yokai films, this one is probably the best known due to its climax wherein Daimon makes clones of himself, and also transforms into a giant form which all the Yokai gang up on, making it sort of like a Yokai version the same year's *Destroy All Monsters.* Scenes of the Yokai parade marching to confront Daimon are undeniably fun, and the end battle doesn't disappoint. As a matter of fact, this film's climax was so well done it made the next follow up, *Yokai Monsters: Along With Ghosts,* something of a letdown. Furthermore, when the series was remade in 2005 as *The Great Yokai War,* this film was used as the template more so than the others.

Final Word
Though sillier than its predecessor, *Yokai Monsters: Great Yokai War* is easily the best of the original trilogy.

Trivia

- Giant Daimon hand and foot props were built for when the monster grows to giant proportions.

Gamera vs. Guiron (1969)

Alternate Titles: *Gamera vs. Giant Evil Beast Guiron* (Japan) *Attack of the Giant Monsters* (U.S.) *King Kong vs. Godzilla* (Germany)
Release Date: March 21, 1969

Directed by: Noriaki Yuasa
Special Effects by: Noriaki Yuasa
Screenplay by: Niisan Takahashi
Music by: Shunsuke Kikuchi
Cast: Nobuhiro Kashima (Akio) Christopher Murphy (Tom) Miyuki Akiyama (Tomoko) Reiko Kasahara (Flobella) Hiroko Kai (Barbella) Kon Omura (Kondo) Yuko Hamada (Aoki's Mother) Edith Hanson (Tom's Mother) **Suit Performers:** Izumi Umenosuke (Gamera) Uncredited (Guiron) Uncredited (Space Gyaos)

Daieiscope, Eastmancolor, 82 Minutes

Story

When space obsessed boys Akio and Tom witness a UFO land near their neighborhood they take off with Akio's little sister Tomoko in tow to investigate. The two boys find the UFO and board it to play around, and to Tomoko's horror it takes off into the skies. The UFO takes the boys into space where they rendezvous with Gamera, but the ship (on autopilot) outpaces the turtle and they fly off into space. Eventually they land on the planet Tera, inhabited by the knife-headed monster Guiron and a pair of seemingly friendly spacewomen. Things take a turn for the worse when the aliens try to eat Tom and Akio's brains, but luckily Gamera arrives in the nick of time. On Tera he eventually triumphs over Guiron while the boys get the best of the aliens. Gamera flies them in the damaged spaceship back to earth, where Tomoko, their mothers, and a group of reporters witness their return.

Background & Commentary

Though Noriaki Yuasa initially believed *Gamera vs. Viras* to be the final Gamera film, he was relieved when Daei tasked him with doing another. Unfortunately, once again he was only allotted the same ¥20,000,000 budget. Remarkably, one wouldn't know it to look at the finished film. Tactics used to keep the film fresh were inventive to say the least. Rather than rely on rural areas again (such as the beach in the previous film) to keep the budget low, Daiei changed the setting to a rural alien planet. This idea is rumored to have been that of AIP-TV's (which again had a prearranged agreement to distribute the film to U.S. television) who felt an outer space theme would be popular. Whatever the case, the somewhat barren alien planet of Tera was a creative way to utilize the limited means of the studio, because on a psychological level the idea of being lost and away from home is scary for all children—in this case stranded on another planet where absolutely no one but Gamera can save them.

One concept that did have to be scrapped was that of an additional monster: Monga. Described as a blue furred kaiju with membranes between its arms and legs (making it a sort of giant alien flying squirrel), it greatly resembled Toho's Varan but featured a horned head and a tail ending in a spiky mace. But, Monga was axed and instead the old Gyaos suit was dusted off and spray painted silver to create a new monster: Space Gyaos. For the main opponent Akira Inoue created what he describes as his favorite among the Gamera pantheon: Guiron, a knife-headed monster meant to represent something children shouldn't play with. Guiron puts his head to good use cutting Space Gyaos into several pieces in his introductory scene. The sequence is surreal and Guiron is methodical in the way he slowly chops the monster into pieces. It's hard to believe the scene is part of a children's film, and in some countries it was excised. When parts of Space Gyaos are severed, like the proverbial chicken with its head cut off, they still pulsate with movement. Later Guiron attempts to cut Gamera in half in a sequence frightening for younger viewers—in this way the film is undeniably the pinnacle of the notorious gore and bloodshed in the series. It also represents the pinnacle of outlandish battle techniques on Gamera's end. At one point the monster does a series of acrobatic flips inspired by similar maneuvers from the Mexico City Olympics of that same year, and later Gamera deflects some ninja throwing stars with a rock in a nod to

Daiei's popular samurai franchise, *Zatoichi, the Blind Swordsman.*

The film was another hit in Japan, and easily outclassed Toho's Godzilla entry for that year *All Monsters Attack,* which itself drew inspiration from the Gamera series. In the tradition of AIP's "monster series" this was released to U.S. TV as *Attack of the Monsters.*

Final Word

One of the best Gamera films in the series thanks to the screenwriter who knew how to write around the limited budget.

Trivia

- Reiko Kasahara, who played the kindly older sister in *Gamera vs. Gyaos,* here plays one of the villainous alien sisters.

- Guiron was mistakenly drawn with a tail in some magazine illustrations.

- Originally the role of Akio was supposed to go to Yoshinobu Kaneko of the popular *Watari, Ninja Boy* (1966) but the young actor was too busy with school.

- Guiron was considered as an opponent for what eventually became *Gamera 2: Advent of Legion* (1996). His knife-head was rumored to have influenced Legion's pointy snout.

- Though most English fans translate the katakana for the monster as gu-i-ro-n, according to *G-Fan* editor J.D. Lees, Noriaki Yuasa said it was intended to be Guillon (l and r are represented by the same symbol) because the name referenced a guillotine!

Yokai Monsters: Along with Ghosts (1969)

Japanese Title: *Tokaido Haunted Journey*
Release Date: March 21, 1969

Directed by: Kimiyoshi Yasuda & Yoshiyuki Kuroda
Special Effects by: Yoshiyuki Kuroda
Screenplay by: Tetsurô Yoshida & Shozaburo Asai
Music by: Michiaki Watanabe
Cast: Kojiro Hongo (Hyakasuro) Pepe Hozumi (Shinta)
Masami Burukido (Miya) Bokuzen Hidari (Jinbei)

Daieiscope, Eastmancolor, 78 Minutes

Story
When young girl Miyo's grandfather is murdered by a
corrupt clan owner who runs her town, the Yokai Monsters
take note. When the clan owner finds out that Miyo has proof
of his corruption, he locks her up with her long lost father as
one by one the Yokai hunt down the murderers and
eventually free Miyo and her father.

Background & Commentary
Often regarded as the weakest entry in the Yokai Monsters
trilogy, *Along with Ghosts* lacks a strong monster villain as
seen in the previous film and harkens back more to the first
film with the Yokai tormenting evil doers. On top of this, the
spooks are not seen nearly as much as they were in the second
film either. In fact, it takes the Yokai nearly 30 minutes to
show up at all, and considering the production was intended
as a spring break children's film to be double billed with
Gamera vs. Guiron, that is quite the cinema sin. However, this
likely wasn't due to ineptitude on the part of the writers, but
rather Daiei's budget woes of the time period.

Basically, the film plays as a typical Japanese period
melodrama but with Yokai thrown into the mix and much of
the film is comprised of the human cast wandering through
the forest. Gamera stalwart Kojiro Hongo, sitting out his
first Gamera movie in three years, plays the lead male
character in the film and, as usual, makes for a likeable lead.
As stated earlier, the Yokai are seen fleetingly (nor does the

loveable water Kappa of the second film reappear) and the ending, featuring a pair of supernatural dice, is a bit too abrupt to prove terribly satisfying.

For this entry, the original director Kimiyoshi Yasuda was brought back alongside the last film's director Yoshiyuki Kuroda, who pulled double duty by also helming the film's SPFX work. Kuroda said that for this film he thought of the Yokai as having individual personalities just like people and that, "It is a story to feature the yokai in an ordinary period drama and destroy evil." As Daiei was entering into financial difficulties (likely the main reason the Yokai are used sparingly in this film) around this time, the studio decided not to make another sequel, and as with Daimajin before it, the Yokai series ended as a trilogy.

Final Word

Though not a bad film, it is easily the weakest entry of the Yokai Monsters trilogy.

Trivia

- The main Yokai melody composed for this film was later adapted by composer Watanabe and used in Toei's *Android Kikaida* series.

Latitude Zero (1969)

Alternate Titles: *U 4000: Panic in the Deep Sea* (Germany) *Where the World Ends* (Spain)
Release Date: July 26, 1969

Directed by: Ishiro Honda
Special Effects by: Eiji Tsuburaya
Screenplay by: Shinichi Sekizawa, Ted Sherman & Warren Lewis
Music by: Akira Ifukube
Cast: Joseph Cotton (Capt. McKenzie) Caesar Romero (Malik) Patricia Medina (Lucretia) Richard Jaeckel (Perry Lawton) Akira Takarada (Dr. Ken Tashiro) Masumi Okada

(Dr. Jules Mason) Linda Haynes (Dr. Ann Barton) Hikaru Kiroki (Capt. Kroiga) **Suit Performers:** Haruo Nakajima (Giant Rat/Bat Man/Black Moth) Harekichi Nakamura/Hiroshi Sekida (Giant Rat/Bat Man)

Cinemascope, Eastmancolor, 89 Minutes

Story

Reporter Perry Lawton descends to the bottom of the sea in a bathysphere with two scientists, Dr. Jules Mason and Dr. Ken Tashiro. The trio finds themselves in peril when an underwater volcano erupts and are rescued by the futuristic submarine Alpha under the leadership of Captain McKenzie. After a duel with a rival sub, the Black Shark created by McKenzie's arch-nemesis Malik, the Alpha docks in Latitude Zero, an idyllic city at the bottom of the ocean comprised of the world's leading scientists. When one of the scientists, Dr. Okada, is kidnapped by Malik, McKenzie assembles a hastily made rescue team in the form of Lawton, Mason and Tashiro. The men storm Malik's island base, Blood Rock, and rescue Dr. Okada. However, Malik releases his monster Black Moth to attack McKenzie in the Alpha. Instead Black Moth turns on Malik and attacks him in the Black Shark, destroying the submarine. Back in Latitude Zero, Perry Lawton decides to return to the surface while Mason and Tashiro decide to stay behind. When Lawton surfaces the world remains skeptical to his story, and Lawton wonders if it was all a dream.

Background & Commentary

Latitude Zero has its origins as an NBC radio serial from the 1940s by Ted Sherman. When Sherman began shopping the rights to a Latitude Zero movie it got picked up by Don Sharp, who in turn took the production to Japan in 1969 teaming with Toho to handle the SPFX. Unfortunately for Toho, Sharp encountered financial difficulties and backed out of the production, leaving Toho to foot the bill just as the film's American stars arrived in Tokyo. And these weren't the usual American imports, but distinguished actors Joseph Cotton (*Citizen Kane*), his wife Patricia Medina, and Caesar Romero (the Joker on TV's *Batman* among other roles). Though initially the trio refused Tomoyuki Tanaka's request that he pay them six months after the picture had come out, they decided not to be "ugly Americans" and agreed to help out the stressed Tanaka. According to Patricia Medina in *Monsters Are Attacking Tokyo*, "the producer" was so relieved he burst into tears and fell to the floor. Whether or not this was for sure Tanaka is unknown, but he likely would have been the one negotiating.

Remarkably, the finished film still has the sheen of a fairly high production (for Japanese standards at least) and the screenplay is fantastic, always moving at a brisk, adventurous pace. A near constant supply of SPFX eye candy is on display on the screen more often than not, as is a constant barrage of fantastical gadgets and futuristic technology that was sure to have delighted the audience of the time, though it is naturally somewhat dated by today's standards. Sadly, since Toho had to foot the entire production bill once the American co-producers bailed out, this meant certain aspects of the SPFX budget had to be cut. This is most apparent during the climax involving the film's giant monster: a Frankenstein-like combination of a lion, a hawk, and a human brain made by Malik. Though it resembles a griffin, it is called the Black Moth for some reason. Unfortunately this monster would look more at home on the Island of Misfit Toys rather than a Toho SPFX film, and knocks the film down a notch. However, the miniature sets and submarines are all fantastic for the most part. The American stars are also all fantastic and chew their respective scenery well, particularly Caesar Romero as Malik, and Richard Jaeckal provides a solid lead in Perry Lawton. Also of interest is the fact that Akira Takarada (and Akihiko Hirata in a small role) speak their lines in English and weren't dubbed. Sadly, Joseph Cotton became ill during production and barely managed to finish the shoot. Patricia Medina remains grateful to Tanaka for helping them quickly get back to the states, and also for delivering them their pay six months after the film's release as promised.

This was not surprisingly under the circumstances Toho's last major U.S.-Japanese co-production. Nor was the film a big hit in America as hoped, though it did decent in International markets. Budgeted at ¥360,000,000, it was not surprisingly hard for Toho to recoup their investment in the film.

Final Word
Warts and all, *Latitude Zero* is an undeniably fun picture. It would be interesting to see how the film turned out had the American Producers not backed out on Toho.

Trivia

- The original ending would have seen Perry Lawton returning to the surface world to find that 50 years had passed since he had been in Latitude Zero.

- Fans have speculated that Lucretia is a vampire due to the way she crumbles into dust at the point of her death. Apparently, in one version of the script, she was to be able to turn into a "zombie bat" according to the film's Japanese Wikipedia page, though this could be an error in translation.

- The Black Shark is actually the Moonlight SY3 from *Destroy All Monsters* repainted.

- One of the Bat Men suits would appear as a giant monster in Toho's TV series *Go! Godman* (1973).

- Malik's "ringtone" for his phone at Blood Rock is King Ghidorah's roar.

All Monsters Attack (1969)

Alternate Titles: *March of the Monsters* (Japan) *Minya: Son of Godzilla; Godzilla's Revenge* (U.S.) *Godzilla on the Island of Monsters* (Spain)
Release Date: December 20, 1969

Directed by: Ishiro Honda

Special Effects by: Eiji Tsuburaya & Ishiro Honda (uncredited)
Screenplay by: Shinichi Sekizawa & Ishiro Honda
Music by: Kunio Miyauchi
Cast: Tomonori Yazaki (Ichiro) Eisei Amamoto (Inami) Sachio Sakai (Bank Robber #1) Kazuo Suzuki (Bank Robber #2) Kenji Sahara (Ichiro's father) Machiko Naka (Ichiro's mother) Midori Uchiyama (Voice of Minilla)
Suit Performers: Little Man Machan (Minilla) Haruo Nakajima (Godzilla) Hiroshi Sekida (Gabara)

Cinemascope, Eastmancolor, 69 Minutes

Story

Young boy Ichiro leads a lonely life in Kawasaki and is frequently bullied by a gang of boys lead by Gabara. Both Ichiro's parents work late and he rarely sees them. Looking after him is a kindly neighbor, Inami, who makes toys for a living. The neighborhood is also falling victim to a series of robberies. In his dreams Ichiro escapes to Monster Island, home of Godzilla, his son Minilla, and several other monsters including one named Gabara. Ichiro befriends Minilla, who is bullied by Gabara himself. During several dream time visits, Ichiro witnesses battles between Godzilla and other monsters, and also fights between Minilla and Gabara. In the real world Ichiro is kidnapped by the crooks responsible for the robberies. Escaping to his dreams once again, Ichiro watches as Minilla finally overcomes Gabara with help from Godzilla. A newly inspired Ichiro escapes from the robbers and even causes them physical harm before being rescued by police. Ichiro then stands up to his Gabara and ends up taking over his gang.

Background & Commentary

Though Tomoyuki Tanaka had claimed 1968's *Destroy All Monsters* was to be the final Godzilla film, by the next year he had already changed his mind and put a new G-film into production. What likely caught Tanaka's eye was the popularity of Toei's Manga Film Festivals for children, which packaged together several cartoons aimed at a child audience providing nearly a whole day's worth of entertainment which was held three times a year, typically around the out of school holidays. Tanaka conceived of the Toho Champion Matsuri Festival for Children, which would revolve around a new G-film aimed at kids to anchor the event along with a secondary feature and a few cartoons. Though it was always written around the dreams of a young boy, initially the film wasn't as heavy on stock footage, and Godzilla would have battled the Odako prop at one point in addition to Rodan making an appearance (chasing Ichiro no less). It was only later to cut costs that these scenes were replaced by stock footage, and Rodan's part by Kamacuras.

Although disdained universally by most G-fans, *All Monsters Attack* is surprisingly embraced by many of the series' serious scholars, and not without good reason. On the surface the production may seem like a cheap stock footage opus, but upon closer inspection the film has relevant social commentary pertaining to the real world in which it is set. While it's never confirmed whether Godzilla and co. are the far away residents of Monster Island or fictional movie characters the latter is most likely. The stock footage sequences in Ichiro's dreams, it could be argued, are his memories of G-films seen in theaters mixed in with his own imaginary experiences. For someone who has never seen a G-film, it makes for a rather lively affair, chock full of SPFX footage, though it can be jarring since the G-suit changes from battle to battle. Because of the island locale the film can borrow only from *Ebirah, Horror of the Deep* and *Son of Godzilla* and a few brief snippets of *Destroy All Monster*s Monsterland scenes. Making stock footage cameos are Anguirus, Gorosaurus, Manda, Ebirah, Kumonga and Kamacuras—Rodan is conspicuously absent, though Ichiro does drop his name. The film does feature some amusing new FX footage, and there was even a new monster created for the picture: Gabara. The final battle between Godzilla and Gabara, in which Minilla amusingly comes to his father's aid, was a lively affair with Gabara getting thrown over Godzilla's shoulder judo-style. This foreshadows further gravity defying antics to come in the 1970s, as did the film's short running time to fit in with the Champion Festival. Also, a line in this film's title song proclaims that "pollution is the real monster" foreshadowing the heavy ecological themes of the 1970s. Just as the film's story was a rather downbeat affair, so it was behind the scenes also. An ailing Eiji Tsuburaya was unable to work on the film, and in his place Ishiro Honda himself directed much of the SPFX footage. Tsuburaya's credit on this picture was purely out of respect, as most of the stock footage used was in fact directed by Sadamasa Arikawa and the new footage by Ishiro Honda with Teruyoshi Nakano. Tsuburaya had several new projects in development and was looking to the future when he passed away in 1970, shortly after the film's release. Akira Ifukube didn't return for the film either, though this likely was for the best as his heavy themes would've been inappropriate for the playful atmosphere. In his place Kunio Miyauchi, composer of the *Ultraman* series, does a splendid job. Honda's direction of scenes in the industrial city of Kawasaki, a rather uninviting place to be a child, are top notch. As many critics point out, Ichiro and his father are rarely presented in the same frame of film together. In the one scene that they are, Ichiro's father is high above him in the train, his son down on the ground running to keep up. Although the ending in which Ichiro befriends Gabara seems to be a happy one with its upbeat music, it is in fact a thinly veiled tragedy. Ishiro is still separated from his parents and now runs afoul with a gang of hooligans.

Oddly, in Japan the film sold 1,480,000 tickets which put it on par with the last two films despite being inferior to *Destroy All Monsters*. In America, the film was briefly released by Maron Films under the more appropriate title *Minya: Son of Godzilla* before being re-titled *Godzilla's Revenge* in 1971. The new moniker, like *Godzilla vs. the Thing* before it, was merely created to generate more interest in the film. It was double billed somewhat inappropriately with *Island of the Burning Damned* starring Christopher Lee and Peter Cushing.

Final Word
As a child's film it is an artistic success. Though Toho calls

it *All Monsters Attack,* perhaps a better title in light of its reappraising is *Ishiro Honda's Dreams?*

Trivia

- Eisei Amamoto (Inami) and Tomonori Yazaki (Ichiro) both appeared on Toei's TV series *Kamen Rider* together.

- Ishiro Honda originally wanted the film to end on a shot of Ichiro's mother crying, and in an abridged version of the movie edited by Honda this is how the story ends.

- Supposedly Tomoyuki Tanaka took note of Daiei's "success" in utilizing stock-footage for *Gamera vs. Viras* when he thought of this film.

- Gabara's head was made from an old Godzilla suit's head.

- Ichiro's mother, Machiko Naka, was a regular on both the *Young Guy* and *Company President* series. Though this was her first Godzilla film, she appeared in guest spots on *Ultra Q* and *Ultra Seven.* In the 2000s she had a recurring role on *Kamen Rider Kuuga.*

- While ironically Bandai has received petitions for an Ichiro figure, Gabara, being an unpopular kaiju, never got a Bandai figure (a rite of passage for Toho monsters) made in its likeness.

- Some sources claim Gabara is a mutated bullfrog. This was the character's origin in an episode of Toho's 1972 TV series *Go! Godman,* but not this film. Interestingly, Gabara appears human-sized in this series, which is unrelated to the Godzilla canon unlike Toho's other SPFX TV series *Zone Fighter.*

Gamera vs. Jiger (1970)

Alternate Titles: *Gamera vs. Demon Beast Jiger* (Japan) *Gamera vs. Monster X* (U.S.)
Release Date: March 21, 1970

Directed by: Noriaki Yuasa
Special Effects by: Noriaki Yuasa
Screenplay by: Niisan Takahashi
Music by: Shunsuke Kikuchi
Cast: Tsutomu Takakuwa (Hiroshi) Kelly Burris (Tommy) Catherine Murphy (Susan) Flame Sanshiro (Keisuke) Junko Yashiro (Miwako) Kon Omura (Ryosaku) **Suit Performers:** Izumi Umenosuke (Gamera) Uncredited (Jiger)

Daieiscope, Eastmancolor, 82 Minutes

Story

When a mysterious statue on Wester Island is removed and transported to Japan to be a part of Expo 70 in Osaka, the ancient monster Jiger awakens. Gamera tries to keep the monster at bay on Wester Island but is unsuccessful and Jiger heads to Osaka where she wreaks havoc. When Gamera battles the monster in the city the beast impregnates him with an embryo and Gamera collapses into the water. Two boys in a mini-sub travel inside Gamera where they discover the Jiger larva and manage to kill it with radio waves. Gamera revives and uses the statue from Wester Island to kill Jiger, finally ending the monster's reign of terror.

Background & Commentary

Having utilized alien invaders twice in a row now, Daiei felt it was time to bring Gamera back down to earth. As boys' magazines with stories on ancient civilizations were popular, the plot was constructed around an ancient monster from the lost continent of Mu. Daiei also managed to secure a cross promotion with Expo 70, which was currently taking place in Osaka. As such, they were able to film extensively on location at the Expo. On the downside, the Expo 70 committee would not allow Daiei to destroy any miniatures representing the Expo. That didn't stop Yuasa from engaging in some good old urban destruction though, and the new kaiju Jiger destroys a good portion of Osaka even if she doesn't damage any attractions at the Expo 70 site. This welcome return in miniature destruction was the result of an increased budget of ¥35,000,000, quite a surprise considering Daiei's financial troubles of the time.

Particularly frightening is the triceratops-like Jiger, who in each battle seems to come up with a new power to stump Gamera. And unlike many quadruped monsters, Jiger does not crawl on its knees, a testament both to the actor in the suit and the suit designer. Gamera in some ways returns to his earlier roots in this film too, spending quite a bit of time in his quadruped stance in addition to menacing the human cast, chasing after fire, and flying via his old spinning form from time to time. One of the two titular beasts is almost always on screen, and as in *Gamera vs. Gyaos*, Gamera battles Jiger three times during the film with each battle providing plenty of entertainment. During the second battle, Jiger actually stings Gamera with her tail embedding a Jiger larva inside his body! Through this screenwriter Takahashi scores a homerun in the form of his subplot for the child heroes, Tsutomu and Tommy, when the duo board a miniature submarine and sail it inside Gamera's mouth for a *Fantastic Voyage*-like adventure to destroy the Jiger larva. This film might well have struck a perfect balance between adults and children, who are again central to the story but not at the expense of the adult characters' dignity. Particularly enjoyable in this outing is the loveable Kon Omura as Hiroshi's inventor father, who turns in a hilarious performance without coming off as a buffoon.

In Japan, the film was another success and was double billed with Yoshiyuki Kuroda's fantasy film *The Invisible Swordsman*. Sadly, despite being one of the best and most ambitious Gamera films, the movie still went straight to U.S. TV rather than theaters. On the bright side though, it was the first film since the original that was billed as a Gamera film in America, titled *Gamera vs. Monster X* by AIP-TV. However, it was also the last Gamera film that they would distribute to U.S. television.

Final Word

Easily on a par with *Gamera vs. Gyaos* as one of the best Showa Era Gamera films even though it is not as well known.

Trivia

- At the Japan World Exhibition, Toho and Daiei teamed up and offered live shows wherein Haruo Nakajima donned the Godzilla suit to battle Umenosuke Izumi as Gamera.

- Was one of the only Showa Gamera films along with *Gamera vs. Viras* and *Super Monster Gamera* not to receive a VHS release through Sandy Frank. As such many U.S. fans had to rely on bootleg VHS copies to see the film.

!!!!!!!!!!!!!!!!!!!Bonus Review!!!!!!!!!!!!!!!!!!!!!

The Vampire Doll (1970)

Japanese Title: *Fear the Ghost House: The Bloodsucking Doll*
Release Date: July 4, 1970

Directed by: Michio Yamamoto
Special Effects by: Teruyoshi Nakano
Screenplay by: Ei Ogawa & Hiroshi Nagano
Music by: Riichiro Manabe
Cast: Yukiko Kobayashi (Yuko) Atsuo Nakamura (Kazuhiko) Kayo Matsuo (Keiko) Akira Nakao (Hiroshi) Yoko Minakaze (Yuko's Mother) Jun Usami (Doctor)

Cinemascope, Eastmancolor, 71 Minutes

Story

A young woman, Keiko, goes in search of her missing brother, last seen at the estate of his dead fiancé Yuko, now inhabited only by her somber mother and mute groundskeeper. There she and her beau Hiroshi are menaced by a ghostly young woman until they finally realize it is the dead Yuko, hypnotized when she was at the point of death and thusly now exists as a vampire. In her final act of vengeance Yuko kills the doctor responsible for her hypnosis.

Background & Commentary

According to director Michio Yamashita in *Monsters Are Attacking Tokyo*, he was at a party talking about how he would like to make a horror thriller like *The Birds*. This conversation was overheard by Toho producer Fumio Tanaka who subsequently tasked Yamashita with making a Japanese version of Hammer's Dracula films. As it was, after Great Britain and America, Japan was the country where Hammer horror films grossed the most—in fact, Hammer sometimes shot extra footage just for the Japanese releases. Reluctant to imitate Hammer's Dracula films, Yamashita decided to meet Tanaka in the middle and came up with a vampire story which took its inspiration from Edgar Allen Poe's short story *The Facts in the Case of M. Valdemar.*

The simply plotted film, part haunted house mystery and part vampire movie, begins in the penultimate cliché of the dark and stormy night, and it is only one of many to follow. The audience is clued in to the film's contemporary setting in the first shot as glimpsed through a car's windshield with the wipers going at full blast. The modern setting was the only innovation Toho had on Hammer which wouldn't try the same until the insistence of Warner Brothers in *Dracula AD 1972. Count Yorga, Vampire,* the original modern vamp-film, was only released in America one month before this film debuted in Japan, so it's doubtful it had any influence on Toho either. Unfortunately in Toho's case, the modern setting is a result of budgetary necessitation rather than creativity, of which there isn't much. The unimaginative script fails to take advantage of the modern setting, and the story could have just as easily taken place in the 1800s. In spite of this, the film does come up with a few striking visuals. The main set, a western-style estate adorned with various European artwork, is quite lavish. The most memorable aspect is the female vampire Yuko, who sets herself apart from other vampires with her reflective eyes (minus pupils) that appear silver in the moonlight and golden by candlelight. The character was effectively portrayed by Yukiko Kobayashi, one of Toho's "new faces" when she played the female lead in *Destroy All Monsters* (1968), and she also appeared in *Space Amoeba* the same year as this film. In the film's only bloody scene, Yuko slashes the villain's throat with a knife in which SPFX director Teruyoshi Nakano uses a blood-spraying effect to the extreme (an effect he would utilize again in 1974's *Godzilla vs. Mechagodzilla*). The film's most gruesome shot is when the heroine discovers her decayed dead brother sitting upright in a chair not unlike Norman Bates' mother in *Psycho* (likely this scene's direct inspiration as Yamamoto was a fan of Hitchcock). Some of the scares make no sense at all though, and at one point a manikin—an inanimate decoy for the vampire's absent body—jumps out of a coffin with no explanation for how it did so. The film is convoluted to the extreme, and a long sequence of exposition by the film's surprise villain (the hypnotist responsible for Yuko's vampiric condition) is badly crammed into the story. While meant to be a twist ending it is more akin to a badly told ghost story.

Released during the summer (which is the ghost season in Japan rather than fall) the film was a moderate success. Known internationally as *The Vampire Doll*, this was the only entry of the trilogy not to be dubbed into English or get a U.S. television broadcast though it did receive some limited theatrical showings in Los Angeles and New York in subtitled format.

Final Word

Though the film didn't mimic Hammer as closely as its two sequels, *Vampire Doll* is oddly the dullest film of what was eventually dubbed "The Bloodthirsty Trilogy." Ultimately one can only be glad when the film's scant 70 minute running time comes to an end.

Trivia

- The gold contact lenses were the idea of director Yamamoto, and Yukiko Kobayashi claimed she couldn't see a thing in them.

Space Amoeba (1970)

Alternate Titles: *Gezora, Ganime, Kamoebas: Decisive Battle! Giant Monsters of the South Seas* (Japan) *Yog Monster from Space* (U.S.)
Release Date: August 1, 1970

Directed by: Ishiro Honda
Special Effects by: Sadamasa Arikawa
Screenplay by: Ei Ogawa
Music by: Akira Ifukube
Cast: Akira Kubo (Kudo) Atsuko Takahashi (Ayako) Yoshio Tsuchiya (Dr. Mida) Kenji Sahara (Obata) Yukiko Kobayashi (Saki) Noritake Saito (Rico) **Suit Performers:** Haruo Nakajima (Gezora/Ganimes) Haruyoshi Nakamura (Kamoebas)

Cinemascope, Eastmancolor, 84 Minutes

Story

Space flight Helios 7 is hijacked by formless alien life-forms in route to Jupiter. The aliens ride the capsule back to earth where it crash lands on an island inhabited by squid monster Gezora. A group of investors travel to the island to see if it is suitable to become a resort. Along for the ride is photographer Kudo, convinced the island was the landing spot of Helios 7, and Dr. Mida, who believes it to be home to giant monsters. Both men are proved right when the alien possessed squid monster rises from the ocean and attacks the native village. The monster is dispatched by fire, but in its place a crab monster arises. One of the extraterrestrials also possesses Obata, a corporate spy on the island. Soon a giant mutated turtle joins the fray and the humans are able to deduct sonar emitting creatures such as bats and dolphins are the key to defeating the aliens. The giant turtle and crab battle while a swarm of bats circles overhead. The battle causes a volcanic eruption that swallows the monsters. Obata jumps into the volcano as well, taking the alien parasite with him thus saving the earth.

Background & Commentary

While *Destroy All Monsters* is typically thought of as Toho's last big hurrah, that honor belongs to this film. It was Toho's last original monster movie, and the last production to combine the talents of Ishiro Honda, Tomoyuki Tanaka, and Akira Ifukube for several years. Eiji Tsuburaya was also involved in the pre-production of this film, but died soon after filming had commenced briefly halting production. Overall it is not one of the team's better efforts when put in context with the rest of their collaborations, but it's not a bad film by any means. Despite its far out plot, *Space Amoeba*, better known as *Yog Monster from Space*, is a thoroughly enjoyable story. The plot represents an interesting combination of two of the genre's most overused staples: a tropical island of prehistoric monsters and alien invaders. In this case, aliens come to an exotic South Seas isle and possess the monsters. To some degree all the kaiju are variations of things we've seen before. Gezora, the giant squid, was preceded by numerous giant octopi; Kamoebas is a more realistic version of Daiei's Gamera; and the not one, but two, crab monsters called Ganimes are naturally reminiscent of Ebirah. While the turtle and crab monsters are mutated into their monstrous forms by the aliens, Gezora, interestingly enough, is implied to already be a giant monster before it is possessed by aliens. Gezora is also the film's most interesting kaiju, but unfortunately is killed before the end battle. This colossal cuttlefish was not a marionette but a man in a suit, walking upright on its tentacles. Toho's most outlandish suit creation, it was played by Godzilla himself, Haruo Nakajima.

After the passing of Tsuburaya, Sadamasa Arikawa was brought in as the senior SPFX director, a job he had been doing for the most part since *Ebirah, Horror of the Deep*. However, this was his last Toho production as he left the studio soon after in part due to Toho's dismantling of their SPFX department. As for the cast, this too was the last film made with Toho contracted actors and the familiar faces of the 1960s. Making their exits are Akira Kubo, a favorite lead of Toho's for some time, and Yoshio Tsuchiya, who was a regular for playing hot heads or alien possessed scientists in Toho sci-fi pictures. However in this film it is Kenji Sahara's smarmy con man Obata who gets possessed by aliens (reportedly this part was to go to Tsuchiya as was typical, but Tsuchiya let Sahara have the role). Although he began his career as the heroic lead in *Rodan*, Sahara eventually developed a penchant for playing slimy villains and this film marked his seventeenth Toho SPFX production to date. Unlike Sahara's other villains, Obata is repentant proving he has a heart when he takes his own life to defeat the aliens in the tradition of Dr. Serizawa and other tragic characters directed by Honda.

Unfortunately the film wasn't a big hit in Japan, a fact Arikawa's SPFX successor Teruyoshi Nakano blames on the monsters and their silly names. Also, when Toho neglected to attach an "in memory of Eiji Tsuburaya" card on the film as he requested, Ishiro Honda left the studio in anger to go work at Tsuburaya Productions. Happily, the film did garner a theatrical release in America as *Yog Monster from Space* in a time when many of the non-Godzilla films were being sent straight to television. It was double billed by AIP with a re-release of *Destroy All Monsters* in 1971.

Final Word
The film's unique plot makes for a very zany ride that is uniquely Japanese. No American studio in their right mind would have ever been so imaginative.

Trivia

- The island is called Sergio Island because Sergio Leone (director of *The Good, the Bad and the Ugly*) was popular at the time according to producer Fumio Tanaka.

- Originally Ayako was to be played by Noriko Takahashi who backed out when she got married. Ironically Takahashi had also been up for the role of Daiyo in *Ebirah, Horror of the Deep* but got appendicitis when production began in 1966.

- The Helios 7 spacecraft model appears as a toy in the Sakimori home in Toho's TV series *Zone Fighter*.

- Toho originally wanted to film in Guam as they did with *Son of Godzilla* but were unable to do so.

- Kamoebas reappeared in an episode of *Go! Godman* in 1972, and more importantly cameos in 2003's *Godzilla: Tokyo S.O.S.* as a dead monster carcass on a beach.

- While filming on Oshima Island, Yoshio Tsuchiya and Akira Kubo thought they had spotted a flying saucer. Later they learned it was only a weather balloon.

- During shooting, Gezora's eyes stopped working, but none of the SPFX crew bothered to fix them according to Fumio Tanaka in an interview with David Milner.

- This film began life in 1966 as *Giant Monster Assault* and was believed to have been the 7th Godzilla film at one point.

Voyage Into Space (1970)

Broadcast Date: 1970

Directed by: Minoru Yamada
Special Effects by: Masao Ichikura, Yasuo Ogawa & Nobuo Yajima
Screenplay by: Masaru Igami
Music by: Takeo Yamashita
Cast: Mitsunobu Kaneko (Johnny Sokko) Akio Ito (Jerry Mano) Jerry Berke (Narrator) **Suit Performers:** Toshiyuki Tsuchiyama (Giant Robot)

Academy Ratio, Color, 95 Minutes

Story

After a mysterious UFO lands on earth, an ocean liner is attacked by a giant monster. The only two survivors, young boy Johnny Sokko and secret Unicorn agent Jerry Mano, wash up on a desolate island. The island is overrun by the alien invaders, the Gargoyle Gang, who are forcing scientist Dr. Lucius Guardian to build a giant destructive robot with which they can destroy the earth. Dr. Guardian rescues Jerry and Johnny just as the robot is about to go online. As the robot will obey the first voice that it hears, Johnny shouts into the radio control watch given to him by the doctor and he becomes the only one capable of controlling the robot. As such, Johnny is made an agent of Unicorn himself and he and Giant Robot begin defending Japan from the Gargoyle Gang's various monster attacks. In the end, when Giant Robot confronts the alien leader, Emperor Guillotine, it is learned that the giant alien mastermind has the destructive power of an atomic bomb capable of destroying the whole earth in his body. As such, acting under his own influence rather than Johnny's, Giant Robot grabs Guillotine and flies him into space where the two collide with a comet.

Background & Commentary

Though popularly known as *Johnny Sokko and His Flying Robot* on American television in the late 1960s, the series true name was *Giant Robot* and it naturally hailed from Japan. It was created by Toei Studios and aired on TV Asahi from October 11, 1967 to April 1, 1968. In America, it began airing in 1969 successfully through AIP-TV, who also decided to edit five episodes of the series together into a 95 minute feature film curiously titled *Voyage Into Space* (1970).

As a compilation film comprised of the pilot episode, the second episode, two random middle episodes, and the series finale, naturally the beginning and the ending fare well while the middle sags and drags along. The first episode has a fun *Ebirah, Horror of the Deep* vibe to it as Johnny and Jerry find themselves stranded on a deserted island full of militaristic alien despots—and, to top it all off, the island is even set to explode in an atomic explosion. The narrative doesn't become muddied until the third episode begins which features some new villainous alien characters sans any real explanation. Still, the monster battles are naturally entertaining to watch with the main middle portion being taken up by Nucleon, Gargoyle Vine and Lygon.

As to why this film wasn't simply called *Johnny Sokko and His Flying Robot: The Movie*, is anyone's guess, though perhaps AIP was doing their best to hide the fact that this wasn't an all new feature. Instead, the film derives its title from the story's final moments wherein Giant Robot flies Emperor Guillotine into space where the two collide with a meteor in an act of self-sacrifice on the part of the former. Though in the Japanese TV series finale it is clear that Giant Robot isn't coming back, the narration for the U.S. version gives things an optimistic twist stating, "And so the saga comes to an end, Giant Robot sacrificed himself to save the earth from the terrible Guillotine. But know knows? When Johnny desperately needs him again, perhaps, like a miracle, he will come back out of the sky."

Final Word

As a whole, *Voyage Into Space* is mostly worth watching for nostalgic value for those that grew up watching it on TV, or for those who wish to see a "digest" version of *Johnny Sokko and His Flying Robot*. For anyone else, they would be better off sticking with the full TV series.

Trivia

* A condensed 10-minute version of *Voyage into Space* was released for the Super 8 home-movie market by Ken Films in the early 1970s.

* As it turned out, this film was something of a trendsetter as in the mid-1980s Sandy Frank would do the same thing to several Tsuburaya TV series: *The Monkey Army* which became *Time of the Apes*; *Star Force: Fugitive Alien* based off of *Star Wolf* from 1978; and 1968's *Mighty Jack* was turned into a TV movie of the same name in 1987.

!!!!!!!!!!!!!!!!!!!Bonus Review!!!!!!!!!!!!!!!!!!!!

The Bloodsucking Eyes (1971)

Japanese Title: *Lake of Dracula*
Release Date: June 16, 1971

Directed by: Michio Yamamoto

203 / 呪 い の 館 血 を 吸 う 眼

Special Effects by: Teruyoshi Nakano
Screenplay by: Ei Ogawa & Hiroshi Nagano
Music by: Riichiro Manabe
Cast: Shin Kishida (Vampire) Choei Takahashi (Saeki)
Midori Fujita (Akiko) Koyoshi Sanae (Natsuko) Shuji Otaki
(Vampire's Father)

Cinemascope, Eastmancolor, 82 Minutes

Story
What a young woman believes to only be a vivid childhood
dream about vampires comes back to haunt her when a real
bloodsucker arrives in her small lakefront town. With her
friends being vampirized one by one, she fears her memory
isn't merely a dream and turns to her fiancé Natsuko, a doctor
who doesn't believe in superstition, to confront the vampires.
The duo eventually trail the vampire to an old gothic house
where they meet the creature's father, who reveals he and his
family are the descendants of Dracula. When the vampire
returns, he and Natsuko begin to struggle, and Dracula's
descendant is killed when he is impaled on a stair post.

Background & Commentary
After *Vampire Doll* proved to be a "bit hit" in Japan, an
enthusiastic Fumio Tanaka commissioned a sequel again to
be helmed by Yamashita. Though Yamashita had managed
to avoid Dracula in the first film, this time Tanaka insisted
the film (initially called *Phantom of the Vampire*) feature
Dracula. When actor Masumi Okada (Dr. Jules Mason in
Latitude Zero) proved unavailable to play Dracula, Yamashita
suggested his longtime friend Shin Kishida, who reminded
him of the count, for the role.

The first shot of the film atmospherically presents a
rocky beach at dusk with splashing waves and a vibrant
sunset, one of many striking images that the film's storyline
fails to compliment. That being said, it is a marked
improvement over the last film and adheres more closely to
traditional vampire myths. It contains five vampires no less
lead by the imposing figure of Kishida who makes for a
fantastic Dracula, or Dracula type as he plays an unnamed a
descendant of the count. He too possesses the golden

mirrored eyes seen in the last film, hence the title *The Bloodsucking Eyes.* Though in the next film he would be even more Dracula-like, complete with spooky old house and red lined cape, his restrained performance here is better minus the cartoonish grunts and growls he would emit in the next. That all being said, the vampire's origins are explained in yet another tedious info-dump of exposition in the last ten minutes of the picture. This vampire is a case of genetics, as the family is descended from Dracula himself, though this affliction apparently skips a generation. Further confusing the matter is the vampire's father, inexplicably still alive though in a state of corpse-like decomposition, who is not implied to be a vampire himself. He too seems to be hanging around to give the film a "twist" ending that only confuses rather than enlightens. The climax is taken directly from Hammer's *Dracula Has Risen from the Grave* (1968). The male lead and Kishida wrestle endlessly atop a staircase until finally Kishida falls and is impaled by a stair post from behind. Nakano's version is bloodier and gooier, but nonetheless inferior. Kishida's disintegration is a near shot for shot mirror of Christopher Lee's death scene from 1958's *Horror of Dracula* that begins with a glimpse of Kishida's deflating hand, and then switches to him clawing at his face and the shot goes on for too long. As a result the flaws in the makeup are too clearly visible, and it seems as though Kishida is just screaming whilst waiting for director Yamamoto to finally, mercifully, yell "Cut!" The female vampire then drops dead when he finishes expiring, as if the screenwriters felt they had written enough pages and needed to end the film.

On the production side the film is well directed by Yamamoto, and at one point Kishida's lack of reflection in a mirror makes for a particularly good scare. Due to the isolation of the film's lead female character (who everyone thinks is crazy) the scares in this entry are the most effective of the entire trilogy. The merits of Riichiro Manabe's weird scores were unusual for *Godzilla vs. Hedorah,* and debatable at best for *Godzilla vs. Megalon,* but in this film his odd instruments actually excel. Sections of his score here are evocative of Robert Cobert's *House of Dark Shadows* which came out in March of 1971 in Japan, three months before

Bloodsucking Eyes June release. The film was released to American television in 1980 as *Lake of Dracula*, a moniker it successfully retained on home video, though it was also notoriously called *Japula* in a nod to *Blackula*. Oddly the climax, the film's main highlight, was severely edited for airing on television in a time when most of Hammer's horrors were shown uncut in terms of gore to a certain degree. As a result, this sequence was also missing from the U.S. home video release. To make matters worse, Kishida's vampire was dubbed with a thick European accent.

Final Word
The best of Yamamoto and Ogawa's Bloodthirsty Trilogy.

Trivia

- Shin Kishida was too short to play Dracula and so wore lifts in his shoes. He liked them so much he made them a permanent part of his wardrobe.

Gamera vs. Zigra (1971)

Japanese Title: *Gamera vs. Deep Sea Monster Zigra*
Release Date: July 17, 1971

Directed by: Noriaki Yuasa
Special Effects by: Noriaki Yuasa
Screenplay by: Niisan Takahashi
Music by: Shunsuke Kikuchi
Cast: Eiko Yaname (the Spacewoman) Yasushi Sakagami (Kenny) Gloria Zoellner (Helen) Kei'ichi Noda (Voice of Zigra) **Suit Performers:** Uncredited

Daieiscope, Daieicolor, 88 Minutes

Story
Alien-shark Zigra attacks a base on the Moon and abducts a Japanese woman to become his emissary on earth. His ship hides beneath the ocean where he remotely triggers

earthquakes that devastate Japan. Two marine biologists and their children, Kenny and Helen, are out investigating ocean pollution and are abducted by the ship but manage to escape back to the surface where they are saved by Gamera. The military then attacks Zigra with fighter planes which he easily destroys. On land, the spacewoman has pursued Kenny and Helen to Sea World where the military is convening to discuss Zigra. Gamera engages in an underwater dogfight with the ship which explodes releasing Zigra. The two take their battle on land where Zigra morphs into a bipedal form and hypnotizes Gamera with his ray. The giant turtle, now in a comatose state, falls into the ocean while the Spacewoman is caught by the military and is snapped out of her trance. The two marine-biologists then descend in a bathysphere, in which Kenny and Helen are also stowaways, to try and revive Gamera. Zigra then snatches it and holds them for ransom. Lightning strikes Gamera, who awakens, and saves the bathysphere. Zigra follows him to the surface, the two monsters battle, and this time Gamera is victorious.

Background & Commentary

Gamera vs. Zigra was the beginning of the end for the first cycle of the Japanese monster movie, and is one of the genre's worst offerings. Although it starts promisingly with Zigra destroying a base on the Moon, once the story comes down to earth the action is mainly confined to the Sea World Amusement Park in Kamogawa (which Daiei had a cross promotional agreement with). Sequences such as the complete destruction of Tokyo in a Magnitude 18 earthquake take place entirely off-screen, with only brief snippets of the aftermath shown. Likewise, there is one short military battle against Zigra's spaceship, while other battles (worldwide no less) are mentioned but never seen.

Though the protagonists of the series had always been children, this film aims for an even younger demographic with actors only seven years old to portray Kenny and Helen. Not surprisingly, the two solve several problems that the adults can't making buffoons out of them. They also run afoul of Zigra's henchwoman in a scene that is no doubt a delight for the younger crowd. That being said, there are many lazy plot devices inexcusable even for a children's matinee. People hypnotized by the space woman can be shocked out of their catatonic state simply by listening to people shouting into walkie-talkies. In a long monologue by Zigra—voiced by *Goke, Body Snatcher from Hell*'s voice actor Kei'ichi Noda—we are lead to believe his lone spacewoman is going to wipe out earth's entire population. Then Zigra, who can be repelled by something as simple as the bathysphere's bright lights, convinces the people of earth that they are powerless to stop him. Even the intentional humor is so bad it can only generate unintentional laughs, such as the snoring Zigra. The bizarre proceedings are climaxed by Gamera breaking the fourth wall by playing the notes of his theme-song along Zigra's dorsal fins as though they were piano keys. After this humorous scene he graphically proceeds to roast Zigra alive with his flame-breath (at the children's insistence naturally). The film, already rife with heavy handed ecological messages, manages to squeeze one more in when Kenny throws a pop bottle on the beach giving his father an excuse to go into a long lecture to close the film. This was the first monster film in a trend to begin emphasizing the dangers of environmental pollution over that of nuclear testing. In the story it is stated that the ocean of Zigra's home planet was polluted to the point that he had to search out a new planet, Earth, but even its oceans are becoming polluted fast. Aliens in the Godzilla series would likewise also claim to have come to save earth from its own environmental destruction and this film was released only a week before the similarly minded *Godzilla vs. Hedorah*.

Zigra has an interesting design and the idea of a shark monster is utilized well (at one point he uses his dorsal fin to slice an oil tanker in half). According to Yuasa, the inspiration for Zigra was a shark attack in Japan that made the national news. While often times monsters are the brainless muscle of invading aliens, in Zigra's case he is the invading alien. As such he possesses superior intelligence and the ability to speak, but the monster never gets a city destruction scene due to the budget. Also, due to its limited mobility, it is difficult for the suit to provide interesting battles for Gamera compared to the knife-headed monster he faces in *Gamera vs. Guiron* or the alien squid from *Gamera vs. Viras*. On that note, Gamera doesn't suffer any notorious beatings in this film either. He was impaled by Viras, nearly cut in half by Guiron, and in *Gamera vs. Jiger* he gets impregnated with a larva! Gamera gets off easy here as he merely gets hypnotized into a coma. Although Godzilla would continue to trudge on until 1975, this would be Gamera's last feature for some time. In an age ruled by television superheroes such as Toei's *Kamen Rider* and Tsuburaya's many *Ultraman* sequels, Godzilla and Gamera were the only kaiju still surviving on the big screen. However, this film was still a moderate success and Daiei had planned to continue with *Gamera vs. Wyvern,* wherein the turtle would fight a two headed menace similar to King Ghidorah. It was not to be however, Daiei filed for bankruptcy and Gamera was no more.

Final Word

Though not technically the last Gamera film, it is more or less the last entry in the classic Gamera series. This was also the first Gamera film not to immediately reach American television and did not do so until the 1980s.

Trivia

- Supposedly this film had the same ¥35 million budget of *Gamera vs. Jiger.* However, none of the money is apparent on screen and some theorize "cooking of the books" was going on behind the scenes.

- Zigra's design is based off that of a goblin shark and a sailfish.

Godzilla vs. Hedorah (1971)

Alternate Titles: *Godzilla vs. the Smog Monster* (U.S.) *Frankenstein's Battle Against the Devil's Monster* (Germany) *Godzilla: Fury of the Monster* (Italy)
Release Date: July 22, 1971

Directed by: Yoshimitsu Banno
Special Effects by: Teruyoshi Nakano

Screenplay by: Yoshimitsu Banno & Kaoru Mabuchi
Music by: Riichiro Manabe
Cast: Hiroyuki Kawase (Ken Yano) Akira Yamaguchi (Dr.
Yano) Toshio Shibamoto (Keuchi) Keiko Mari (Miki)
Toshie Kimura (Toshie Yano) **Suit Performers:** Haruo
Nakajima (Godzilla) Kengo Nakayama (Hedorah)

Cinemascope, Eastmancolor, 85 Minutes

Story

Dr. Yano and his son Ken have discovered a strange new
species of tadpole in Suruga Bay. Dr. Yano goes on a scuba
diving mission to study the creatures and is attacked by one
of the larger ones. Although he survives, his face is badly
burned. From the incident he determines the monsters are a
strange sludge-like lifeform that feeds upon pollution. The
creatures soon merge together growing to gigantic size. The
monster, which Ken calls Hedorah, surfaces in Tokyo where
it attacks a nightclub and clashes with Godzilla. The next
day the monster returns in yet another form, flying through
the air poisoning thousands with its noxious gas. Godzilla
again confronts the monster, but even he chokes on the
monster's fumes. As people ponder what form it will take
next, Dr. Yano determines a way to kill Hedorah and alerts
the military. Hedorah appears in its final form (now bigger
than Godzilla) at a Mt. Fuji youth rally where it begins
killing the partiers until Godzilla intervenes. Japan's
defender fights the monster all the way to a pair of electrical
grids the military has constructed to fry the monster. When
Hedorah flies away and escapes, Godzilla himself takes flight
and catches up with the monster and drags it back to the
grids where it is destroyed.

Background & Commentary

While it's no longer regarded as the worst Godzilla movie, it
is still regarded as the strangest. Whether this is a merit or
a detriment is still the subject of debate, but views have
tempered towards the former in recent years. The previous
entry, *All Monsters Attack*, was strictly for kids and took place
in the real world where Godzilla and company were movie
monsters that appeared strictly in the young protagonist's

dreams. Although in this film Godzilla is presented as "real" it doesn't exactly bring Godzilla back to the real world. With strange dream scenes, hallucinations, and even animated vignettes, *Godzilla vs. Hedorah* is decidedly surreal. And, although it contains a child protagonist as did the previous entry, this is by no means a child's film. Main characters are killed and maimed throughout the proceedings, often gruesomely, and young Ken stumbles across horrifically deformed dead bodies in the streets. Godzilla swings Hedorah by the tail slinging chunks of his slimy body off as they twirl, one of which crashes through the window of an upstairs mahjong game dissolving the participants. Oddly, in the same scene, a kitten survives being coated in the monster's sludge. Other weird touches abound including the beginning of the youth rally presented in black and white rather than color. Strange elderly vagabonds watch the youthful characters from a distance as soft guitar music plays. The lead teen character strikes an energetic chord on his guitar and the proceedings jump back to color.

Godzilla vs. Hedorah is certainly a youth film full of new ideas thanks to its young creative team of director Yoshimitsu Banno, chosen for his work on the Expo 70 film *The Birth of the Japanese Islands*, and new SPFX director Teruyoshi Nakano, formerly Eiji Tsuburaya's assistant. Tomoyuki Tanaka was hospitalized during the making of the film and as the saying goes, while the cats are away the mice will play. Although critics initially considered this film to be a far cry from the original 1954 *Godzilla*, it was the very film Banno and Nakano hoped to emulate, serving as a warning against rampant pollution rather than nuclear experimentation. What many critics hate about the film is also what others love about it. Hallucinations of dancing skeletons, humans with fish heads, and trippy picture-in-picture shots of crying babies and irate citizens are some of the highlights. The biggest offense for most is when Godzilla flies which he accomplishes via his atomic ray. Some say this was in response to Godzilla's true nemesis at the time: Daiei's flying turtle Gamera. However, Banno and Nakano said they felt they owed the light-hearted scene to the children who had sat through all of the depressing gore and gloom. An alternate take was shot with Godzilla running to catch

Hedorah, but the flying scene being more interesting was the version decided upon by Tanaka's assistant in his absence. After seeing the finished results Tanaka was so disgusted he forbade Banno from ever making another G-film, though Banno himself refutes this saying he turned in screenplays for the next Godzilla film at Tanaka's behest. The screenplays were only rejected because they proved too expensive Banno said in a 2015 interview with *Sci-Fi Japan TV*. Whether he disdained the film or not, Tanaka was for a fact disappointed in the film's box-office haul which would ironically turn out to be the second highest grossing Godzilla film of the 1970s.

 Godzilla vs. Hedorah was successfully released in the U.S. by AIP in 1972 as *Godzilla vs. the Smog Monster* and was fittingly put on a double bill with *Frogs*, an ecologically themed "animals attack" horror film. *Smog Monster* features an excellent English rendition of *Hedorah's* theme song called "Save the Earth" recorded in Los Angeles by Adryan Russ under producer Guy Hemric, who had worked on such films as *Muscle Beach Party* (1964). The song remains popular today, but can only be found on VHS, as all DVD releases utilize the International Dub. For many years *Smog Monster* had a bad reputation and was included as one of the *Fifty Worst Films of All Time* in the book of the same name. However, there are plenty of other films far more deserving of that "honor" than this one.

Final Word
Love it or hate it—it's usually one or the other—it's significant for being the first "art house" monster film.

Trivia

* After the initial 35 day filming schedule was completed Ishiro Honda was called in to watch a rough cut of the film at the behest of Tomoyuki Tanaka. Banno then persuaded Honda to go to Tanaka to ask for an extension of filming on his behalf, to which Tanaka obliged.

- The film is notorious in American fan circles for being the first film in which Godzilla toys were glimpsed on screen, which made American children envious as very few Godzilla toys existed in the States outside of Aurora model kits. Among the toys visible onscreen are those for Godzilla, King Ghidorah, Baragon and Ultraman.

- Tanaka walked in on the strange nightclub sequence with the fish heads and was said to be more perplexed by this sequence than Godzilla's flight later in the film.

- Banno filmed the movie's underwater scenes, and also doubled for Akira Yamaguchi (Dr. Yano) during his scuba diving scenes. In fact the actor was cast in part due to his physical resemblance to Banno for the sake of said scuba scenes.

- The scene of the girls collapsing during the outdoor aerobics class from smog was inspired by real events in July of 1970.

- Contrary to reports that Banno wanted to film a sequel wherein Godzilla battles Hedorah in Africa, in a recent interview with *Sci-Fi Japan TV*, Banno said he never wrote any such script. He did mention interest in working on a sequel of sorts without Godzilla, where Hedorah would battle a good algae monster named Midora.

- Hiroyuki Kawase was the star of the Japanese version of *Sesame Street*.

- The sludge placed in the big pool began to stink badly as the film's summer shoot dragged on.

- The baby placed in the sludge was the grandchild of one of the staff from the lighting department.

Godzilla vs. Gigan (1972)

Alternate Titles: *Earth Destruction Directive: Godzilla vs. Gigan* (Japan) *Godzilla on Monster Island* (U.S.) *Objective Earth Mission Apocalypse* (France) *War of the Monsters* (UK) *Godzilla Against the Giants* (Italy) *Frankenstein's Brood of Hell* (Germany)
Release Date: March 12, 1972

Directed by: Jun Fukuda
Special Effects by: Teruyoshi Nakano
Screenplay by: Shinichi Sekizawa
Music by: Akira Ifukube
Cast: Hiroshi Ishikawa (Gengo) Yuriko Hishimi (Tomoko) Tomoko Umeda (Machiko) Minoru Takashima (Shosaku) Kunnio Murai (Shima) Toshiaki Nishizawa (Kubota) Zan Fujita (Fumio) **Suit Performers:** Haruo Nakajima (Godzilla) Yukietsu Omiya (Anguirus) Kengo Nakayama (Gigan) Kanta Ina (King Ghidorah)

Cinemascope, Eastmancolor, 89 Minutes

Story

A woman recruits a cartoonist named Gengo, recently hired by Children's Land, to help look for her brother Shima, who she believes to have been kidnapped by the amusement park's mysterious directors. Gengo discovers the directors are actually aliens bent on destroying Monster Island when he steals a strange recording from them that lures Anguirus to the mainland. Gengo and his friends go to rescue the kidnapped Shima and instead become trapped inside the Children's Land Godzilla Tower with the aliens who have just unleashed their monsters Gigan and King Ghidorah on Tokyo. Godzilla and Anguirus show up to battle them while Gengo and his friends rescue Shima from the tower which turns out to be a secret weapon against Godzilla, now battling Gigan in the amusement park. Godzilla is overwhelmed by the tower's laser beams, so Gengo and the military sneak in and use explosives to destroy it. Free of the tower's rays, Godzilla and Anguirus are able to vanquish Gigan and Ghidorah.

Background & Commentary

After the box-office returns of *Godzilla vs. Hedorah* proved disappointing, Tomoyuki Tanaka began a concentrated effort to return Godzilla to the glory days of the 1960s. His first order of business was the commissioning of a story revolving around the return of King Ghidorah. Two drafts were written, with Kaoru Mabuchi penning *Godzilla vs. the Space Monsters* and Shinichi Sekizawa concocting *The Return of King Ghidorah*. Both scripts featured Godzilla, Gigan and King Ghidorah with an assortment of additional friends and foes that never made it into the finished film. Elements of both screenplays were scaled down for the sake of the budget and combined into one script by Sekizawa, his last produced screenplay for the series. The final touch was the return of a proven director in the form of Jun Fukuda, marking the first of three G-pictures in a row that he would helm. The film is also bright and colorful to contrast with *Hedorah*'s somewhat muted color pallet. However, the film again harkens to environmental pollution as the invading cockroaches had to flee their planet when it was destroyed by the pollution of the dominant species. Tanaka also wanted Ifukube to score the picture, but when the maestro declined, feeling his themes were ill-suited for a cyborg monster, Tanaka instead commissioned the use of some of Ifukube's best known stock tracks. The swelling music elevates the final battle to grander heights than Riichiro Manabe's scores could've ever done, and for many fans unaware that this was stock music it was considered one of Ifukube's greatest scores.

Despite Tanaka's efforts to make this a better film than *Hedorah*, it is marred by some jarring stock footage. Godzilla frequently changes back to his mid-1960s suits in the midst of battles with King Ghidorah by way of *Ghidorah, the Three Headed Monster* and *Invasion of Astro-Monster*. And as for the monster whom this film was originally written around, King Ghidorah makes what unfortunately amounts to one of the shoddiest appearances in his career, including his guest appearance on *Zone Fighter*. Like the Godzilla suit, falling apart on the screen after four consecutive films of abuse, the Ghidorah suit is only a shell of its former self (though it sports a shiny new paint job) and suffers from limited mobility. This was not necessarily the suit's fault, but rather a lack of SPFX workers at Toho to operate the wireworks. Through the script's different drafts Rodan and Varan were meant to return as allies to Godzilla, but Anguirus was chosen instead because his suit from 1968's *Destroy All Monsters* was still in good condition. Gigan, the only new monster in the film, sports scythe-like arms and feet, a single visor for an eye, wind sails along his back, and a buzz saw in his stomach. In this sense the new creation is truly a monster for the 1970s. However, he is still a considerable notch above the many monsters on Superhero TV shows of the time, which he would eventually join when he guest starred on *Zone Fighter* along with Godzilla the following year. Kudos must go to the film's final battle as Godzilla nearly bites the dust and is the recipient of several Gamera-style beatings (this film coincidentally also ends with a Godzilla theme song). The monster is mercilessly drubbed by laser beams from the aliens' Godzilla Tower, Gigan cuts into him numerous times with his buzz-saw, and also bashes Godzilla's head with his hooks. In this sense, the staff made a concentrated effort to instill some suspense into the final battle for once. Nakano was even quoted in an interview as saying it would've been interesting to make a film where Godzilla loses. As the overmatched Godzilla, Haruo Nakajima turned in one of his best performances as the monster and the actor retired after the film's release.

Godzilla vs. Gigan elevated attendance by only 40,000 tickets over *Hedorah*'s in Japan. In America, due to AIP cancelling its plans to release this film in 1973, the movie was beaten to theaters by its own sequel *Godzilla vs. Megalon*. As a result, *Godzilla on Monster Island* as it was called, featured no "new" monsters to the American public and wasn't the great success that *Godzilla vs. Megalon* was in the States. In some instances the film was part of a triple feature with *Megalon* and *Godzilla vs. the Cosmic Monster*, which also beat it to theaters. The movie carried some notoriety as the first film in which Godzilla talks. While in the Japanese version comic book-like word bubbles were used to translate what Godzilla and Anguirus say to one another, in the American version they were instead dubbed into English themselves!

Final Word

Though this film was created in direct opposition to *Godzilla vs. Hedorah*'s experimental techniques; the former film has since emerged as the more memorable of the two.

Trivia

- Godzilla and Anguirus's respective suit performers, Haruo Nakajima and Yukietsu Omiya, both cameo together as JSDF officers during the military scenes. Nakajima has an additional cameo earlier in the film as a manga editor.

- Yuriko Hishimi (Tomoko) also played Anne Yuri in Tsuburaya Production's *Ultra Seven*, a role she reprised in many other Ultra sequel series.

- *Godzilla vs. Gigan* borrows footage from *Rodan*; *The Mysterians*; *The Last War*; *Mothra vs. Godzilla*; *Ghidorah, the Three Headed Monster*; *Invasion of Astro-Monster*; *Ebirah, Horror of the Deep*; *War of the Gargantuas*; *Son of Godzilla*; *Destroy All Monsters*; *All Monsters Attack* and *Godzilla vs. Hedorah*.

- Some of the better Ifukube tracks in this film are taken from *The Birth of the Japanese Islands* (1970) directed by none other than Yoshimitsu Banno. Some of these tracks were ironically also used in the trailer for *Godzilla vs. Hedorah*.

- Teruyoshi Nakano had to work hard to persuade Haruo Nakajima to play Godzilla one more time.

- During shooting this film's title was *Earth Destruction Directive: Godzilla vs. King Ghidorah* before Tomoyuki Tanaka decided Gigan should be touted as "the monster to beat."

- Zan Fujita's (the Chairman) moon-shaped office chair was the actual moon prop from Toho's *Battle in Outer Space* (1959) of which this film borrows stock music from.

- Toshiaki Nishizawa (Kubota) had a prominent role in the Japanese version of the *Spiderman* TV series.

- *Godzilla vs. Gigan* was produced during what was known as the "second giant monster boom" of Japan (though this boom centered more so on TV superheroes which fought giant monsters than their big screen rivals). As by this point the Godzilla films were partially produced just to sell toys and other merchandise, Shinichi Sekizawa comments on the marketing of the monsters via Children's Land Amusement Park, which plans to commercialize the denizens of Monster Island by killing and replacing them with giant replicas.

- *Godzilla vs. the Space Monsters* featured an ally, Majin Toul, to Godzilla inspired by Daiei's *Daimajin* films, which would come to life in the amusement park to aid Godzilla and Anguirus.

- Kunio Murai (Shima) dubbed Harrison Ford into Japanese for the Indiana Jones films.

- Shinichi Sekizawa's third draft for *Return of King Ghidorah* featured Godzilla, Anguirus and the Mothra larva battling King Ghidorah, Gigan and Megalon.

Daigoro vs. Goliath (1972)

Japanese Title: *Great Deadly Monster Battle: Daigoro vs. Goliath*
Release Date: December 17, 1972

Directed by: Toshihiro Iijima
Special Effects by: Teruyoshi Nakano

Screenplay by: Kitao Chiba
Music by: Toru Fuyuki
Cast: Hiroshi Inuzuka (the Inventor) Akiji Kobayashi (Zoo Keeper) Shoji Kobayashi (Suzuki) Minami Shinzuki (Kumo Goro) **Suit Performers:** Tetsuo Yamamura (Daigoro) Kotobuki Kato (Goliath/Daigoro's Mother)

Academy Ratio, Eastmancolor, 85 Minutes

Story

A submarine accident awakens a huge monster that goes on a rampage. After it is killed by the military, the female creature's infant son Daigoro is discovered nearby. Instead of killing it, the Japanese government raises it on an island. With no mother to teach it to hunt for food, the creature is content to be fed by his human supervisors. Soon Daigoro becomes too expensive to feed and the government decides to feed him a growth inhibitor. At the same time the monster Goliath is released from a meteor that has fallen into the ocean. Daigoro does his best to fight the monster but is badly beaten. The humans rally around Daigoro to try and get him well, while others debate using the A-Bomb on Goliath who is ravaging cities. Daigoro begins practicing for a rematch and learns that he can breathe fire. Eventually the two monsters cross paths again, and Daigoro manages to deliver a knockout to the larger monster in the form of his fiery breath. Goliath is strapped to a rocket and shot back into space, and Daigoro, having earned his place in the world, is allowed to eat all the food he wants should Japan need defending again.

Background & Commentary

If one didn't know better they might think *Daigoro vs. Goliath* was a live action Disney film made in Japan. Produced by Tsuburaya Productions, the humor, music, and even the actors, all seem to be right out of films like *Herbie Rides Again* and other 1970s Disney fare. While usually attempts at humor in these films are groan inducing, *Daigoro vs. Goliath* can't help but make one smile, and at times even laugh. Much of the humor is at the expense of the main character, an inventor whose creations include a flying motorcycle among others. The inventor was played by Hiroshi Inuzuka of the Japanese comedy team the Crazy Cats, stars of many successful farces for Toho in the 1960s. Providing the heart of the film is the zoo keeper that has raised Daigoro. In a touching scene, he breaks down and is unable to feed Daigoro food tainted with a compound that will stunt his growth.

Oddly, the child characters are kept at a distance and the emphasis is mostly on the inventor and Daigoro's zoo keeper. Although one would suspect the light film would stray from any nuclear subtext, the characters have a long debate as to whether or not to drop the A-Bomb on Goliath. There is also the obligatory "preserve the environment" sermon in a long sequence of shots showcasing the beauty of the earth. The SPFX and monster suits are atrocious, but being a comedy they don't need to emulate any sense of realism. Oddly enough, it is Daigoro's mother that fares the best in her scenes, which serve as a brief flashback to her death. While it is implied the audience should feel sympathy for her, she comes across as the film's scariest creation with her flowing white hair and snarling visage. The Goliath suit on the other hand has stiff, overlong arms and is your basic giant lizard. Daigoro has the most interesting, albeit goofy, design with a hippo-like appearance, complete with whiskers and a short, stubby tail.

There are alternating stories as to this film's genesis, but the accepted belief is that this began life as a Godzilla film to be titled *Godzilla vs. Redmoon*. Having a close relationship with Toho Studios, Tsuburaya Productions obtained permission to borrow Godzilla for their 10th Anniversary film and constructed suits for three monsters: a mother, father, and an infant that is killed by humans causing the parents to go bad. According to legend, Godzilla was mysteriously dropped and the script was re-written to become *Daigoro vs. Goliath*. An inverse to this story claims that *Daigoro vs. Goliath* had already been made when the *Godzilla vs. Redmoon* script was written, the plan being to reuse the Goliath and Daigoro mother suits as enemy monsters to battle Godzilla. In any case, one should be thankful the proposed feature never materialized. It would've made for an awful G-film, and this delightful children's picture may have never been made.

Final Word

Although not well known for lack of exposure outside of Japan, it represents how to do a children's monster/comedy film right and is the best of the small sub-genre.

Trivia

- A life-sized Goliath head and back prop were created so as to allow the actors climb onto it for certain scenes.

- The Daigoro suit is made with parts of an old Red King suit, one of the more popular monsters in the *Ultraman* franchise.

- Some scholars don't believe the Goliath suit was ever meant to portray the titular villain in *Godzilla vs. Redmoon*, as artwork for that film shows the monster to have wings and doesn't resemble Goliath. However, this artwork was done years later by Hurricane Ryu.

Godzilla vs. Megalon (1973)

Alternate Titles: *King Kong: Demons from Space* (Germany) *Gorgo and Superman Fight in Tokyo* (Spain) *Godzilla 1980* (Belgium) *To the Limits of Reality* (Italy) *Titans from Space* (Mexico)
Release Date: March 17, 1973

Directed by: Jun Fukuda
Special Effects by: Teruyoshi Nakano
Screenplay by: Jun Fukuda
Music by: Riichiro Manabe
Cast: Katsuhiko Sasaki (Goro) Hiroyuki Kawase (Rokusan) Yutaka Hiyashi (Jinkawa) Robert Dunham (Emperor Antonio) **Suit Performers:** Shinji Takagi (Godzilla) Tsugitoshi Komada/Masachika Mori (Jet Jaguar) Hideo Date (Megalon) Kengo Nakayama (Gigan)

Cinemascope, Eastmancolor, 82 Minutes

Story

Inventor Goro Ibuki's new super robot Jet Jaguar is hijacked by agents of the underwater kingdom of Seatopia. Angry at the surface world for inadvertently destroying part of their country in an underground nuclear test, they are using Jet Jaguar to guide their monster Megalon to Tokyo. Goro intercepts Jet Jaguar in a helicopter and overrides his commands, ordering him to go to Monster Island to get Godzilla, which he does. Arriving in Japan before Godzilla, the robot increases his size to match Megalon's and the two battle in the countryside. Seatopia requests that their allies, the Space Hunter M Nebula aliens, send Gigan to aid Megalon. Hopelessly outmatched, Jet Jaguar is rescued by Godzilla who arrives in the nick of time. In an all-night battle the duo overcome Megalon and Gigan, both of whom retreat. Godzilla returns to the sea, and Jet Jaguar shrinks back down to size so he can reunite with his creator.

Background & Commentary

If the theme of *Godzilla vs. Hedorah* was pollution, and that of *Godzilla vs. Gigan* commercialism of the monsters, the theme of *Godzilla vs. Megalon* seems to be Japanese superhero TV shows. This is essentially what the film amounts to: an hour-plus long episode of such a program. With most of the feature revolving around the robot Jet Jaguar, Godzilla seems thrown into the film as though he was an afterthought (conflicting stories say this was actually the case).

The film, which began life as *Godzilla vs. the Megalon Brothers: The Undersea Kingdom's Annihilation Strategy*, was hastily shot in only three weeks. To save money most of the actors' scenes were shot outside, therefore only two sets (excluding the miniature ones) were constructed for production: Goro's lab and the Seatopian square. The film is also padded with stock footage from a total of nine other films to illustrate various scenes, including the all-important city destruction sequences. However, this film isn't as careless as its predecessor *Godzilla vs. Gigan*, which features accidental "cameos" by Rodan and Mothra when stock footage from *Ghidorah, the Three Headed Monster* is used during the end battle. In a clever move, Megalon's beam weapon was even made to be identical to Ghidorah's so footage of the aforementioned film could be used for this picture's city destruction scenes. As for Megalon himself, the kaiju was a leftover creation cut for budgetary reasons from early script versions of *Godzilla vs. Gigan*. The title kaiju from that film reappears as well, and it must be said the two monsters compliment one another's designs nicely. While Gigan has scythe-like arms the insectoid Megalon (designed after the Japanese beetle) has drill-like appendages. Toho finally constructed a new Godzilla suit after the one utilized in the past four films literally fell apart filming the previous picture. The new suit has a friendly countenance with its oversized eyes and a peppy walk (the role having been taken over by Shinji Takagi). As for the film's real star, Jet Jaguar, the robot was the result of a publicity contest between Toho, Tsuburaya Productions and Seiyu Department Stores wherein children submitted designs for a new robot hero which would appear in a Toho film. The winner, Red Arrow, featured the body of Jet Jaguar but with bat-like wings and a monstrous head. Toho redesigned and renamed the automaton Jet Jaguar proving it was all just a publicity stunt. The end "tag team" battle between the four kaiju is creatively choreographed and is still thoroughly enjoyable despite the barren country setting and the monsters' skippy antics. Actually, the best fight in the film is easily the solo match between Jet Jaguar and Megalon before their two co-stars, added in for marquee value, show up.

While *Godzilla vs. Gigan*'s attendance had went up from *Godzilla vs. Hedorah*'s, this film severely tanked with only 980,000 admissions. Consequently, *Megalon* didn't reach U.S. screens until 1976 after Godzilla's retirement in Japan and was a big success for distributer Cinema Shares making over $5 million (the press even claimed it had the biggest opening for an independent film at the time in New York). Part of this surprise success may have been due to the fact that it was the first G-film to be released in U.S. theaters in four years, but it is more likely because of Cinema Share's spunky advertising; cleverly consisting of a "Godzilla for President" campaign and a poster that falsely depicts the monsters battling atop the World Trade Centers. The film's exposure didn't end there. It was the first G-film aired on prime time television by NBC, which also included host segments of John Belushi in a Godzilla suit. In the days of VHS cassette tapes, *Megalon* was in the public domain and as a result became one of the best—if not the best—known G-films in the states.

Final Word

Although regarded as one of the worst Godzilla films, it remains culturally significant due to its wide exposure in the States. The widescreen uncut Japanese version is actually superior to the pan and scanned Cinema Shares cut and is a fun film when viewed in the right frame of mind.

Trivia

- The Megalon that appeared in the scripts for *Godzilla vs. the Space Monsters* and *Return of King Ghidorah* was described as a tactile, smog-emitting creature and bears no physical similarities to the insectoid kaiju in this film.

- To keep the actors warm during the opening scene (filmed outside in winter) at Lake Motosu, Jun Fukuda gave each a shot of whiskey.

- This film establishes that Monster Island and *Destroy All Monster's* Monsterland are two separate places, as Monster Island in this film is said to be in the South Pacific, while Monsterland is part of the Bonin Islands near Japan.

- Rumors circulated that a photograph of Kengo Nakayama in the Megalon suit exists, however, Nakayama says he never played Megalon and that he and Hideo Date look quite similar, hence the confusion.

- Though no connections are implied between Seatopia and *Atragon*'s Mu Empire, a 1973 manga featuring Godzilla battling Manda on Easter Island (a Seatopian base in *Godzilla vs. Megalon*) exists.

- Supposedly most of the film's budget was eaten up by production of the monster suits, all of which were brand new including Gigan, as the monster's costume got damaged during the previous film. The film's other big expenditure was the elaborate destruction of Okouchi Dam.

- Katsuhiko Sasaki is the son of Minoru Chiaki from *Godzilla Raids Again* (1955) and his grandfather also had a small role in *Invasion of Astro-Monster* (1965).

- This film is based off of a story concept by Shinichi Sekizawa, who didn't have time to write the script leaving director Jun Fukuda to do it instead.

- Robert Dunham (Emperor Antonio) doubled for the helmet clad Seatopian agent on the motorcycle that chases down Yutaka Hiyashi (Jinkawa).

- This film had a tie in with Honda Motor Company as Goro takes the Seatopian sand sample to the Honda Motor Industrial Technology Research Institute.

- Shortly after this film's release, Godzilla showed up on the small screen making guest appearances on Toho's SPFX TV series *Zone Fighter*. The monster wasn't a last minute addition to boost ratings and the pilot episode originally featured Godzilla and Gigan both until Godzilla's first guest spot was pushed back to the fifth episode, and Gigan eventually appeared in the eleventh episode. *Zone Fighter* is surprisingly considered "in canon" with the Godzilla films and also featured a two-part episode guest starring King Ghidorah, minus Godzilla. Like the many "transforming hero" programs of the time, Zone Fighter was a friendly alien who protected earth from the evil Garoga aliens. How Zone Fighter and Godzilla became allies is never explained.

!!!!!!!!!!!!!!!!!!!Bonus Review!!!!!!!!!!!!!!!!!!!!!

Submersion of Japan (1973)

Alternate Titles: *Tidal Wave* (U.S.)
Release Date: December 29, 1973

Directed by: Shiro Moritani
Special Effects by: Teruyoshi Nakano
Screenplay by: Shinobu Hashimoto & Sakyo Komatsu
Music by: Masaru Sato
Cast: Hiroshi Fujioka (Toshio Onodera) Tetsuro Tamba
(Prime Minister Yamoto) Ayumi Ishida (Reiko) Kenji
Kobayashi (Dr. Tadokoro) Shogo Shimada (Prince Watari)
Nobuo Nakamura (Australian Ambassador)

Panavision, Eastmancolor, 140 Minutes

Story
When an island mysteriously sinks into the ocean overnight,
Dr. Tadokoro is sent to investigate. In a submarine piloted
by Onodera, Tadokoro makes a startling discovery in the
Japan Trench. The doctor hypothesis that within a matter of
years Japan will sink into the ocean. However, it becomes
apparent the submersion will happen much sooner than that
when an earthquake devastates Kanto. Preparations are
made to evacuate as many Japanese to other nations as
possible. As Japan continues to sink into the sea, Dr.
Tadokoro decides to die with the nation he loves, while
Onodera searches for his missing fiancé, Reiko, in an
unknown country.

Background & Commentary
In March of 1973 was published Sakyo Komatsu's landmark
novel *Submersion of Japan*. However, even before the book
became a bestseller, Tomoyuki Tanaka had already optioned
it for a film. The production values are incredibly high when
compared to the Godzilla films of the same era, and features
a cast of superstars such as Tetsura Tanba as the Prime
Minister and *Kamen Rider's* Hiroshi Fujioka as Onodera.

Kenji Kobayashi gives an excellent performance as Dr. Tadokoro, the scientist who first learns that Japan is doomed to sink into the ocean. The scene where he tries to convey the gravity of this fact to his colleague is one of the thespian highlights of the film. Another excellent scene occurs when Onodera, sworn to silence by the government, walks down a crowded street in Osaka tormented by the fact he can't warn his fellow countrymen as to Japan's fate.

The film is easily the crown jewel of SPFX director Nakano's works. One of the highlights is certainly the earthquake that decimates Kanto. It is truly horrific as people catch fire and others are graphically injured by showering shards of glass that rain down on them from a skyscraper. In one scene an old man fearfully frets about the fires that started in the Kanto earthquake of 1923 only to be swallowed up by a massive wall of water. The aftermath of this scene is also impressive, as helicopters try to put out fires in the decimated city. The rest of the destruction is limited mostly to urban areas, and though it is fascinating to watch for fans of miniature effects, the Kanto earthquake remains the film's best scene. But, *Submersion of Japan* is not merely a SPFX film, but a solid disaster movie reminiscent of American films such as *Earthquake*. Actually, it could be said this film surpasses many of the American made disaster films in terms of story, atmosphere, SPFX and cinematography. A shot of Onodera running into the sun, obscured by volcanic ash, is particularly outstanding, especially because it was created with practical effects. Somewhat misplaced is Sato's score which lacks the gravity of Ifukube's works. While it is by no means a bad score (in fact, it's quite poignant) it simply isn't downbeat enough most of the time, and fans of the Godzilla series will find sections reminiscent of *Godzilla vs. Mechagodzilla* which Sato would score the next year.

The merits of the film's last act are debatable. It is somewhat flawed in that it totally loses track of Onodera. However, this could have been the intent of director Shiro Moritani as Onodera has himself lost track of his lover Reiko and many of Japan's citizens are being scattered across the globe. And, although the last act is peppered with various scenes of destruction, it lacks a final set-piece to truly cap-off the film. Instead, the climax is an emotional one as the Prime

Minister has one last meeting with Dr. Tadokoro, who delivers a touching eulogy of sorts to Japan. The final scene shows both Onodera and Reiko inside trains on different sides of the world, letting the audience leave the film wondering if ever the two shall meet again. Released in December of 1973, it garnered 8.8 million admissions and became the highest grossing Japanese made film of the 1970s. It was released in America by Roger Corman's New World Pictures as *Tidal Wave* in 1975 with new footage of Lorne Greene as the U.S. ambassador to Japan inserted into the proceedings.

Final Word
With its cornucopia of excellent effects shots coupled with excellent direction and acting, *Submersion of Japan* may well be THE special effects film of its decade.

Trivia

- The Kermadec submarine uses some of the same sound effects used for Jet Jaguar in *Godzilla vs. Megalon* the same year. This sub was later reused as the Akatsuki in *Terror of Mechagodzilla* (1975).

- Author Sakyo Komatsu has a cameo alongside Hiroshi Fujioka and Kenji Kobayashi early in the film. Recently retired Godzilla suit actor Haruo Nakajima has a cameo as one of the Prime Minister's men.

- The film was followed by a TV series adaptation of the novel produced by Tomoyuki Tanaka and broadcast on TBS from October 1974 to March of 1975.

- A proposed sequel to the film, the title of which was *After Japan Sinks* according to *Famous Monsters*, was planned but never actually materialized.

Jumborg Ace and Giant (1974)

Alternate Titles: *Yuk Wud Jaeng vs. Jumbo A* (Thailand)
Mars Men (France)
Release Date: March 16, 1974

Directed by: Sompote Sands & Shohei Tojo
Special Effects by: Kazuo Sagawa
Screenplay by: Bunzo Wakatsuki & Hiroyasu Yamaura
Music by: Toru Fuyuki & Masanobu Higure
Cast: Naoki Tachibana (Naoki Tachibana) Anon Pricha
(young boy) Chaiya Suriyan (Thai woman) **Suit
Performers:** Uncredited

Chaiyoscope, Color, 93 minutes

Story

As the earth is beset upon by an army of monsters, pilot
Naoki Tachibana rams his Cessna into one of the monsters.
Tachibana is saved by a benevolent alien who gives him the
power to turn his Cessna into the giant robot Jumborg Ace
and his Honda Z into Jumborg 9, both of which he uses to
battle the monsters. The monsters are the result of an alien
invasion led by Demon Go-Ne, who sends one of her cronies
to steal a magical gem from Wat Arun. On the moon, Demon
Go-Ne is using a giant mirror weapon (powered by the stolen
gem) to cause an eclipse that plunges the world into
darkness. A guardian statue, Giant, then flies to the moon
with Jumborg Ace close behind him. Together the heroic duo
defeat Demon Go-Ne and her monsters and take the gem
back to Wat Arun.

Background & Commentary

In the early 1960s, Sompote Sands (the anglicized name of
Sompote Saengduenchai) came to Japan to study under Eiji
Tsuburaya through a government scholarship from his
homeland of Thailand. Taking what he learned back to
Thailand, Sands founded his own production company,
Chaiyo Studios, and produced a Thai monster film of sorts
revolving around legendary giant statues battling one
another called *Tah Tien* in 1971. In 1973, Sands approached

the late Eiji Tsuburaya's son, Noboru, to acquire distribution rights in Thailand for the first six Ultraman TV series and *Jumborg Ace*—Tsuburaya's new TV series about a transforming airplane that battles monsters.

As it turned out, *Jumborg Ace* became quite a hit in Thailand, and Sands then approached Tsuburaya about co-producing a film together about the giant robot. Tsuburaya Productions agreed and has been haunted by the decision to this day. In later years, after Noboru Tsuburaya passed on, Sands came forward with what many people consider to be a forged document that alleges Noboru gave Chaiyo Studios exclusive distribution rights to the first six Ultraman series and *Jumborg Ace* outside of Japan. As such, Tsuburaya Productions has since disavowed the two films they produced with Chaiyo. And it's a shame too, because the two films that the studios produced make for some interesting curiosities from both a historical perspective and for their wild entertainment value. Of the two produced films (the latter of which was *6 Ultra Brothers vs. the Monster Army*), *Jumborg Ace and Giant* is easily the more inferior of the two. The main reason for this is that, unlike the following film comprised mostly of original footage, *Jumborg Ace and Giant* is something of a patchwork film that combines footage from the TV series with new footage shot by Chaiyo. As such, the story is hard to follow as it jumps back and forth between what is obviously new footage shot in Thailand, and the footage from the TV series. That being said, the new footage of the two stone statues from *Tah Tien* coming to life to battle the glam-rock-star-looking aliens from *Jumborg Ace* is delightful. Of the two statues, Yuk Wud Jaeng, or "Giant", gets the most attention and Wad Pho was essentially thrown in because his suit was still in good enough shape to use. His scene confronting Jumkiller Jr. is one of the film's best for several reasons. First off, the miniature set of Bangkok is well done, and second, Wad Pho and Jumkiller Jr. size each other up and argue like a couple of road rage fueled cabbies before they begin their wrestling match. The film's final battle is probably most comparable to that of *Godzilla vs. Megalon's* with a heavy emphasis on tag team comradery between the titular characters. However, before they team up, they are tricked into battling one another on the surface of the moon. Later, the duo joins forces on earth to battle Demon Go-Ne and her monsters. The battle, high on monster violence, is a taste of what's to come in the next film as Giant impales one of the monsters on his scepter and then causes two of the monsters to explode into oblivion.

After its successful release in Thailand, the film strangely never saw release in Japan, but did find its way to Taiwan in 1976. There, director Hung Min Chen removed the Thai actors, cut much of the original *Jumborg Ace* TV series footage, and created his own version called *Huo xing ren*. From there, the film was released in France as *Mars Men* in what is probably its most widely seen version. Reportedly, little to no translation was applied to this version, and the new distributor only loosely followed the original storyline of *Jumborg Ace and Giant* for their dub.

Final Word

As a practice run between Tsuburaya and Chaiyo Studios the film isn't bad, but it doesn't hold a candle to its follow-up *6 Ultra Brothers vs. the Monster Army*.

Trivia

- First and only feature film appearance of Jumborg Ace in his traditional form. The robot appears in *Ultraman Zero: The Movie* in a rebooted form called Jean Bot.

Godzilla vs. Mechagodzilla (1974)

Alternate Titles: *Godzilla vs. the Cosmic Monster* (U.S.) *King Kong vs. Godzilla* (Germany) *Godzilla vs. Robot* (Italy) *MechaKing vs. Godzilla* (Mexico) *Godzilla vs. the Mechanical Monster* (France) *Godzilla vs. Cyber Godzilla: The Destruction Machine* (Spain)
Release Date: March 21, 1974

Directed by: Jun Fukuda
Special Effects by: Teruyoshi Nakano
Screenplay by: Jun Fukuda & Hiroyasu Yamaura
Music by: Masaru Sato

Cast: Masaaki Daimon (Keisuke) Reiko Tajima (Saeko)
Kazuya Aoyama (Masahiko) Goro Mutsumi (Alien
Commander) Akihiko Hirata (Prof. Miyajima) Hiroshi
Koizumi (Prof. Wagura) Shin Kishida (Agent Nanbara)
Beru-Bera Lin (Minami) **Suit Performers:** Isao Zushi
(Godzilla) Kazushige Mori (Mechagodzilla) Mamoru
Kusumi (Anguirus/King Seesar)

Cinemascope, Eastmancolor, 84 Minutes

Story
A cave in Okinawa tells of a prophecy involving a monster
that will destroy the world if not opposed by King Seesar and
another mystery monster. Godzilla then emerges from Mt.
Fuji and uncharacteristically beats up pal Anguirus and
begins destroying Tokyo. Soon the real Godzilla emerges to
stop him, and the beast is revealed to be a Mecha-Godzilla
created by aliens. After being damaged by Godzilla, the
aliens force earth scientist Dr. Miyajima to repair
Mechagodzilla. In the meantime, Miyajima's companions
escort the King Seesar statue back to Okinawa while alien
agents try to thwart their plans. Miyajima is rescued by his
friends with the help of INTERPOL just as the aliens re-
launch the robot. At the same time King Seesar awakens and
battles the monster just as the prophecy said, with the real
Godzilla also entering the fray. Miyajima and the
INTERPOL agent destroy the aliens' base as Seesar and
Godzilla destroy the robot.

Background & Commentary
Just as *Godzilla vs. Gigan* was made in response to *Godzilla
vs. Hedorah*'s "failures," *Godzilla vs. Mechagodzilla* was a
result of *Godzilla vs. Megalon*'s abysmal box office returns.
And, as the 20th Anniversary G-film, Tomoyuki Tanaka
wanted to do something to celebrate the series. As Toho had
been pining to use Okinawa (re-unified with Japan in 1972)
in a film since the aborted *Godzilla vs. Redmoon*, the first
official draft for the film was titled *Monsters Converge on
Okinawa: Showdown in Cape Zanpa*. It featured Godzilla,
Mothra, and Anguirus against Garugan—a mechanical
monster controlled by aliens. As the Mothra Imago prop was

by now unusable, and perhaps dissatisfied with Hiroyasu Yamaura (future pen of the *Star Wolf* TV series) and Jun Fukuda's attempt at the script in general, Tanaka had the men change the script drastically to excise the big moth and replace her with King Barugan—a precursor to King Seesar said to sport horns. Recalling the popularity of Mechanikong from *King Kong Escapes*, Tomoyuki Tanaka and Teruyoshi Nakano came up with the idea of a Mechagodzilla as the new antagonist replacing Garugan.

Mechagodzilla showcased a stunning design, an overkill of futuristic weaponry and is clearly the star of the show. Its unveiling in the oil refinery is on a par with King Ghidorah's fiery birth in its debut film ten years earlier. The other show stopper occurs when the robot releases all of its arsenal at once on Godzilla and his new sidekick, the leonine King Seesar (based upon Shisha statues). Just as *Godzilla vs. Megalon* revolved around sidekick Jet Jaguar, this film too revolves around King Seesar to a degree, specifically a game of keep away involving a statue of the monster. Godzilla is somewhat better integrated into the story here though, and the *Megalon* suit was refitted to give him a more serious appearance. Toho gets some more mileage out of the Anguirus suit that originated in *Destroy All Monster* six years ago which makes its final appearance when it battles the disguised Mechagodzilla at Mt. Fuji. Nakano, hot off his successful work on 1973's *Submersion of Japan*—which this film borrows some B-roll outtakes from—demonstrates some of the greatest pyrotechnics of his career in the nighttime battle between the two Godzillas at the oil refinery, the striking well-lit imagery reflecting on the waterfront. Also having worked on 1971's *The Bloodsucking Eyes*, Nakano utilizes a blood-squirting effect during the final battle which is extreme to say the least. Overall, the cast for this film is a notch above the last with Akihiko Hirata and Hiroshi Koizumi returning to the series in addition to a cameo from Kenji Sahara. Goro Mutsumi also does a fine job as the leader of the ape-like aliens, inspired by both the *Planet of the Apes* films as well as the villains from the popular Japanese TV series *Spectreman*.

The new monster and increased production values were enough of a draw to lure in 1.3 million attendees into theaters rebounding the series. Mechagodzilla quickly gained popularity as the favorite new Godzilla opponent second to King Ghidorah. In the U.S., Cinema Shares tried to release the film as *Godzilla vs. the Bionic Monster* but were stopped by a lawsuit from Universal claiming it infringed upon their popular *Six Million Dollar Man* and *Bionic Woman* series. Instead it was released as *Godzilla vs. the Cosmic Monster* to lesser fanfare than *Godzilla vs. Megalon's* U.S. release.

Final Word
The final pairing of Jun Fukuda, Masaru Sato and Teruyoshi Nakano is one of the team's best efforts. Sadly, when asked years later in an interview which of his Godzilla films were his favorites, Jun Fukuda responded, "None of them." He should have mentioned this film.

Trivia

- Producer Tanaka's first story concept for the film involved Godzilla facing doubles of himself in the form of two new Godzillas created by atomic testing by both the Chinese and the U.S. This idea was deemed too political and dropped according to Bob Eggleton's article, "*Godzilla vs. Mechagodzilla*: Technological Terror Meets the King of the Monsters!" In *Famous Monsters of Filmand's* Sep/Oct 2013 issue.

- Lead actor Masaki Daimon won the Nippon Award for Best Newcomer in 1974.

- When Shinichi Sekizawa was approached to write this film, according to Guy Mariner Tucker's *Age of the Gods*, his response was, "There aren't any monsters left!"

- The King Seesar suit was put on display during Expo 75 in Okinawa.

- Despite his death in the *Zone Fighter* TV series, Gigan was originally scripted to return in this film as an ally to Mechagodzilla under the control of aliens from the Planet R.

- Reiko Tajima and Goro Mutsumi both lent their voices to the anime *Space Cobra*.

- The Ape Alien shot by Agent Nanbara is portrayed by Takanobu Toya, the same actor who portrayed the Ape Alien Dr. Gori in TV's *Spectreman*.

- The character of Minami appeared in the *Monsters Converge on Okinawa* script.

- Godzilla's head rising over the hill in Okinawa was meant to emulate his introduction on Oto Island from the original *Godzilla* (1954).

- The same year as this film's release, Tsuburaya Productions produced *The Monkey Army*, a *Planet of the Apes* inspired TV series. *The Monkey Army* was re-edited into a TV-movie for America called *Time of the Apes*.

- Beru Bera Lyn (Minami) has a small filmography consisting of erotic thrillers. The actress's real name is in fact Chung Yu-his and she hails from Taiwan.

- The film's opening scene with Anguirus is said to be set in Siberia. The reason for this hails all the way back to publicity material for *Godzilla Raids Again* (1955) which stated Anguirus originated in Siberia.

- The jewels that represent King Seesar's eyes are made from the taillights of a car.

- Isao Zushi, who plays Godzilla in this film, had played the monster before on *Zone Fighter*. He also played King Ghidorah on the same series giving him the distinction of playing both Godzilla and King Ghidorah, an honor shared by Tsutomo Kitagawa many years later when he played the dragon in *Mothra 3: King Ghidorah Attacks* (1998) and the Big G in *Godzilla 2000* (1999). In addition to this, Zushi also played Gigan fighting against Godzilla on yet another episode of *Zone Fighter*!

- The hand of the transforming ape-man that grows hair is that of Eiichi Asada, future SPFX director of some of the 2000 era Godzilla films.

- Though he looks ancient in his elaborate makeup, actor Masao Imafuku (Nami's grandfather) was in fact only fifty years old.

!!!!!!!!!!!!!!!!!!!!Bonus Review!!!!!!!!!!!!!!!!!!!!!

The Bloodsucking Rose (1974)

Alternate Titles: *Evil of Dracula* (U.S.)
Release Date: July 20, 1974

Directed by: Michio Yamamoto
Special Effects by: Teruyoshi Nakano
Screenplay by: Ei Ogawa & Hiroshi Nagano
Music by: Riichiro Manabe
Cast: Toshio Kurosawa (Akira) Shin Kishida (Principal) Mariko Mochizuki (Kumi) Mika Katsuragi (Principal's Wife) Katsuhiko Sasaki (Prof. Yoshi) Mio Ota (Yukiko)

Cinemascope, Eastmancolor, 83 Minutes

Story

A new teacher, Akira, arriving at a secluded all girls' school is surprised to learn the news that he will soon succeed the school's eccentric principal. Strange occurrences plague the school, with girls becoming pale and anemic until finally it is learned the current principal and his "dead" wife, both vampires, are to blame. Akira stabs the principal through the chest with a poker and kills him.

Background & Commentary

Though he had been offered a chance to direct a third vampire film hot off the success of *The Bloodsucking Eyes*, Michio Yamamoto was initially hesitant to do another. Producer Fumio Tanaka had also been transferred to Toho's TV department after that film's release, but by 1974 Tanaka had been moved back to the film division and production on a third vampire movie was pushed by Toho due to the recent crop of successful horror films in America.

Opinions on the finished film vary, with some calling it the best of the trilogy and others the worst. One thing is certain, the film has more gore than its predecessors, and in a first, nudity. It also has the most vampire content and serves as a hodgepodge of homage shots to Hammer's vampire films. Kishida (NOT portraying the same vampire as in the last film) is more Dracula-like than ever, his introduction identical to Christopher Lee's charming walk down the staircase to meet Harker in the 1958 *Horror of Dracula*. The antiquated European style estate that serves as the principal's home comes complete with a cellar, where his "dead" wife lies in state. The film's other major setting is an all-girls school dormitory inspired by *Lust for a Vampire* (1970) where see-through nightgowns and breasts abound. When Kishida appears to terrorize the girls they, like Lee's victims began to do in the mid-1960s, react with delight upon being bitten. Later in the film, bite marks are revealed to be closer to the breast than the neck. The first film had reoccurring imagery of dolls to back up its title; this film not surprisingly does the same with roses. Throughout the film there is a white rose that slowly turns red as the vampires feed, though the link is never explained. For once the origin of the vampire is not confusing, and is revealed midway through the story to be a shipwrecked foreigner that has survived in Japan for generations feeding on blood. To conceal his identity, he and his bride can take on the form of their victims. When this becomes known it explains an earlier scene between the new teacher and the principal wherein Kishida's dialogue, "You are my successor," takes on a new meaning. Though Kishida looks good in his red-lined black cloak, he plays the vampire in an over the top fashion that descends the film into unintentional camp, a bad contrast in a story that strives for seriousness. Although *Lake of Dracula* utilized its contemporary setting well, this film, like the first, has no benefits from its modern placing. Manabe's score is a step down here too. Though his compositions always carried their fair share of notoriety, in this piece in some instances they can't even be called compositions but long stretches of annoying noises akin to a cat's screech.

The artfully done ending, in which the principal and his wife both crawl to one another in the midst of decomposing until finally their skeletal hands touch, was for the most part unscathed when it aired on American television in 1981 as *Evil of Dracula*. Unlike its two predecessors, *The Bloodsucking Rose* was not a success at the Japanese box office, thus ending Toho's exploits with "Dracula."

Final Word
Toho's Bloodthirsty Trilogy had come to a close, and, for the most part, the films' merits for movie buffs exist only in seeing a famed Japanese studio pay homage to a famous British one.

Trivia

- Shin Kishida had a small but important role in *Godzilla vs. Mechagodzilla* (1974) and was also a *Return of Ultraman* television series cast member. In addition to this, he was also in installments of the *Lone Wolf and Cub* and *Lady Snowblood* series. The actor passed away in the early 1980s. Reportedly, one of the last people to see him alive was his good friend (and co-star in *Godzilla vs. Mechagodzilla*) Goro Mutsumi.

- Katsuhiko Sasaki, who plays this film's version of Reinfeld, was the lead in last year's *Godzilla vs. Megalon* and would also head up *Terror of Mechagodzilla* (1975).

- Toshio Kurosawa was extremely reluctant to star in the film, and reportedly never watched the finished product.

Great Prophecies of Nostradamus (1974)

Alternate Titles: *The Last Days of Planet Earth* (U.S.) *Prophecies of Nostradamus (Catastrophe 1999)* (International Version)
Release Date: August 3, 1974

Directed by: Toshio Masuda
Special Effects by: Teruyoshi Nakano
Screenplay by: Yoshimitsu Banno, Toshio Masuda, Toshio Yasumi & Tsutomu Goto (novel)
Music by: Isao Tomita
Cast: Tetsuro Tamba (Dr. Ryogen Nishiyama) Toshio Kurosawa (Akira Nakagawa) Kaoru Yumi (Mariko Nishiyama) Yoko Tsukasa (Nobuo Nishiyama) So Yamamura (Prime Minister) Katsuhiko Sasaki (Nishiyama's assistant) **Suit Performers:** Isamu Sugii & Nobuyuki Nakano (Soft-Bodied Humans)

Panavision, Eastmancolor, 114 Minutes

Story

In the year 1999 the world is choked by horrible pollution. Dr. Nishiyama tries to advise the government to limit the pollution caused by factories but is unsuccessful. As the pollution worsens, strange disasters due to climate change befall the world. When a team sent to investigate a radioactive cloud over New Guinea disappears, Dr. Nishiyama volunteers to join a rescue party that goes after them, only to discover they have turned into zombie-like cannibals. Back in Japan, a jet explodes and tears a hole in the ozone layer causing the countryside to erupt in flame. Then, a food shortage causes the populace to riot as the world continues to spiral out of control. In an impassioned speech, Dr. Nishiyama warns the government what will happen if they don't take precautions. During the meeting, the participants envision a world ravaged by nuclear war and inhabited by mutant survivors, and hopes that it never comes to pass.

Background & Commentary

After the monster success that was *Submersion of Japan*, Tomoyuki Tanaka set his sights on yet another film adaptation of a popular novel, in this case *Great Prophecies of Nostradamus* by Tsutomo "Ben" Goto published late in 1973. Tanaka instructed Yoshimitsu Banno to pen a script based off of the book following a similar narrative to *The Last War* (1961)—so much so that its writer, Toshio Yasuda, even gets a screenplay credit though he had nothing to do with this film.

The resulting film is essentially any apocalyptic disaster film fan's paradise as it manages to work nuclear annihilation, food shortages, global warming, zombies, massive flooding, super powered children, mass suicide, cannibalism and giant mutant creatures into one coherent narrative. Of interest to kaiju fans are the aforementioned mutants, starting off with a quartet of giant slugs that mysteriously appear with no explanation early in the proceedings. The scene is brief, and the creatures are roasted by flamethrowers (at one point said flames are shot directly into the camera lens to great effect) courtesy of the JSDF. The slugs are followed by some poorly executed giant bats in the New Guinea scenes alongside some giant leeches whose bite can turn people into zombies. The film's two scariest suitmation creations (designed by Toro Norita, who also created Sanda and Gaira in *War of the Gargantuas*) are the two mutated humans that appear in a prophetic dream scene in a post-apocalyptic wasteland where they wrestle to the death over a mutated slug—their only source of food. The scene is quite disturbing, even for 1974 standards, and the grotesque depiction of the mutants would eventually doom the film to obscurity in the future.

The film was another huge success, and ended up ranking as the #1 grossing Japanese made film of 1974 with Toho's *ESPY* in second place. However, trouble soon beset the film due to a "No Nukes Group" protesting the mutant scene, along with a cannibal sequence that occurs in New Guinea. Toho removed some of the footage and released a new 90 minute version entitled *Prophecies of Nostradamus (Catastrophe 1999)*. The full uncut version was last seen during a 1980 TV broadcast in its entirety and was slated for a Toho Video VHS release in 1986 which was cancelled. Today, the only way to see the film is through its badly cut 83 minute American TV version by UPA, *The Last Days of Planet Earth*, released to VHS by Paramount Home Video in the 1990s. The film's standout soundtrack by the legendary Isao Tomita has been re-released several times on CD it is so popular, however.

Final Word

Great Prophecies of Nostradamus is undoubtedly one of the greatest banned films of all time, and it's a true shame many fans will never see its uncut version.

Trivia

- The protective radiation suits worn in the New Guinea scenes are those worn by the ape aliens in *Godzilla vs. Mechagodzilla* while the helmets come from the Moonlight SY3 crew from *Destroy All Monsters*.

- A shot of a traffic jam that goes awry and turns into a pyrotechnic tour de force was reused as stock footage many times, namely in *The War in Space* (1978), *Deathquake* (1980), and *The Return of Godzilla* (1984).

6 Ultra Brothers vs. the Monster Army (1974)

Alternate Titles: *Hanuman vs. 7 Ultraman* (Thailand)
Release Date: November 26, 1974 (Thailand); April 28, 1979 (Japan)

Directed by: Sompote Sands & Shohei Tojo
Special Effects by: Kazuo Sagawa
Screenplay by: Bunzo Wakatsuki
Music by: Toru Fuyuki & Masanobu Higure
Cast: Ko Kaeoduendee (Koh) Anan Pricha (Anan) Yodchai Meksuwan (Dr. Wisut) Pawana Chanajit (Marisa) **Suit Performers:** Uncredited

Chaiyoscope, Color, 103 minutes

Story

During a time when the sun drifts dangerously close to the earth, the world suffers through an intense drought and heat wave. At the same time, a young boy named Koh doing a rain dance spies thieves breaking into a sacred temple. Koh attempts to stop them, and is killed in the process. In the Land of Light, Mother of Ultra observes this and revives Koh as the mythical monkey hero Hanuman who crushes the bandits. When a scientist fires a missile to induce rain into the air, there is a malfunction and one of the missiles explodes prematurely. The explosion awakens five mighty monsters from beneath the ground, and when Hanuman is overwhelmed by their numbers, the Ultra brothers travel to Earth to aid him. Together Hanuman and the Ultra brothers defeat the monsters.

Background & Commentary

Strangely enough, the first full-length original feature film in the Ultraman franchise has its origin in Thailand. In the early 1960s, Sompote Sands had traveled to Toho Studios in Japan to learn under Eiji Tsuburaya through a Thai government scholarship. Sands returned to his homeland and began producing his own SPFX films via his Chaiyo Studios. In 1973 he reached out to Noboru Tsuburaya about Tsuburaya Productions co-producing several films together, eventually resulting in *6 Ultra Brothers vs. the Monster Army*.

The Thai Ultraman movie is bizarre for a number of reasons. Primarily the most distracting factor is the stark contrast between the goofy, low brow child humor and the disturbing violence. Case in point, young boy Koh fights off a band of thieves admirably for the amusement of the target audience until he is shot point blank in the head by one of the thieves. Young Koh is then revived by Mother of Ultra in the Land of Light (using footage from the pilot episode of *Ultraman Taro*) to become Hanuman, a mythical monkey deity from the Hindu religion. The Hanuman suit is bizarre in of itself, as it has no semblance to realism and looks to be a man in costume wearing a ceremonial mask—though perhaps this was the intent. The titular six Ultra Brothers don't arrive on scene until the picture's climactic battle, which it has to be admitted is actually spectacular. Kazuo Sagawa, of Tsuburaya Productions, puts together a pyrotechnic spectacle similar to the works of Teruyoshi Nakano when a missile base serves as the battle field for the climax. The contrast between bizarre violence and comedy reemerges in the finale, when Hanuman defeats the five monster army in methods both unique and disturbing. Two of the monsters have their appendages sliced off one by one, another is skinned alive by Hanuman and Ultraman, and Gomora is sliced in half.

The film reportedly did very well upon release in Thailand, though the film was curiously not released in Japan until a full five years later on April 28, 1979. The Japanese version wisely excised the film down to 80 minutes, cutting out some of the violence and overtly Thai elements in the process. Sands would later try to claim Noboru Tsuburaya had given him all rights to the Ultraman franchise outside of Japan, resulting in years of unfortunate legal turmoil for Tsuburaya Productions. On top of this, footage from *6 Ultra Brothers vs. the Monster Army* was re-edited to become an atrocious made for TV movie in the U.S. by Sands in 1985 entitled *Space Warriors 2000*.

Final Word
If not for the negative and scandalous consequences of this film's production, it would likely be regarded as a classic curiosity amongst the Ultraman franchise rather than the blemish it has become.

Trivia

- Sompote Sands next approached Toei about teaming Hanuman with the Kamen Riders. When they declined his offer, Sands pilfered Toei's film *Five Riders vs. King Dark* and produced *Hanuman and the Five Riders* anyway in 1975.

- The five monster army comprises of Gomora from *Ultraman*, Dustpan from *Mirrorman*, and Astromons, Tyranto and Dorobon from *Ultraman Taro*.

- The reason in Thailand that this film is titled *Hanuman vs. 7 Ultraman* is because the number 6 is pronounced the same was as "falling" in Thai and has a negative connotation to it, therefore Mother of Ultra was decided to be the 7th "Ultraman" hence the title.

!!!!!!!!!!!!!!!!!!Bonus Review!!!!!!!!!!!!!!!!!!

ESPY (1974)

Alternate Titles: *E.S.P./Spy* (U.S.)
Release Date: December 28, 1974

Directed by: Jun Fukuda
Special Effects by: Teruyoshi Nakano
Screenplay by: Ei Ogawa
Music by: Masaru Sato
Cast: Hiroshi Fujioka (Yoshio Tamura) Yumi Kaoru (Maria Harada) Masao Kusakari (Jiro Miki) Tomisaburo Wakayama (Wolf) Katsumasa Uchida (Goro Tatsumi) Yuuzou Kayama (Houjou) Goro Mutsumi (Teraoka) Eiji Okada (Sarabad) Andrew Hughes (ESPY International Manager)

Cinemascope, Eastmancolor, 94 Minutes

Story

Yoshio Tamura and Maria Harada are two of the top members of ESPY, a secret government agency comprised of psychic spies. To stop an assassination attempt on the Bulgarian Prime Minister by the evil Counter-ESPY ran by Wolf, they recruit the help of psychic race car driver Jiro Miki. It is Wolf's hope that the assassination will incite World War III, and to deal with the agents of ESPY he sends psychic assassin Goro to take care of them. After defeating Goro and thwarting the assassination via Yoshio's new ability to teleport, together the trio track Wolf to his castle where he is defeated once and for all.

Background & Commentary

After completing work on the relatively low budget *Godzilla vs. Mechagodzilla*, Jun Fukuda was rewarded with the job of directing Toho's big budget New Year's Blockbuster *ESPY*. Based upon a manga written by Sakyo Komatsu in the 1960s, the film differs only slightly from the source material, excluding some alien villains and also adding in a new character, Jiro Miki.

The resulting film is reminiscent of a James Bond movie, right down to an ambitious pre-credit scene where Katsumasa Uchida (Murakoshi in *Terror of Mechagodzilla*) uses his psychic abilities to assassinate four delegates on a train rushing through Switzerland. The globetrotting doesn't stop at Switzerland, and on location filmed action scenes also take place in Paris and Turkey as well. The Turkey sequence contains a notorious striptease where Maria is manipulated into dancing. When she is approached by one of Wolf's henchmen, Yoshio psychically rips his tongue out in a scene naturally cut for the U.S. TV version aired years later in the 1980s. The highlight of the film for many SPFX buffs occurs when a jumbo jet (piloted by *Godzilla vs. Megalon's* Robert Dunham) is psychically induced to crash into some mountains before Yoshio takes the controls and saves the day. Fans of Teruyoshi Nakano may notice that his rocky landscape used for the plane scene is awfully familiar to the Siberia set, sans the snow, used in the same year's *Godzilla vs. Mechagodzilla* and could have been the same set only redressed. The film's climax, where Yoshio gains the ability to teleport just as the car he is trapped in explodes, is also excellently done and exciting.

The previous year had seen a massive success in the form of Sakyo Komatsu's *Submersion of Japan,* and once again Komatsu's *ESPY* was a huge hit for Toho, coming in as the #2 highest grossing film of 1974 behind *Great Prophecies of Nostradamus*. However, Komatsu himself was supposedly dissatisfied with this adaptation.

Final Word

Though one of Toho's best action films, unfortunately a few too many clumsy scenes make it rife for the picking for the likes of MST3K or Rifftrax.

Trivia

- In addition to future *Terror of Mechagodzilla* star Katsumasa Uchida, Goro Mutsumi (the alien leader in both *Mechagodzilla* films) has a small role in *ESPY* as Teraoka.

- One draft of the script featured a satellite, and a satellite can be glimpsed in the film's release poster.

Terror of Mechagodzilla (1975)

Alternate Titles: *Mechagodzilla's Counterattack* (Japan) *The Terror of Godzilla* (U.S.) *Konga, Godzilla, King Kong: Brood of the Devil* (Germany) *Destroy Kong: The Earth is in Danger!* (Italy) *Monsters from an Unknown Planet* (UK) *Ogres from Space* (France) *Mecha-Kong* (Mexico)
Release Date: March 15, 1975

Directed by: Ishiro Honda
Special Effects by: Teruyoshi Nakano
Screenplay by: Yukiko Takayama
Music by: Akira Ifukube
Cast: Tomoko Ai (Katsura) Katsuhiko Sasaki (Ichinose) Akihiko Hirata (Dr. Mafune) Goro Mutsumi (Mugal) Tohru Ibuki (Tsuda) Katsumasa Uchida (Murakoshi)
Suit Performers: Toru Kawai (Godzilla) Katsumi Nimiamoto (Titanosaurus) Ise Mori (Mechagodzilla II)

Cinemascope, Eastmancolor, 83 Minutes

Story

The Black Hole aliens save the life of earth scientist Dr. Mafune's daughter Katsura, turning her into a cyborg. To return the favor, Dr. Mafune agrees to help the spacemen repair their robot Mechagodzilla and also lends the assistance of his dinosaur slave Titanosaurus in their impending invasion. On the trail of the dinosaur, who has attacked several submarines in search of Mechagodzilla's remains, is marine biologist Ichinose and INTERPOL agent Murakoshi. Ichinose falls in love with Katsura, unaware she is a cyborg holding the Mechagodzilla II controls inside her. The spacemen unleash Titanosaurus and Mechagodzilla II on Tokyo leaving Godzilla hopelessly outmatched when he intervenes. In a skirmish between the spacemen and INTERPOL Dr. Mafune is killed and Katsura regains her humanity in the arms of Ichinose. In an act of self-sacrifice she commits suicide, short circuiting Mechagodzilla II allowing Godzilla to defeat his old nemesis and Titanosaurus in the process.

Background & Commentary

In an era where Godzilla flew, made guest appearances on a children's TV show, and even talked, *Terror of Mechagodzilla* is a sheer anomaly among the 1970s G-films and remains an island of dignity. This is all thanks to Tomoyuki Tanaka who wished to return Godzilla to his roots along with Ishiro Honda, who returned to the director's chair, and Akira Ifukube, who returned to the music studio. The more serious atmosphere is also largely attributed to new screenwriter, Yukiko Takayama, the first woman to ever script a G-film. She was the winner of a contest to script a sequel to last year's successful *Godzilla vs. Mechagodzilla*. Takayama introduces a cyborg girl, Katsura, who is forced to work with the spacemen as is her peaceful dinosaur pet Titanosaurus at the mercy of her father—bent on revenge against the world who mocked him. Her tragic death scene (cut from the U.S. version) ranks as the most touching self-sacrifice since Dr. Serizawa's in the original *Godzilla*, ironic considering Katsura's father is portrayed by Akihiko Hirata in his last G-series performance as Dr. Mafune.

Decidedly adult oriented with a grim tone and a bleak ending, the film contains brutal scenes of human violence and even a breast shot. In sharp contrast to this is the kid friendly Godzilla suit. Clearly wanting to save money, Toho had never built a new suit since *Godzilla vs. Megalon*, though they did at least attempt to make its facial features fiercer. There are also a few battle sequences that defy gravity but the rest of the effects work is stellar and Nakano reaches the apex of his career in his pyrotechnic tour de force destruction of Tokyo by Mechagodzilla II. It looks a like a 1970s version of Roland Emmerich's *Independence Day* with several city blocks worth of buildings exploding in tandem. Originally, Tokyo was scripted to be destroyed entirely, but the budget wouldn't allow so Nakano achieved more spectacle on a limited budget by filming the same buildings exploding from different and reverse angles. The new monster Titanosaurus was also originally scripted as two long-necked monsters called the Titans that became violent and enraged when their necks wreathed together, but was later simplified into one monster. The creature became a fan favorite in America long after the film's release and also represents the original series' most realistic looking suit since Gorosaurus. Its colorful, glistening hide truly looks alive in some sequences. Nakano said in a *G-Fan* interview the only type of dinosaur Toho had yet to create a kaiju out of was something akin to a plesiosaur. Being bipedal Titanosaurus is by no means a plesiosaur, but he is aquatic and has a long neck and fins. Even the film's climax centers more so on the battle between Titanosaurus and Godzilla than it does his mechanical doppelganger, and, refreshingly, Titanosaurus proves to be one of Godzilla's toughest opponents despite a lack of beam weapons.

Terror of Mechagodzilla tanked in Japan with an attendance even lower than that of *Godzilla vs. Megalon* with tastes in SPFX features tempering towards disaster films such as 1973's *Submersion of Japan*. Many scholars cite this as the reason for the end of the original series, but others think Mickey Mouse was the cause of the monster's retirement. As Toho had just struck a distribution deal with Disney, the next year's Champion Festival was comprised completely of Disney cartoons such as *Peter Pan* and there was no need for a new SPFX picture. By February of 1978, Tanaka and Toho were already planning Godzilla's return. Among the projects that never materialized were many iterations of what was initially called *Godzilla Resurrected* that eventually turned into *The Return of Godzilla*. In America in 1978 *Terror of Mechagodzilla* saw a very limited release in theaters as the badly butchered *The Terror of Godzilla* through Bob Conn Enterprises. Oddly, it simultaneously broadcast on TV (with a newly created five minute prologue) as *Terror of Mechagodzilla* at the behest of Henry G. Saperstein.

Final Word

One of the best films of the original series even if its charms weren't recognized at the time. If nothing else, it provided a graceful exit for Godzilla who, accompanied by Ifukube's poignant score, wades into the silver tinted surf in what ultimately became the final frame of the original series.

Trivia

- As with the previous film's Isao Zushi, Godzilla suit performer Toru Kawai had played the role before on *Zone Fighter*.

- Tomoko Ai auditioned for the role of Katsura in her MAC (Monster Attacking Crew) costume from *Ultraman Leo*, which she was currently appearing in as the character Matsuki.

- Katsumi Nimiamoto, the suit performer who played Titanosaurus, also played the titular hero in *Ultraman Leo* that same year and also played the triceratops in Tsuburaya Production's *The Last Dinosaur* (1977).

- The Mechagodzilla II suit is new apart from the head which is the same one from the previous film. That film's suit was used for the battle damaged Mechagodzilla that has its head ripped off by Godzilla.

- Jun Fukuda refused to direct this film after finally having had enough of the series. Before Ishiro Honda agreed to return rumors persist Yoshimitsu Banno was also asked to direct due to Tomoyuki Tanaka being pleased with his work on *Great Prophecies of Nostradamus* (1974).

- Apparently one early version of the script would have had Mechagodzilla II revert to his old trick of posing as Godzilla with fake skin according to *Toho Special Effects Movie Complete Works*.

- Originally the first scripted scene was to be the submarine Akatsuki on the surface prepping for its voyage to find Mechagodzilla's remains until Honda suggested the film start with the Akatsuki already in the water.

- The Super Geiger Detector used by Mugar is in fact Goro Ibuki's TV from *Godzilla vs. Megalon* (1973).

The Iron Super Man (1975)

Alternate Titles: *The Iron Giant* (Taiwan) *Robot of the Stars* (Germany) *Mazinger: The Robot of Stars* (Spain)
Release Date: July 21, 1975

Directed by: Kwok Ting-Hung & Hiroyuki Maekawa
Special Effects by: Unknown
Screenplay by: Kwok Ting-Hung, Koichi Takano & Kiyoshi Sizuki
Music by: Bobu Sakuma
Cast: Stephan Yip (Kai) Maggie Li Lin-lin (Su) Kim-Ming (The Professor) Paul Chun (Inspector)
Suit Performers: Uncredited

Academy Ratio, Color, 84 Minutes

Story
While crossing the Bermuda Triangle aboard an ocean liner with his parents, young boy Kai ends up the lone survivor when the ship is destroyed by a gigantic robot. As an adult, Kai joins the organization KSS (Kokusai Scientific Salvage) to battle the aliens that control the robots. Piloting the robot Mach Baron, he battles many of the alien robots that emerge from the ocean depths. When a member of KSS is kidnapped,

the team leader/professor trades himself to the enemy in return for their safety. There, the professor builds the aliens a new more powerful robot that defeats Mach Baron in combat. The professor manages to fake his death and escape the alien lair. Back on the outside, he tells Kai how to defeat the new super robot. Mach Baron defeats the machine and exterminates the rest of the aliens.

Background & Commentary

Since *Giant Robot* had *Voyage Into Space* (1970), and many Tsuburaya TV shows had their episodes edited into compilation movies like *Time of the Apes* (1987), many westerners have no doubt wondered why the popular Japanese TV series *Super Robot Red Baron* never had a similar compilation film. The truth is that it did (or rather its sequel series, *Super Robot Mach Baron*) in Taiwan as *The Iron Giant* produced by Chang Films, Co. Director Kwok Ting-Hung wrote his script based upon the Japanese TV series, and most sources imply that the film was produced with the cooperation and blessing of the Japanese creators. This is likely the case, for the finished film utilizes reproductions of the sets and uniforms from the TV series with lookalike Chinese actors. If one compares them back to back it is almost humorous.

It is implied this film was edited from episodes 1, 2, 9, 11 and 12 of *Super Robot Mach Baron*, which aired in Japan from 1974-1975. However, despite recreating elements of the series, certain elements of the storyline were changed, with the Robot Empire becoming space aliens (via dubbing, not reshot footage). In the series, the villain has some sort of ties to Germany and has white hair that stands on end due to radiation exposure and changes color when angry. For people unaware that this movie is in fact the compilation of a TV show, they are in for quite the wild ride as it features the aforementioned crazy haired villain, a floating balloon-bicycle riding inspector, a group of heroes in garish clothing that inhabit an underwater base, and the giant, red, toy-like Super Robot Mach Baron. However, most people are usually aware of what they are getting into with a film like this, and what they want (giant robots fighting other giant robots in wild fashion) is delivered in spades.

The film was released in Taiwan in 1975 on July 21st and only three days later it was seized by the film censors board. The film was next released in Germany as *Robot of the Stars* in 1976, and, supposedly, this version was dubbed with no script! Today, this German dub with English subtitles can be found on Amazon Prime under the title *The Iron Super Man*.

Final Word

As compilation movies go, this one is a little more nonsensical than the rest. But, on the other hand, if you are an English only speaking fan who wishes to see the as of yet un-subtitled *Super Robot Mach Baron*, this may be your only chance.

!!!!!!!!!!!!!!!!!!Bonus Review!!!!!!!!!!!!!!!!!!!!

The Super Inframan (1975)

Alternate Titles: *Inframan* (U.S.) *Chinese Superman* (China)
Release Date: August 1, 1975

Directed by: Hua Shan
Special Effects by: Michio Mikami
Screenplay by: Kuang Ni
Music by: Frankie Chan
Cast: Danny Lee (Rayma/Inframan) Terry Liu (Princess Dragon Ma) Hsieh Wang (Prof. Ying-Te) Man-Tzu Yuan (Mei-Mei) Wen-Wei Lin (Chu Ming) Bruce Le (Lu Xiao-long) Dana Shum (Witch Eye)
Suit Performers: Uncredited

Panavision, Color, 84 Minutes

Story

When the evil Princess Dragon Ma awakens from a 10 million year slumber deep under the earth, she immediately begins trying to conquer the Earth by destroying several major cities in China. At the Science Headquarters Professor Ying-Te, creates the android superman Inframan. Powered by solar energy, Iframan is in fact high ranking Science Headquarters member Rayma. As Inframan, Rayma destroys the various monsters dispatched by Princess Dragon Ma to conquer earth. Princess Dragon Ma then steals the professor's blueprints for Inframan to discover his weakness. Next she captures the professor's daughter in an effort to blackmail him into creating a new Inframan for her. At her headquarters inside Mount Devil, Rayma leads a rescue party to recapture the professor and his daughter. Inframan defeats Princess Dragon Ma, and the day is saved.

Background & Commentary

Though one would think this relatively big budget film was inspired by blockbusters like *Star Wars* and *Superman: The Movie*, it in fact predates them. As China's first ever superhero movie, *The Super Inframan* essentially amounts to "Super Sentai: The Movie." This should come as no surprise though, as both Tsuburaya's *Ultraman* and Toei's *Kamen Rider* franchises were both incredibly popular in China at this time and, as such, the titular character is essentially a combination of both heroes. The monster costumes and designs are appropriately of the quality of a Japanese Super Sentai series. The suits were even made by Ekisu Productions, which had constructed many of the suits for Toei's SPFX series. The production values in the form of the design and execution of the sets—miniature and otherwise—are spectacular though. And, scenes of the earth cracking apart are nearly on par with the earthquake scenes of *Superman: The Movie*. It's only in the form of the monster suits that the film falters. But, in some respects, they match the storyline, which swings back and forth between being legitimate, goofy fun, while at other times it seems not only to have been written for children, but by children as well.

The true extent of the film's zaniness is perhaps best summed up in a shot of Professor Ying-Te riding in a speedboat casually flanked on either side by two of the film's poorly executed monsters. Actor Hsieh Wang looks back and forth between the two rubber-suited monsters and one can only assume he's thinking to himself, "What has my career come to?" Perhaps even more ludicrous is the fact that Princess Dragon Ma has a speedboat with a red dragon mounted on it. The scene feels as though the viewer has just channel surfed onto the most bizarre James Bond movie of all time. Perhaps not coincidentally, it's around this point that *Super Infra-Man* truly becomes worth watching. The climax is classic Shaw Brothers only with garishly costumed monsters and super heroes duking it out outside of Princess Dragon Ma's skeletal fortress. Oddly, the entire climactic battle stays human sized and there are no giant monster battles to cap it all off and it's still quite entertaining.

The film saw a decent release in America from Joseph Brenner, who titled it *Inframan* and tried to capitalize on the success of *The Six Million Dollar Man* by giving it the tagline, "The Man Beyond Bionics!" Amazingly, the film seemed even to strike Roger Ebert's funny bone who gave the film a very kind three out of four stars and wrote in his review, "It's a classy, slick production by the Shaw Brothers, the Hong Kong kung fu kings. When they stop making movies like *Infra-Man*, a little light will go out of the world." Oddly enough, the film was never released theatrically in Japan.

Final Word
Though this film deservedly holds a soft spot for those who saw it at a young age, for anyone over the age of ten the film can be a hard pill to swallow.

Trivia

- The Shaw Brothers used a hot air balloon to promote the film in China.

- Supposedly the first time the Shaw Brothers ever storyboarded one of their films.

Legend of Dinosaurs and Monster Birds (1977)

Alternate Titles: *The "Legend of Dinosaurs"* (U.S.)

Release Date: April 29, 1977

Directed by: Junji Kurata
Special Effects by: Fuminori Obayashi
Screenplay by: Masaru Igami, Isao Matsumoto
& Ichiro Otsu
Music by: Masao Yagi
Cast: Tsunehiko Watase (Ashizawa) Nobiko Sawa (Akiko)
Tomoko Kiyoshima (Junko) Shotako Hayashi (Akira)
Fuyukichi Maki (Muku) **Suit Performers:** Uncredited

Panavision, Color, 91 Minutes

Story

An ice cave full of prehistoric eggs is rumored to lie beneath
the forests of Mt. Fuji which brings Tokyo geologist
Ashizawa to the area. During his investigation Ashizawa
meets an old flame, Akiko, a photographer scuba diving in
the lake with her friend Junko. It becomes apparent that
something is lurking in the waters after several mysterious
deaths occur including Junko's. Soon Lake Sai is besieged by
scientific equipment and investigators who have no luck in
finding the monster, alleged to be a plesiosaurus. In the ice
cave one of the eggs hatches a Rhamphorynchus that kills
two spelunkers. Determined to see the dinosaur in the lake
for himself, Ashizawa and Akiko go scuba diving. With no
luck finding the monster, they travel up an underwater
passage into the ice cave where they find the broken egg and
the grizzly remains of the two victims. Back on the surface,
the newly hatched Rhamphorynchus kills several of the
town's populace and then returns to the forest. Making their
way outside the cave, Ashizawa and Akiko are shocked to see
the Plesiosaur roaming the woods. Soon it battles the
returning Rhamphorynchus as Mt. Fuji begins to erupt. The
two dinosaurs, and presumably the lovers, are killed in the
massive eruption.

Background & Commentary

This film serves as a strange transitional bridge between old
school Japanese monster films and gory big-budget horror
like *Jaws*, which the film strives to become the Japanese

equivalent of but doesn't quite succeed. Toei Studios clearly had high hopes for the film though, as it was their highest budgeted feature ever up to that time. The direction, editing and music are all excellent with stylish shots and music in abundance. It is in the SPFX department that the film tragically fails. Had the high budget effects been executed properly the horror could have worked. For instance, at one point a giant claw bursts out of an egg providing a good scare. The problem is the claw is as big as the egg, an unforgivable error in scale. Severed limbs abound, a girl's half eaten torso (inexplicably still alive) grabs for a raft in the water, and a headless horse is found in the tree tops among other things, but the bloody horror is in stark contrast to the unconvincing dinosaur props. The full sized plesiosaur looks intimidating in the water, but on land the smaller suit is positively goofy looking. The Rhamphorynchus doesn't fare any better. While it has a decent design it is far too stiff to convince the audience that it is anything other than a lifeless prop. At one point there is also a close up of the plesiosaur blinking in bemusement at the flying Rhamphorynchus suggesting an attempt at humor that has no place in the gloomy film.

The film has one saving grace where all of the elements work together: the atmospheric raft scene in the middle of the movie. Set in a secluded foggy spot of the lake, the tension mounts as the plesiosaur watches Junko from a distance. In a famous shot it bursts from the water and bites her leg, dragging her high into the air before dropping her back into the water, deliberately toying with its prey. After a few more frightening instances of the monster tormenting Junko (some versions shortened this sequence), the scene slowly transitions to minutes later when Junko's fate is confirmed by a horrified Akiko. The only thing detracting from the sequence is that the audience had already seen a clear shot of the monster earlier where its flaws were not obscured by the fog. After this the film manages a few more good scares but its best scene is behind it. Even Kurata's artful direction grows a little thin as the film plods towards the obligatory monster vs. monster climax. Between the out of place looking Plesiosaur and the stiff Rhamphorynchus, there isn't much to recommend in what should have been a stand out sequence.

The last scene is in an interminably long montage of the lovers reaching for one another across a chasm during the eruption of Mt. Fuji, the scene's length dictated by the Japanese love ballad playing on the soundtrack. As the song ends and the two lover's hands finally meet, the audience can only speculate their fate is bittersweet as they are surrounded by rivers of lava.

Though Toei had hoped that this film would see distribution in 40 countries (including America) it was a failure at the Japanese box office and instead went straight to U.S. television in 1983. Soon after it was released uncut in all its gory glory to home video in 1987 via King Features Entertainment's "Just For Kids!" label traumatizing a whole generation of unsuspecting children.

Final Word

As a horror picture this movie had potential to be a classic, but the dinosaur props maul the movie just as badly as they do their on-screen victims.

Trivia

- Final dai-kaiju eiga project of Fuminori Ohashi.

- Before this, Toei had teamed with Amicus Films in England to produce *Kongorilla*, a rip-off of the looming 1976 *King Kong* remake before they were stopped by Dino DeLaurentiis's lawyers. Toei also toyed with making another monster film called *Devil Manta*. Similar to *Dogora, the Space Monster*, a giant alien stingray descends upon earth from "the void" in outer space to wreak havoc. Upon the release of *Star Wars* in 1977, *Devil Manta* was dropped in favor of *Message from Space* (1978).

- The plesiosaur was brought to life with full scale head, neck, fin and tail props created by Fuminori Ohashi, who created the first Godzilla suit. There was also a plesiosaur suit used for the land scenes and a small plesiosaur doll used for one of the final shots where it perishes in the lava. Similarly, a scale beak and claws were built for the Rhamphorynchus along with a full body marionette to match the plesiosaur for their battle scenes.

- Around this same time, Toho Studios had teamed with Hammer Studios in England to produce *Nessie*, a film about a giant plesiosaur going on a rampage. Some speculate Toei pushed *Legend of Dinosaurs and Monster Birds* into production to compete with Toho. They needn't have worried as production on *Nessie* collapsed before filming began, though Teruyoshi Nakano had created a full scale plesiosaur prop for filming.

- Some people mistakenly believe the plesiosaur prop was later used in Tsuburaya's TV series, *Dinosaur Task Force Koseidon*. Sometimes images of the two plesiosaur props from the aforementioned TV series pop up on U.S. VHS box art for *The Legend of Dinosaurs*.

!!!!!!!!!!!!!!!!!!!Bonus Review!!!!!!!!!!!!!!!!!!!!

Mighty Peking Man (1977)

Alternate Titles: *King of the Orangutans* (China) *Goliathon* (U.S.)
Release Date: August 11, 1977

Directed by: Ho Meng-hua
Special Effects by: Sadamasa Arikawa
Screenplay by: Kuang Ni
Music by: Frankie Chan
Cast: Evelyn Kraft (Samantha) Danny Lee (Johnny Feng) Hsiao Yao (Huang) Ku Feng (Lu Tien) Lin Wei-tu (David Chen) **Suit Performers:** Uncredited

Panavision, Color, 90 Minutes

Story
A crew of Chinese anthropologists journey into the Himalayan Mountains in hopes of finding a legendary giant

known as the Mighty Peking Man. When the party of explorers abandons one of their own, Johnny Feng, the lone anthropologist ends up discovering the giant ape and also a jungle girl raised by the monster named Samantha. As Johnny and Samantha fall in love, Johnny convinces her and her giant pet to travel with him to civilization. Things take a turn for the worse when Johnny's partners begin exploiting Mighty Peking Man, who grows angry and escapes in Hong Kong. Samantha and Johnny do their best to save the giant ape, who has climbed atop a skyscraper, but it is to no avail and the beast is pummeled with bullets, some of which also hit Samantha. Mighty Peking Man falls to his death as Johnny scoops up an unconscious Samantha in his arms, her fate uncertain.

Background & Commentary

If *Legend of Dinosaurs and Monster Birds* was a subtle answer to *Jaws*, then *Mighty Peking Man* is a blatant attempt to cash in on Dino De Laurentiis's *King Kong*. The film wasn't alone as its brethren included the Korean made *A*P*E* and *Queen Kong*. Produced by Chinese powerhouse Shaw Brothers Studios, the film was shot over the course of one year on a budget of $6 million with on location filming taking place in both Hong Kong and Mysore, India (for some of the jungle sequences). The SPFX were handled by none other than the retired Toho veteran Sadamasa Arikawa with some help from Koichi Kawakita. In the lead is Danny Lee (not surprisingly a vet of many Kung Fu films whom the Shaw Brothers hoped at one time could replace Bruce Lee) while the true star of the film, the jungle girl Samantha, was played by Swiss sex symbol Evelyn Kraft.

The finished film is both undeniably campy and also irresistibly fun as the story is not just a remake of *King Kong*, but Tarzan as well in the form of jungle girl Samantha who falls in love with a man from modern civilization. In this sense, the human storyline, silly though it may be just like the rest of the film, has a certain endearing quality to it. And for those that want to read something deeper into the story it presents a well done take on the greed of civilized life versus an innocent rural existence. If nothing else, Samantha provides eye candy for the target male audience in between SPFX scenes. As for Mighty Peking Man, he is more Yeti than giant ape, and has a more humanoid face than King Kong which gives him a somewhat creepy countenance despite his sometimes sympathetic portrayal. Also strange is the monster's roar, which at times sounds more like a shrieking woman. Overall the SPFX scenes are abundant, and the miniature work when Mighty Peking Man attacks Hong Kong is quite expansive, even if Arikawa's miniature work hadn't progressed much in the past six years. It would seem the Shaw Brothers were determined to eclipse the climax of De Laurentiis's film, and though they obviously don't succeed on a technical level, the titular monster's death is quite spectacular. The Mighty Peking Man is brought down not only by bullets, but also a massive explosion. As such his flaming body plummets off of the roof of the skyscraper and crashes spectacularly into another building below. Sadly, it's never clear whether Samantha is unconscious or dead when the film ends.

The film was released in the U.S., first as *Goliathon* in 1980, and then under its rightful name by Quentin Tarantino's Rolling Thunder Pictures in 1999. Roger Ebert even gave the film a favorable review though, not surprisingly, it tanked at the box-office.

Final Word
Among all the 1976 inspired *King Kong* rip-offs, *Mighty Peking Man* is easily the best.

Trivia

- There is a rumor that Teruyoshi Nakano was supposed to handle the SPFX for the film but his contract ran out so he was replaced by Sadamasa Arikawa.

The Last Dinosaur (1977)

Japanese Title: *Polar Probe Ship Polar Borer*
Release Date: September 10, 1977

Directed by: Tom Kotani & Alex Grasshoff
Special Effects by: Kazuo Sagawa
Screenplay by: William Overguard
Music by: Maury Laws
Cast: Richard Boone (Mason Thrust) Joan Van Ark (Frankie) Steven Keats (Chuck) Luther Rackley (Bunta) Tetsu Nakamura (Dr. Kawamoto) Masumi Sekiya (Hazel) William Ross (Expedition Captain) **Suit Performers:** Toru Kawai (Tyrannosaurus) Katsumi Nimiamoto/Uncredited (Triceratops)

Widescreen, Color, 106 Minutes

Story

Wealthy industrialist Mason Thrust is the head of a large company which has discovered an oasis in the Arctic while drilling for oil there. The oasis is said to be home to a large T-Rex, which big game hunter Thrust can't resist seeing despite claiming he has no plans to kill the beast. Boarding the Polar Borer with female photographer Frankie, scientist Dr. Kawamoto, African tracker Bunta, and the lone survivor of the last mission, Chuck, Thrust journeys to the oasis. There he finds not only the T-Rex, which absconds with the Polar Borer, but several other prehistoric monsters. Stranded there for months, Mason and the others band together to battle not only the T-Rex, but prehistoric cavemen as well. When Chuck manages to recover the Polar Borer he and Frankie return to civilization, while Thrust refuses and decides to stay behind until he has killed the gigantic dinosaur of his obsession.

Background & Commentary

This co-production between Tsuburaya Productions and Rankin/Bass was originally meant to be a theatrical feature in America, that is, until the first viewing of the final product. Instead it went straight to U.S. television on February 11, 1977. This was a wise choice as the film was itself rendered a dinosaur in the aftermath of big-budget 1970s hits such as *Jaws* (1975), *King Kong* (1976) and *Star Wars* (1977). The film was considered good enough to go to theaters in Japan, but like its contemporary *Legend of Dinosaurs and Monster Birds*, the film was a flop.

The film is mainly notorious for its casting of an inebriated Richard Boone in the lead. The fact that Boone is either drunk or hungover in many of his scenes is painfully obvious for those wanting to take the film serious, while those watching it for laughs can find much to delight in. Boone also phones in the exposition scenes so badly that it's obvious he must be reading his lines off-screen somewhere. Humorously, the only times that Boone sounds genuine is when he's angry or yelling. Joining Boone in the prehistoric setting is future star of the *Dallas* spin-off *Knott's Landing*, Joan Van Ark. In a 2010 *G-Fan* interview with Brett Homenick, Van Ark reminisced that the on-location shooting was dreadful due to the weather, though she enjoyed working with Boone even if he was inebriated. The two stars' chemistry together is fairly good and Van Ark's love triangle with Boone and Steven Keats is more compelling than love triangles presented in similar films.

As for the production values the direction is so-so, but the music score by Maury Laws is top notch. The film also has a title song not unlike one from the James Bond series written by Jules Bass and sung by Nancy Wilson that actually manages to get the film's title in the lyrics making it unintentionally hilarious, if not also a little catchy. As for the all-important SPFX scenes, the suitmation dinosaurs are nearly on par with past creatures such as Gorosaurus in *King Kong Escapes* (1967) and Titanosaurus from *Terror of Mechagodzilla* (1975). Coincidentally, Katsumi Nimiamoto, who played Titanosaurus in the aforementioned film, here spars as a triceratops with the T-Rex, played by that film's Godzilla performer, Toru Kawai. The battle, filmed in a foggy boneyard, is easily the film's highlight and has a surreal quality to it. Other prehistoric creatures glimpsed include a type of rhino, a giant turtle, and a pterodactyl. The film's "jungle" oasis seems to have been inspired by the 1975 *The Land That Time Forgot* and, like that film, the miniature prehistoric sets don't match up with the actual on location filming locales (Kamikochi, Nagano, in Japan to be exact).

Final Word

For those wanting a quality dinosaur picture the film is a disappointment, but for lovers of unintentionally hilarious 1970s cinema this film is a gold mine.

Trivia

- Candice Bergen was the original choice for Frankie because of her love of photography.

- The T-Rex suit was immediately reused in Tsuburaya Productions TV series *Dinosaur War Aizenborg* the same year as the main villain Ururu, and after that played Tyrannosaurus Jackie in 1978's *Dinosaur Task Force Koseidon*.

- Rankin/Bass had hoped that the dinosaurs could be stop-motion animated initially before suitmation was used instead.

- The Tyrannosaurus emits a bevy of different monster roars including Gaira's from *War of the Gargantuas* and a Gamera-like shriek. One of his roars was later adapted as Godzilla's roar in the 1990s.

- Several members of *Legend of Dinosaurs and Monster Birds* English dub cast have roles in this film.

The War in Space (1977)

Japanese Title: *The Great Planet War*
Release Date: December 17, 1977

Directed by: Jun Fukuda
Special Effects by: Teruyoshi Nakano
Screenplay by: Shuichi Nagahara & Ryuzo Nakanishi
Music by: Toshiaki Tsushima
Cast: Kensaku Morita (Miyoshi) Yuko Asano (June) Ryo Ikebe (Prof. Takigawa) Masaya Oki (Reisuke) Hiroshi

Miyauchi (Morrei) David Perin (Jimmy) Goro Mutsumi (Hell Commander) Akihiko Hirata (Defense Forces Commander) **Suit Performers:** Mammoth Suzuki (Space Beastman)

Panavision, Color, 87 Minutes

Story

When former fighter pilot Miyoshi returns to Japan, he finds not only that his old sweetheart June is engaged to his best friend Reisuke, but also that hostile aliens from Venus are planning on conquering Earth. As the alien ships destroy cities across the world, Miyoshi and Reisuke form a crew with June's father, Professor Takigawa, who has built a super space ship called the Gohten, and takes the ship to Venus to fight the aliens. Along the way, June is kidnaped by the Hell Commander. Upon arriving on Venus, Miyoshi rescues June from the aliens' main ship, a gigantic galleon, while Reisuke fights the aliens from the air but is killed in the process. The Gohten and the galleon engage in a spectacular aerial battle, but it is apparent to Professor Takigawa that only his secret super weapon can destroy the enemy ship. Takigawa bids his daughter farewell and then flies the superweapon into the galleon, destroying it and also the planet Venus itself, while Miyoshi, June and the surviving crew escape in the Gohten.

Background & Commentary

The War in Space is both a throwback to Toho's alien invader epics of the late 1950s and, at the same time, an offshoot of *Star Wars*, the success of which Tomoyuki Tanaka had witnessed firsthand while he was visiting Hawaii with Teruyoshi Nakano. Like many other studios across the world, Tanaka quickly rushed his own version of *Star Wars* into production hoping that he could beat the real thing to Japan. However, unlike an outer space fantasy like *Star Wars*, Tanaka wanted his film to be an outer space remake of the classic *Atragon* (1963). This wasn't the only Toho classic the film was meant to pay homage to, as it was also conceived of initially as *Battle in Outer Space 2*, a direct sequel to the 1958 film of the same name, though this concept was eventually dropped.

Just as with *Atragon*, production was extremely rushed beginning in the fall and just barely making the crank-in to become the New Year's Blockbuster. With a ¥500,000,000 budget, most of the effects work is quite good, though sadly outdated and outclassed when compared to its more expensive American contemporary. And, in their haste, Toho raided their classic library of films to portray the city destruction scenes, utilizing clips from relatively recent films like *Submersion of Japan* (1973) and *Conflagration* (1975) and even ones as old as *The Last War* (1961) and *Battle in Outer Space* (1959). The models for the Gohten and the alien galleon, called the Daimakan, are pleasing to the eye, especially the Daimakan which was innovative for a spaceship (impractical though it may be). The Gohten looks similar to the one from *Atragon* and still somewhat resembles an ocean going vessel (though this idea was also inspired by the popular anime *Space Battleship Yamato* more so than *Atragon*). The real stars of the movie are the sets, miniature and otherwise. For Venus, Nakano creates a red-rocked world spewing with sulfurous vapors. The sequence of the Gohten entering the planet's stormy atmosphere is easily a main highlight of the film. Also fantastic is the interior set of the Daimakan. It's somewhat reminiscent of the ancient yet advanced Mu Empire from *Atragon*, and also has a golden serpent near the Hell Commander's throne. The film is also somewhat notorious for the inclusion of an evil Chewbacca rip-off with horns called the Space Beastman. The suit is overall poor and would have looked more at home on *Sesame Street*, though the beast's axe which can shoot a laser is somewhat interesting.

Once again Tanaka turned to director Jun Fukuda to direct his new SPFX film, his last work having been 1974's *ESPY* for Toho about psychic spies. For this, which ended up being his final feature film, Fukuda delivers another fast-paced, fun-filled adventure that never lets up. Under his direction are mostly new faces, though appropriately Ryo Ikebe, the lead in both *Gorath* and *Battle in Outer Space*, returns to play a prominent role and Akihiko Hirata has a small part as an Earth Defense Force Commander. Working with Fukuda yet again as another alien commander is Goro

Mutsumi, who had played a similar part in both of his Mechagodzilla films. Though his screen time is relatively short, he adds a much needed villainous weight to the proceedings. As for the music, though it is certainly dated by this point, for those who enjoy 1970s cinema it's quite enjoyable. Though the film likely wasn't the huge hit Toho was looking for it did manage to gross ¥300 million more than it cost to make and also beat *Star Wars* to Japanese theaters.

Final Word

Though most of the effects work is top notch, it is still badly marred by comparison to the film which inspired its inception: *Star Wars*. Aside from that, *The War in Space* is an undeniably fun romp and a fitting farewell to Toho's "old school" of SPFX.

Trivia

- In interviews Teruyoshi Nakano claims he was already hoping to do an outer space epic before he had even seen *Star Wars*.

- Some fans theorize this film is a sequel to *Gorath* (1961) as the Tera Station from that film is present, and the moon (destroyed in *Gorath*) is never glimpsed or mentioned in the film.

- Initially Sakyo Komatsu, the author of *Submersion of Japan,* was approached to come up with a space-fantasy. When he proved too slow, Tanaka came up with the idea of remaking *Atragon*. Komatsu's concept eventually turned into *Sayonara Jupiter* (1984).

- Daimakan best translates into English as "Giant Demon Warship" according to Toho Kingdom.

- Some sources claimed that the Ghoten was the redressed Alpha from 1969's *Latitude Zero*. However, Nakano refutes this.

Godzilla (1978)

Alternate Titles: "Cozzilla"
Release Date: 1978

Directed by: Luigi Cozzi, Terry Morse & Ishiro Honda
Special Effects by: Eiji Tsuburaya
& Armando Valcauda (colorization)
Screenplay by: Terry Morse, Takeo Murata, Shigeru Kayama, Ishiro Honda & Luigi Cozzi
Music by: Akira Ifukube & Vince Tempera (as Magnetic System)
Cast: Raymond Burr (Steve Martin) Akira Takarada (Ogata) Momoko Koichi (Emiko) Akihiko Hirata (Dr. Serizawa) Takashi Shimura (Dr. Yamane) **Suit Performers:** Haruo Nakajima/Katsumi Tezuka (Godzilla)

Academy Ratio, Spectrorama 70, 89 minutes

Story

Reporter Steve Martin is in route to Tokyo, unaware that below him a ship has been mysteriously sunk. Martin, who is in Japan to visit an old college friend Serizawa, immediately gets in on the investigation and joins a trip to Oto Island where he witnesses the monster Godzilla first hand. He also witnesses the monster's rampages through Tokyo and barely survives the second encounter as one of the wounded amidst the wreckage. Emiko Yamane tells Steve of his friend Serizawa's powerful new invention the Oxygen Destroyer and Steve persuades Emiko to convince Serizawa to use it on Godzilla. Serizawa agrees to use his weapon to kill the monster in Tokyo Bay, but he also takes his own life in the process.

Background & Commentary

In late 1976, fledgling director Luigi Cozzi acquired from Toho Studios the rights to rerelease *Godzilla* in Italy. The only hang-up was they couldn't offer him the original, uncut Japanese version as he wished, only 1956's *Godzilla, King of the Monsters!* To make matters worse, Cozzi's distributers refused to release the film in black and white, and demanded

Cozzi to colorize it! To think of this film in the same vein as the well done colorized 1933 *King Kong* by Ted Turner would be a mistake, as the same painstaking process was not used on Cozzi's *Godzilla*. This isn't Cozzi's fault, as he didn't wish to colorize the film in the first place, and then only had three months to do so. As such, each scene is color tinted with different colors in different spots of the frame which works well in still shots, particularly one of Oto Island with blue waters and a sandy beach. Scenes with movement, however, are crudely done as the color filter moves awkwardly with the camera. On the other hand, scenes with Godzilla attacking Tokyo are actually intriguing to look at, with interesting tints given to the flames and the sky which add to the apocalyptic feel. Godzilla's ray is also well animated whenever he fires it.

As for the newly added footage, aside from the prologue of the bombing of Hiroshima, it is inserted a little too haphazardly. For instance, in the scene where Godzilla surfaces next to a cruise ship, which he leaves be in the original, new footage is forced in of people boarding life boats—in daylight no less. In an effort to "modernize" the film for 1978, Cozzi also removed many scenes of Tsuburaya's miniature planes and vehicles. The scene where jet fighters attack Godzilla in Tokyo Bay is beefed up considerably with the planes now dropping bombs on Godzilla, and real crashing airplane footage is used instead of the original miniatures. Perhaps the strangest addition occurs when Ogata and Serizawa dive to the bottom of Tokyo Bay, where they witness a shark battling an octopus courtesy of *The Beast from 20,000 Fathoms* (1953). Though creepy due to the sound effects, this new scene adds nothing to the proceedings. And when Godzilla surfaces one final time in his death throes, he is accosted by a fleet of Navy destroyers in Tokyo Bay. Finally, for those no doubt wondering about the new score, there isn't any such thing. Verta added only one new composition, the entirety of which plays exclusively (and somewhat awkwardly) over the Hiroshima prologue.

Toho approved of the colorization and the reedits on the condition that seven years later Cozzi turn over the negatives to them. The film was released as part of a Sci-fi film festival in Italy, and according to Cozzi did moderately well, though other sources claim that it was a flop. The film has never seen any type of VHS or DVD release and is something of a lost film. The only "print" many fans have ever seen is only courtesy of a VHS taping of an old TV broadcast of the film from Italy.

Final Word
Though interesting as a curiosity, the new footage adds nothing to the film, and *Godzilla* is a film meant for black and white.

Trivia

- The film's poster became the debut cover of *Fangoria* #1 in 1979.

- Verta's score was released on a 45 record.

- Though the film is often called "Cozzilla", *Godzilla* is still the official title.

!!!!!!!!!!!!!!!!!!!*Bonus Review!!!!!!!!!!!!!!!!!!!!*

Message from Space (1978)

Release Date: April 29, 1978

Directed by: Kenji Fukasaku
Special Effects by: Nobuo Yajima
Screenplay by: Hiro Matsuda
Music by: Kenichiro Morioka
Cast: Vic Moro (General Garuda) Hiroyuki Sanada (Shiro) Phillip Casnoff (Aaron) Peggy Lee Brennan (Meia) Etsuko Shihomi (Emeralida) Makoto Sato (Urocco) Masazumi Okabe (Jack) Sonny Chiba (Prince Hans) Mikio Narita (Rockseia XII) Tetsuro Tamba (Noguchi) Isamu Shimizu (Beba-2)

VistaVision, Color, 105 Minutes

Story

When the planet Jillucia is conquered by the evil Gavanas Empire, they turn the celestial body into a military fortress. The people of Jillucia send out magical Liabe Seeds to find eight brave warriors to free their planet of the Gavanas. As Princess Emeralida, and the warrior Urocco, of Jillucia follow the seeds through space they find "Rough Rider" pilots Shiro and Aaron, adventurer Meia, the disillusioned General Garuda, his robot servant Beba-2, and the skilled swordsman Prince Han among others. The eight warriors siege the Gavanas Empire as Jillucia approaches Earth. Prince Han fights a duel with the Gavanas ruler, Rockseia XII, and kills him as Jillucia detonates in an explosion. Earth offers the surviving Jillucians solace on Earth, but they decline, instead setting out to find a new planet to call their own.

Background & Commentary

As the second "Star Wars rip-off" to come out of Japan after Toho's *The War in Space*, it's hard to say which one is better. Effects wise, Toei's *Message from Space* just might be the winner, but storyline wise, the film's adaptation of *Nanso Satomi Hakkenden* in space just doesn't work, and unlike *The War in Space*, *Message from Space* wears out its welcome well before the credits begin to roll. There are far more nods to *Star Wars* in this film than Toho's, with several scenes early on mirroring shots from the George Lucas film a little too closely. However, oddly enough, in other ways this film actually pre-dates elements from *Return of the Jedi* (1983). For instance, the final duel between Prince Han and Rockseia XII takes place inside the observatory in this film's version of the Deathstar that is similar to Luke and Vader's final duel in *Return of the Jedi*. Also, the spacecraft must fly inside the planet to destroy it ala the second Deathstar from the aforementioned film. On top of that, this film also has a swell asteroid chase in it pre-dating *Empire Strikes Back* (1980). Furthermore, the planet of Jillucia being converted into a weapon itself even foreshadowed the Starkiller base from *The Force Awakens* (2015).

Though the effects work shines pretty bright compared to *The War in Space*, other elements of the film make it far too silly to be taken remotely seriously. Eisei Amamoto dons drag once again as a character that is essentially an alien version Granny from *The Lost World of Sinbad* (1963). And, one has to feel sorry for Sonny Chiba, who looks absurd in his horned costume as Prince Han—who barely figures into the film and arrives late in the game. On the other hand, perhaps the film's greatest scene (depending on one's tastes) occurs when Chiba chases around Amamoto who rides off in his skeletal motorized wheelchair. Though the ending of the film was fantastic, sadly it had one SPFX scene that had to be cut. In it, after the battle seems won, a giant flaming claw piloted by Amamoto's character gives chase to the main characters. But, the scene proved so difficult during filming not enough usable takes were available to use the sequence.

Before this film got off the ground, Toei had been planning a monster from space film called *Devil Manta* until the success of *Star Wars* inspired them to make their own space opera. The film initially started out as *The Planet Fortress* and was budgeted at a very healthy $6 million—which in fact made it the highest budgeted Japanese feature of all time. Happily, Toei's gamble paid off as the film was a success at the Japanese box office and even secured a U.S. theatrical run that same year where it was a moderate success—though western critics were mostly unkind to it.

Final Word

Though its effects work is slightly superior, *Message from Space's* wonky storyline keeps it from eclipsing its competitor from Toho.

Trivia

- In addition to *Street Fighter's* Sonny Chiba, this film also has *Sister Streetfighter's* Etsuko Shihomi in a prominent lead role.

- Both this film and Toho's *The War in Space* feature a space craft based off of a sailing ship.

- Was followed by a TV series, *Message from Space: Galactic Battle.*

The Bermuda Depths (1978)

Japanese Title: *Mystery of Bermuda*
Release Date: July 20, 1979

Directed by: Tom Kotani
Special Effects by: Kazuo Sagawa
Screenplay by: William Overguard
Music by: Maury Laws
Cast: Connie Selleca (Jennie Haniver) Leigh McCloskey (Magnus) Carl Weathers (Eric) Burl Ives (Dr. Paulus)

Spherical Panavision, Color, 95 Minutes

Story
A young boy named Magnus lives with his father who is studying giant sea life in Bermuda. Magnus befriends a girl named Jennie and together the two raise a sea turtle. One day Jennie slips off into the sea and Magnus's father is killed in an accident. Years later, Magnus returns home as a grown man and tries to unravel the traumatic memories of his childhood. He also reunites with Jennie—who is rumored to be an immortal sea siren who sold her soul for eternal youth—while at the same time trailing a giant turtle at sea with old friends of his father's, Eric and Dr. Paulus. Jennie pleads with Magnus to stop trailing the beast, and when he doesn't relent the giant turtle kills both Eric and Dr. Paulus, though Jennie saves Magnus from the depths. A distraught Magnus leaves Bermuda and vows to never return.

Background & Commentary
With both parties satisfied with the results of *The Last Dinosaur*, in 1977 Rankin/Bass and Tsuburaya begat yet another fantasy film together. The new film, it could be argued, ups the American star factor as it features Leigh McCloskey (1980's *Inferno*), Carl Weathers (Apollo Creed

from the *Rocky* films), Connie Selleca (TV's *Flying High* and *Captain America II: Death Too Soon*) and veteran character actor Burl Ives, while at the same time reducing the amount of SPFX work. For while *The Last Dinosaur* in fact featured multiple dinos, *The Bermuda Depths* features a lone giant turtle which shows up about as much as the shark in *Jaws.* As such, the film is more commendable for the mysterious relationship between Jennie Haniver (an immortal sea siren) and Magnus than it is the monster.

This is also one of the film's main problems: it sets up a bevy of intriguing questions which lack answers. For instance, the giant turtle is at one moment implied to be a prehistoric survivor and later it is hinted at that it was a regular sea turtle hatched by Jennie and Magnus. The giant turtle doesn't get a full on reveal until an hour in when it glides spectrally through the water over the camera's POV. As for the inevitable comparison to Gamera, Tsuburaya Production's unnamed giant turtle undeniably has more of a creep factor to it. For one, it is much more realistic than Gamera, and second, it emits whale songs. Furthermore, the relationship between it and Jennie is almost similar to Mothra and the Shobijin. Scenes on the high seas tracking the turtle are pathetically reminiscent of similar scenes from *Orca* and *Jaws* (the miniature boat is badly done and sticks out like a sore thumb). And, as stated earlier, like "Bruce" the shark in *Jaws*, the giant turtle is used very sparingly and doesn't get many clear shots until the climax. The film—which has relatively good production values including a real helicopter—isn't effectively sunk until the scene where the giant turtle rears its head out of the water and destroys the hovering miniature chopper. The scene is made all the worse by Burl Ives' terrible death scene as the beloved actor screams at the camera as though he is a novice performer. Actually, Ives is effectively wasted in his role for the duration of the film, and like Richard Boone before him in *The Last Dinosaur* appears to be quite bored throughout the proceedings.

One area where the film does get to excel though are the underwater SPFX shots. A shot of Jennie sinking into the blue depths during her origin story flashback is particularly well done. Also haunting is the scene where the turtle drags Eric's lifeless body into the titular depths. The on location shots of Bermuda are also spectacular, and the film opens to wonderful underwater photography and the well done song "Jennie" with lyrics by Jules Bass. Connie Selleca and the mystery regarding her and Magnus's childhood friendship is likewise quite stimulating even if it never is resolved or adequately explained. The climax does little to enhance the story though, so much so that one sits through the epilogue waiting for a surprise twist at the last moment to make it all worthwhile. It never comes, and instead something that the audience has suspected all along—that the giant turtle is the same one from Magnus's childhood—is confirmed as though it warrants itself as some sort of payoff. The film aired on January 27, 1978 on ABC and in Japan was released to theaters the next year.

Final Word
Though the production values are commendable, due to the story's many carelessly unanswered questions it can only be labeled a curious dud for anyone who watches the film for the first time as an adult. That being said, many children who caught it on television throughout the 1980s understandably remain quite enamored with it.

Gamera Super Monster (1980)

Japanese Title: *Space Monster Gamera*
Release Date: March 20, 1980

Directed by: Noriaki Yuasa
Special Effects by: Kazufumi Fuji, Yuzo Kaneko & Noriaki Yuasa
Screenplay by: Niisan Takahashi
Music by: Shunsuke Kikuchi
Cast: Mach Fumiake (Kilara) Koichi Maeda (Keiichi) Keiko Kudo (Giruge) Yaeko Kojima (Marsha) Yoko Komatsu (Mitan)

Widescreen, Daieicolor, 92 Minutes

Story

Young boy Keiichi is a huge Gamera fan, and while visiting a pet shop, the store's kindly owner Kilara gives him a free pet turtle. Unbeknownst to Keiichi, Kilara is actually a refuge from outer space that has made Earth her home along with her two friends Marsha and Mitan. Soon the evil space pirate Zanon arrives in orbit to threaten the planet and destroy the space women. He sends his henchwoman, Giruge, to find the girls while his monster Gyaos ravishes Japan. At home, Keiichi's mother convinces him the turtle would be better off in the river, so he sets him free in hopes he will return as Gamera. His wish seemingly comes true as Gamera soon appears and defeats Gyaos, and afterwards the monsters Zigra, Viras and Jiger. Realizing he can't beat Gamera, Zanon implants a control device onto Gamera and then uses him to destroy cities until Kilara disables it. Flying to the planet where the monsters are being kept, Gamera battles and kills the knife-monster Guiron. Arriving back on Earth, Gamera fights the last monster, Barugon, and is victorious. After a fight with Kilara, Giruge realizes the error of her ways and sides with Keiichi and the space women, but is killed soon after by Zanon. Gamera flies into space colliding with Zanon's ship ending the threat but sacrificing himself in the process.

Background & Commentary

"The Strangest in the universe! Gamera returns again! Entertaining! Spectacular! A fantasy of space!" proclaimed a trade ad for the film. Of all the exclamations it touted, only the first two were true. Although some call this the *Destroy All Monsters* of the Gamera films, it's really more like *All Monsters Attack* as its SPFX scenes are almost all stock footage.

Like a TV series finale comprised of best of clips, *Gamera Super Monster* features all of the giant turtle's previous foes and battles, and the results are decidedly strange. The most bizarre parts of the film concern Kilara (played by female pro-wrestler Mach Fumiake) and her pals who transform into superhero-like space costumes with a few strange hand gestures. The trio can accomplish almost anything, from flying to random teleportation, with little regard to logic, much like children making up the rules of the game as they go along. Surprisingly the flying scenes are quite well done when compared with the other new effects. The film's worst shot occurs when Kilara's van turns into a ball of light and takes flight on the freeway. As for the stock footage battles, which comprise most of the film, they are never the less still interesting to watch, and some are accompanied by newly scored music. The film actually contains one scene that is literally stock footage of stock footage. *Gamera vs. Viras* had utilized a black and white city destruction scene from the original *Gamera* and it reappears in this film when Gamera is being controlled by the aliens. Gamera's new scenes in the film consist only of an upper torso prop flying through the air, as the original suit and accompanying props were destroyed by angry Daiei staff workers when the studio went bankrupt in 1971. However, the filmmakers found the time to construct some Gamera legs (he is seen only from the waist down) to knock over an imitation Godzilla poster during a city destruction scene! The Zanon Pirate ship is well done, however, it is a near exact copy of a Star Destroyer from 1977's *Star Wars*. The first shot of the ship is also exactly like the first scene in *Star Wars* with the model flying endlessly overhead. Considering Daiei hoped this film could get them out of bankruptcy, it's surprising they would so carelessly risk a lawsuit.

It is implied that this film is actually not part of the previous Gamera continuity and his origin in the story is never clear (it's hinted he's a fictional movie monster ala *Godzilla's Revenge*). Perhaps this is for the best, as Gamera's end is undignified to say the least. Although Gamera had been spurting green blood in abundance for years, ironically the giant turtle's death more or less happens off-screen. While the audience waits in anticipation as Gamera flies towards the Zanon Pirate ship, the collision results in little more than a flash of light that lasts nary a second. This scene could've been the film's saving grace had it been executed more touchingly. Even director Yuasa said of this film, "I grieved for my son Gamera—it was a very strange fate."

Final Word

It is significant only as the last traditionally made kaiju film and the death of Gamera both figuratively and literally. Perhaps the real tragedy is that the film was never viewed by *Mystery Science Theater 3000*, it's the one place where it had a lot of potential.

Trivia

- Reiko Tajima (*Godzilla vs. Mechagodzilla*) is rumored to have a cameo in this film.

- The idea to kill Gamera was that of Yuasa's, who felt there would be no further Gamera films after this.

- After this film Yuasa went on to direct episodes of Tsuburaya Productions' then current Ultra series *Ultraman 80*.

- This film was semi adapted into the 1995 video game *Gamera: The Time Adventure* for the Playdia system.

!!!!!!!!!!!!!!!!!!!Bonus Review!!!!!!!!!!!!!!!!!!!!

Deathquake (1980)

Japanese Title: *Magnitude 7.9/Earthquake Archipelago*
Release Date: August 30, 1980

Directed by: Kenjiro Omori
Special Effects by: Teruyoshi Nakano
Screenplay by: Kaneto Shindo
Music by: Toshiaki Tsushima
Cast: Hiroshi Katsuno (Koichi Kawazu) Toshiyuki Nagashima (Masayuki Hashizume) Yumi Takigawa (Tomiko Ashida) Kayo Matsuo (Yuko Kawazu)

Widescreen, Color, 126 Minutes

Story

Young and upcoming geologist Kawazu predicts that an earthquake will strike Tokyo within thirty days due to recent activity at Mt. Mihara. Kawazu's colleagues at the Earthquake Prevention Center are outraged at his bold claims and suppress his theory. Kawazu shares the news with Tomiko, a lab assistant he is having an affair with, who in turn shares it with her reporter friend Hashizume. When Kawazu's wife Yuko, demands a divorce, she also requests to meet Tomiko face to face. On the way to see Tomiko via subway, Kawazu and his wife are trapped underground when the earthquake hits and devastates Tokyo. Kawazu sacrifices himself to save his wife and other survivors, while Hashizume rescues Tomiko amidst a blazing Tokyo.

Background & Commentary

Having been five years since Toho's last big disaster film, 1975's *Conflagration*, it's not certain why the studio decided to produce another big budget disaster film. And, though the film was in danger of treading the same ground as 1973's monumental hit, *Submersion of Japan*, the resulting film manages to set itself apart for various reasons. For one, this film is more of a romantic affair drama than *Submersion of Japan*. In fact, one could argue that the family tension between the main character, Dr. Kawazu and his wife Yuko whom he is cheating on, mirrors that of the impending earthquake. The tension mounts and reaches a fever pitch when Kawazu and Yuko board a subway train to meet his mistress, Tomiko, when the earthquake finally hits.

The film's writer was Kaneto Shindo, a playwright and film director born in 1912. Due to his age, Shindo was old enough to witness the great Kanto earthquake of 1923, and that could have well been part of this story's inspiration. In fact, the main character is the grandson of the man who predicted the Kanto earthquake. Naturally, Teruyoshi Nakano's effects work excels, and it's hard to say whether or not he tops himself on *Submersion of Japan*—which it should be noted that, not surprisingly, this film borrows a few stock footage shots from. The film's standout scene occurs when a jumbo jet lands amidst the earthquake and emerges as the

278 / 地震列島

film's most memorable visual. There are also some great long shots of Tokyo in flames, and though this film fails to eclipse *Submersion of Japan* as a whole, its earthquake scene does at least top the aforementioned film's Kanto earthquake scene.

Like *Earthquake* (1974) and other disaster films, the earthquake itself is not the climactic sequence of the film, but rather comes at the end of the second act. The rest of the film is then spent with the main characters surviving the aftershocks. And, amazingly enough, there is some interesting character development here as Yuko, heretofore portrayed as a cold unattractive character, manages to end the picture with the brunt of the audience's sympathy. Kudos should go to the film's stylist, who made Yuko look somewhat unattractive early on, and yet strangely beautiful after the earthquake is over. The film's other female lead, Yukiko, on the other hand, who starts the picture favorably, begins to lose the audience's sympathy as she constantly pines for Dr. Kawazu despite being rescued by Hashizume (played by Toshiyuki Nagashima, the future star of *Gamera 2: Advent of Legion*). *Deathquake* managed to be a hit at the Japanese box office, and was released to American television in 1982.

Final Word

Though not a critical or commercial success on the level of *Submersion of Japan*, *Deathquake* still emerges as one of the better Japanese disaster films ever made.

Trivia

- The U.S. version was narrated by Hal Linden (*Barney Miller*).

- Daigo Kusano, the "angry man on the train", also portrayed the "angry ape man" on the cruise ship in *Godzilla vs. Mechagodzilla* (1974).

Attack of the Super Monsters (1982)

Broadcast Date: 1982

Directed by: Toru Sotoyama & Tom Wyner
Special Effects by: Shohei Tojo
Screenplay by: Masaki Tsuji, Ifumi Uchiyama, Hiroyasu Yamaura & Tom Wyner
Music by: Toshiaki Tsushima, Seiji Yokoyama & Robert J. Walsh
Voice Cast: Tom Wyner (Narrator) Dan Worren (Jim Starbuck) Robin Levenson (Gem Starbuck) Mike Reynolds (Tyrannos) **Suit Performers:** Uncredited

Academy Ratio, Color, 83 Minutes

Story
Unbeknownst to mankind, the dinosaurs never died and have been evolving underground under the leadership of the evil Emperor Tyrannus. The psychically enabled T-Rex begins sending dinosaur emissaries to the surface world to mutate the surface life, namely dogs, bats and rats. Opposing the mutated animals and dinosaurs is the group Gemini which is successful in fending off all of Tyrannus's attacks.

Background & Commentary
Shortly after completing *The Last Dinosaur*, Tsuburaya Productions decided to craft a new dinosaur driven tokusatsu series entitled *Dinosaur War Izenborg*—the big bad of which would be portrayed by *The Last Dinosaur* T-Rex suit named Ururu (and Emperor Tyrannus in the U.S. TV movie version). The strangest aspect of the series is that although it utilizes live action monster suits and miniatures, the human characters are all anime! The series, which aired from late 1977 into 1978, was popular in Japan and even aired in Arabia and Italy. However, in America the series has only been seen in the form of the movie *Attack of the Super Monsters.*

The film, spearheaded by longtime American anime voice actor and distributer Tom Wyner, is essentially the first five episodes of *Dinosaur War Izenborg* run continuously, and as a result the film is obviously episodic to say the least. However, it is still of interest to Toho/Tsuburaya completests. For instance, the pterodactyl has Rodan's roar, and stock footage from familiar films like *The Last War* (1961) can be glimpsed as well. The dinosaur footage is frequent enough to keep enthusiasts entertained, though they will still no doubt be bored by the anime footage focusing around sibling Jim and Gem Starbuck, whose origins are vague here but are better explained in the original TV series. The brother and sister team merge their cybernetic bodies to pilot a craft not dissimilar to the Gohten from *Atragon*, which comes complete with a drill and a freeze ray. Like many children's tokusatsu TV shows, it is much gorier than American counterparts and features the ship drilling through several of the suitmation saurians.

Attack of the Super Monsters was the first of several Tsuburaya TV series to be edited into a cheap TV/Direct-to-VHS movie. It's too bad instead Tom Wyner didn't utilize footage from Tsuburaya's sequel series, *Dinosaur Task Force Koseidon*, which was 100% live action, actors and all to make his dinosaur compilation film.

Final Word
Of interest only to Tsuburaya and Toho fans, this film is far too childish and silly to be enjoyed for any other reason.

Trivia

- Emperor Tyrannus was named Ururu in the TV series, and is defeated by episode 19 and as such is not actually the series main villain.

Reference Materials

Books

***Monsters Are Attacking Tokyo* by Stuart Galbraith IV (Feral House, 1998)** Features interviews with the actual stars and directors from Toho, Daiei, Toei and even Nikkatsu. All the interviews were tirelessly conducted by Galbraith and his translators.

***The Illustrated Encyclopedia of Godzilla* by Ed Godziszewski (By the author, 1998)** Originally Godziszewski was commissioned to do this book to coincide with the release of Tristar's *Godzilla*. When the publisher backed out he published it anyway. It remains the single most authoritative volume on the G-series detailing its every aspect up to 1994.

***Japan's Favorite Mon-Star: The Unauthorized Biography of the "Big G"* by Steve Ryfle (ECW Press, 1998)** The best critical filmography of the G-series with tons of interesting background information and trivia on the production of the series.

***An Unauthorized Guide to Godzilla Collectibles* by Sean Linkenbach (Schiffer Publishing Ltd., 1998)** An all color photographic guide to Godzilla posters and collectibles from around the world.

***A Critical History and Filmography of Toho's Godzilla Series* by David Kalat (McFarland, 1997)** An excellent review of the series by critic David Kalat which closely analyzes its many themes.

***Eiji Tsuburaya: Master of Monsters* by August Ragone (Chronicle Books, 2007)** The most authoritative English language book on Tsuburaya. It is also the best illustrated book on Toho/Godzilla/Ultraman as it was officially licensed by Toho and Tsuburaya Productions.

Japanese Science Fiction, Fantasy and Horror Films by Stuart Galbraith IV (McFarland, 1994) Features a synopsis and brief analyses of every film under the heading of the title genre up to 1992's *Godzilla vs. Mothra*. Its most useful aspect is the many quotations it contains from critics when the films were actually released in America.

The Official Godzilla Compendium by J.D. Lees and Marc Cerasini (Random House, 1998) A wonderful, though unfortunately out of print, officially endorsed volume on the G-series illustrated with color/b&w photos and illustrations. Written by novelist Marc Cerasini and *G-Fan's* editor himself J.D. Lees.

Essential reading for all fans also includes several notable fanzines (fan produced magazines) either dedicated to kaiju eiga or strongly focused on them which began with Greg Shoemaker's The Japanese Fantasy Film Journal *in the 1970s among others. Below is a list of fanzines still running today.*

G-Fan Magazine
Currently the world's longest running fan made magazine at over 100 issues over the course of twenty plus years published by J.D. Less. In addition to reviews, retrospectives and other features, it contains interviews with stars like Kumi Mizuno and Akira Takarada to bit part American actors to behind the scenes players like Haruo Nakajima, Teruyoshi Nakano, and Shusuke Kaneko to name a few. www.g-fan.com

Daikaiju Enterprises Ltd.
530 Willow Crescent
Steinbach, MB, Canada R5G 0K1

Xenorama: The Journal of Heroes and Monsters
Featuring an eclectic group of pop culture topics from Kung Fu, Swords and Sandals Epics, Superheroes, and more often than not Dai Kaiju Eiga and Sentai series by David McRobie. Xenorama.blogspot.com

Mad Scientist
Covers sci-fi and horror films from the 1950s, 60s, and 70s usually with a high emphasis on Godzilla and other Japanese giants. Published by Martin Arlt.
www.madscientistzine.com

Monster Attack Team
A fanzine that graduated into a sister publication of *Famous Monsters of Filmland* for a time. Focuses predominantly on Super Sentai and Ultraman though Godzilla and co. are usually guaranteed to make an appearance.
www.monsterattackteam.com

Websites

Sci-fi Japan
Boasts all the current news relevant to Japanese sci-fi, anime, and kaiju eiga. Is especially good for new information regarding toys, collectibles and DVD/Bluray releases.

Robojapan.blogspot
A fun blogspot full of collected news stories relevant to kaiju, sci-fi, and horror on both sides of the Pacific.

Facebook Monsterland
The Best FB group devoted to the love of kaiju. Frequent posting of lobby cards and posters.

Toho Kingdom
The single best reference point for films made by Toho Studios, including their non-sci-fi and fantasy films. A virtual Wikipedia of all things Godzilla/Toho.

Godzilla-Germany
Detlef Claus runs this website comprised of images from his extensive German Lobby Card and poster collection which can be viewed there in their entirety.

Dai Kaiju Eiga on DVD and Blu-ray in America

Dai Kaiju Eiga has done surprisingly well for itself on DVD in America, with nearly all the entries in this book (save for a few) having widescreen releases with both Japanese and English language tracks. The original *Gojira* has fared the best and has seen two stellar releases. The first, a two-disc set DVD from Classic Media, presented the first legitimate release of the original Japanese subtitled *Gojira*. On the other disc was *Godzilla, King of the Monsters!* The release featured audio commentaries on both films, as well as a few short documentaries, trailers and a booklet. An even more impressive Blu-ray was released by the Criterion Collection which collects both films to one disc. It has even more special features and commentaries by David Kalat on both versions of the picture.

Classic Media also released widescreen uncut Japanese versions of *Godzilla Raids Again*; *Mothra vs. Godzilla*; *Ghidorah, the Three Headed Monster*; *Invasion of Astro-Monster*; *All Monsters Attack* and *Terror of Mechagodzilla*. All releases came complete with their American versions and commentary tracks by various historians. Classic Media presented their best release in the form of a *Rodan/War of the Gargantuas* double feature that also included a full length documentary: *Bringing Godzilla Down to Size*. Directed by Norman England and produced with the help of Ed Godziszewski and Steve Ryfle, it features interviews with Haruo Nakajima and Akira Takarada to name only a few.

Although they lack extras, Sony Tristar released many classic G-films to DVD in 2004. With excellent prints featuring both Japanese and English language tracks, the releases included *Godzilla vs. Hedorah*; *Godzilla vs. Gigan*; *Godzilla vs. Mechagodzilla*; *Ebirah, Horror of the Deep* (as *Godzilla vs. the Sea Monster*); and *Son of Godzilla*.

Taking up the slack for non G-films was Media Blasters, which released DVDs of *Varan*; *The Mysterians*; *Atragon*;

Frankenstein Conquers the World, *Latitude Zero*, *Matango*, *Space Amoeba*, *Dogora the Space Monster*, Nikkatsu's *Gappa the Triphibean Monster* and Toei's *Legend of Dinosaurs and Monster Birds*. All of these releases came with special features imported over from the Japanese releases, including subtitled commentaries. More recently, Media Blasters released a Blu-ray of *Destroy All Monsters*. They had also planned to bring *Godzilla vs. Megalon* to Blu-ray with extras, but had difficulties getting the special features approved by Toho. Instead they released a "bare bones" DVD. Luckily for fans, there was a misprint which resulted in a select batch of DVDs being printed with extras on them. These can be found for sale on EBay if one is willing to pay extra. Eventually a Blu-ray edition of *Godzilla vs. Megalon* was released sans special features. Kraken releasing has released *Ebirah, Horror of the Deep*; *Godzilla vs. Gigan* and *Godzilla vs. Hedorah* on Blu-ray.

Columbia Pictures released *Mothra* (both Japanese and U.S. versions) in a three pack along with other Toho classics *The H-Man* and *Battle in Outer Space*. *King Kong vs. Godzilla* and *King Kong Escapes* were released in a stellar two-pack from Universal on DVD in 2005, and Blu-ray in 2014. Unfortunately they lack their Japanese versions which differ significantly from the American versions, but the prints are pristine.

As for Shochiku's original *The X From Outer Space*, it can be found in the Criterion Collection's offshoot series in Eclipse Series 37: When Horror Came to Shochiku which also contains *Goke, Body Snatcher from Hell*; *The Living Skeleton* and *Genocide*.

The original Gamera films were for years limited to bargain bin DVD companies that often presented them in pan and scan formats taken from the TV prints under such titles as *Attack of the Monsters*. Shout! Factory thankfully released Daiei's Gamera films in the original Japanese and widescreen, though unfortunately some of them lack their English dubs. *Gamera* (which contains a documentary) and *Gamera vs. Barugon* exist on single discs with commentaries, while double features exist for *Gyaos/Viras, Guiron/Monster X*, and *Zigra/Gamera Super Monster*. ADV released the Yokai Monsters trilogy to DVD in the past, but it is now OOP. Daiei's *Daimajin* trilogy was also released onto Blu-ray via Mill Creek Entertainment, which also released all of the Showa and Heisei era Gamera films in the same format. There also exists a now OOP DVD from Image Entertainment featuring *The Magic Serpent* on double bill with *Return of the Monsters (Gamera vs. Gyaos)*. As such, there is currently no official DVD release for *Magic Serpent* in the U.S.

Yongary, Monster from the Deep is available on Blu-ray from Kino Lorber. Toho's *The War in Space* is available on DVD from Discotek, and Toei's *Message from Space* is available from Shout! Factory. *Terror Beneath the Sea* is on DVD courtesy of Dark Sky Films. *The Last Dinosaur* and *The Bermuda Depths* have both been released on DVD through Warner Archive (though *The Ivory Ape* remains conspicuously absent). Image Entertainment released *The Super Inframan* to DVD and *Mighty Peking Man* is available through Miramax. Both are also currently available for streaming on Amazon Prime along with *The Iron Super Man, Voyage Into Space* and *Warning from Space* (also still available on DVD). Some movies, like *Attack of the Super Monsters*, can be found on YouTube.

As for other films listed in this book, a few are actually banned. *Abominable Snowman* and *Great Prophecies of Nostradamus* have a self imposed ban by Toho, while Tsuburaya Productions no longer acknowledges *6 Ultra Brothers vs. the Monster Army* due to a copyright dispute with Chaiyo Studios. As for films like *The Last War, Submersion of Japan,* and others, they simply lack a U.S. home video release.

Acknowledgments

I know, most people put the Acknowledgements at the front of the book, but I've always felt they should be at the end. That way the people who really appreciated the book can see who they have to thank for it; and vice versa for those who hated it. I'd like to first thank Neil Riebe for being a great friend over the years and finally letting me co-author one of his famous fanfiction stories with him. Oh, and I suppose I should thank him for writing the Foreword for this book along with all the proofing he did. I guess that's important too. Thank you Shane Olive for getting me that cover art done when your good-for-nothing son took too long. And lastly, thank you to Martin Arlt, Mike Bogue, E.J. Wilson, David McRobie, Noe Torres, and Ruben Uriarte for offering those wonderful review quotes!

About the Author

John LeMay is the author of such books as *The Real Cowboys and Aliens: UFO Encounters of the Old West* and *Tall Tales and Half Truths of Billy the Kid*, and his writings have appeared in magazines *G-Fan, Cinema Retro, Mad Scientist, True West* and *Xenorama*. He lives in Roswell, New Mexico.

What other authors had to say about the First Edition:

"With *The Big Book of Japanese Giant Monster Movies*, LeMay takes a fresh look at the daikaiju genre, providing both critical analysis and interesting behind the scenes information on the making of these films. Fans of the genre will find all the usual Godzilla and Gamera films here, along with many lesser-known genre entries finally getting their due."—Martin Arlt, Editor of *Mad Scientist* Magazine

"John LeMay's wonderful *The Big Book of Japanese Giant Monster Movies Vol. 1: 1954-1980* is a love letter to all those great Showa Era sci-fi, fantasy, and horror movies from the Land of the Rising Sun. LeMay's enthusiasm is contagious, his prose pumped, his insights enjoyable. And besides all that, LeMay offers great trivia about these movies, some of which even an oldster like me didn't know! Highly recommended nostalgic fun for new and old fans alike. Now I can't wait for Volume 2!"—Mike Bogue, author of *Atomic Drive-In*

"John LeMay has done it again! *The Big Book of Japanese Giant Monster Movies* is loaded with fun facts, well written reviews and loads of interesting historical footnotes and trivia. John has this informal yet formal writing style that makes the book a breeze to read and yet well layered as well. I kind of hate him for making it look so easy! I highly recommend this book, and hopefully it will come out in a nondigital edition for us old fogies that like to hold actual books when we read them!"—David McRobie, Editor of *Xenorama* Magazine

"John LeMay's *Big Book Japanese Giant Monster Movies* blew me away on many levels! First, it took me back to some of the happiest days of my childhood. I'll never forget the day in 1973 when my brother and I were 13 and our parents needed to do some house-hunting. Did they hire a babysitter? NO, they dropped us at the theater with a couple dollars for snacks and we watched *Godzilla vs. the Smog Monster* ALL DAY! It was EPIC! And since we saw the movie a half-dozen times, we were able to tell all our friends about it in great detail. As an adult, I rekindled my interest in Godzilla while writing my book, *Star Trek: Exploring the Original Series*. As it happens, Mr. Sulu himself, George Takei, got his start in show business working on *Rodan* and *Godzilla Raids Again*. Secondly, I can't say enough about John's amazing research for these movies and this genre. He rigorously covers each film, with a unique talent for history, interesting plot summaries, and great trivia; all born of an obvious love for the art form. Finally, I am supremely impressed with the writing and format of the book itself. Mr. LeMay is a master communicator. His style is so engaging and readable, the book should come with a warning: Impossible to Put Down. If it happens to you, don't dispair; just enjoy it as I did."— E.J. Wilson, author of *Star Trek: Exploring the Original Series*

"As a lifelong Godzilla fan, I count among my most cherished memories having attended an all-night marathon of the Showa period films at a South Texas drive-in theater in the early 1970s. Over the years, the Godzilla myth, in its many variants, has continued to entertain and delight me and my family. Consequently, I was thrilled to discover John's LeMay's *The Big Book of Japanese Giant Monster Movies Vol. 1*, which provides an outstanding overview of Godzilla and his monstrous film cohorts. The book is incredibly well organized and, when loaded onto a mobile device, is the perfect companion while one watches these historic films. I love the trivia, the film summaries, and the effort John makes to provide historical and cinematic context for each of the motion pictures. I heartily recommend this wonderful book for all fans of Japanese monster flicks. The only thing missing is the popcorn...."-Noe Torres co-author of *Mexico's Roswell: The Chihuahua UFO Crash*

"Growing up and watching Godzilla movies on the big screen during the 1950s and 60s were always awe inspiring events during my childhood. I was always amazed seeing Godzilla and the other massive god like creatures crushing buildings and unleashing a terrible path of destruction against humanity. Godzilla would often use his fire breath against Japanese military defenses. Obviously infantry, missiles, tanks and jets were no match against Godzilla and the other monsters. Their strange and powerful roars would always raise the hairs on the back of my neck. Future films included the Big Guy battling against these monsters for supremacy. I loved many of the movies made by Toho Productions. I was always impressed with the miniaturization used as special effects. The movies gave me a cultural appreciation for Japanese Society. Japan's film industry was rapidly growing during post WW2. Perhaps one of the most eerie and depressing images that I can remember were the scenes of children and their families suffering from radiation burns. Godzilla became a metaphor depicting the horrors of an atomic war and man's destructive nature. John LeMay's *The Big Book of Japanese Giant Monster Movies* provides a unique historical perspective on these movies "Biggest" legions on screen. Sci-Fi movies in the future may depict other monsters but there is only one Godzilla that still reigns!"—Ruben Uriarte, co-author of *Mexico's Roswell: The Chihuahua UFO Crash*

"A very readable and informative book on tokusatsu films (mostly kaiju) up to 1980. Synopses are brief and to the point, criticism is interesting and balanced, and there are lots of fun facts. Much research went into this book, and even people with well versed in kaiju eiga will learn new things and have an enjoyable read."—J.D. Lees, Editor of *G-Fan* Magazine

What reviewers had to say about *The Big Book of Japanese Giant Monster Movies Vol. 2: 1984-2014*:

"In Volume 2 of his *The Big Book of Japanese Giant Monster Movies*, author John LeMay gives us an enjoyable look at forty-one kaiju eiga from the years 1984 through 2014. From Godzilla to Ultraman to Gamera, LeMay covers the Heisei Era in the same lively, engrossing manner in which he embraced the Showa Era in Volume 1. Intriguing trivia and keen insight abound—indeed, reading the book is like having a front row seat at a marathon kaiju eiga festival! A must read for all Japanese giant monster fans."— Mike Bogue, author of *Atomic Drive-In*

"The entries for this book are quite diverse. LeMay covers many, many kaiju films in this book, including all of the Godzilla films from *The Return of Godzilla* (1984) on, including the two American films, as well as the four Gamera films, the Mothra trilogy, and quite the collection of lesser-known kaiju films, including *Yamato Takeru* (1994), *Big Man Japan* (2007), *Deep Sea Monster Reigo vs. Battleship Yamato* (2008), and even two short films about giant monsters—*Negadon the Monster from Mars* (2005) and *Gehara the Dark and Long-Haired Monster* (2009), several Ultraman movies, and more."—Nicholas Driscoll, Toho Kingdom

What reviewers had to say about
The Big Book of Japanese Giant Monster Movies: The Lost Films:

"I cannot heartily recommend this book enough."—*Matt Frank, IDW's*
Godzilla: Rulers of Earth
"Great fun and tons of revelations throughout!"—*Mike Bogue, author*
of Apocalypse Then: American and Japanese Atomic Cinema,
1951-1967
"Truly an amazing piece of work."—*J.D. Lees, Editor of* G-Fan
"As close as I have felt to being that kid in the movie store again."—
Colin McMahon, ATTACK! of the B-Movie Monsters

Made in the USA
Middletown, DE
22 July 2023